Evidence and
the Adversarial Process

THE MODERN LAW

Jenny McEwan

BLACKWELL
Business

Copyright © Jenny McEwan, 1992

The right of Jenny McEwan to be identified as author
of this work has been asserted in accordance with the
Copyright, Designs and Patents Act 1988.

First published 1992

Blackwell Publishers
108 Cowley Road
Oxford OX4 1JF
UK

Three Cambridge Center
Cambridge, Massachusetts 02142
USA

British Library Cataloguing in Publication Data

A CIP catalogue record for this book is available from
the British Library.

Library of Congress Cataloging-in-Publication Data

McEwan, Jenny,
Evidence and the adversarial process: the modern
law/Jenny McEwan.
p.   cm.
Includes bibliographical references and index.
ISBN 0–631–15845–6   ISBN 0–631–18316–7 (pbk)
1. Evidence (Law)—Great Britain.   2. Evidence,
Criminal—Great Britain.   3. Adversary system (Law)
—Great Britain.
I. Title.
KD7499. M38   1992
347.41'06–dc20
[344.1076]   91–27597

Typeset in 10.5 on 12.5 pt Ehrhardt
by Graphicraft Typesetters Ltd., Hong Kong
Printed in Great Britain by TJ Press Ltd, Padstow,
Cornwall

This book is printed on acid-free paper

Contents

Preface

Many students of evidence find it hard to see any system or coherence in the mass of apparently arbitrary and inconsistent rules. This book is an attempt to show that the rules are to some extent a natural development of the trial procedures adopted in England and exported to the United States and the Commonwealth. If those trial procedures should be at a critical evolutionary stage at this moment, and be found to be moving further away from the adversarial paradigm, as argued here, there is a pressing need to re-examine the necessity of retaining those rules. In an effort to be concise, I have frequently explained the law in only the briefest of terms; some knowledge of the subject therefore will assist the reader in following the arguments. I have concentrated on those aspects of the exclusionary rules which appear the most absurd, unfair or counterproductive. I hope that the general approach adopted here, which is to discuss them in the light of the philosophy which underpins the adversarial trial, and also of some of the psychological findings on the reliability of evidence, will be of interest and of use to those who study the law of evidence.

In any event I am most grateful for the help I have received in writing the book. My husband Malcolm nobly read and attempted to unscramble the entire text; Graham Davies, Eileen Vizard and Gisli Gudjonsson offered ideas and materials; Margaret Bird prepared the tables. Thanks are also due to Olga Bennett, Jean and Keith McEwan, to Pat and Arthur, and to all those both at the University of Keele and at home who have given moral support throughout. Of my colleagues, particular thanks are due to Dr Abimbola Olowofoyeku, who with endless patience introduced me to the mysteries of word-processing. I am grateful also to Tim Goodfellow at Blackwell Publishers, a most understanding editor, and to Bryan Abraham, who manages to be eagle-eyed and constructive at the same time. None should take the blame for the inevitable deficiencies of the book, the responsibility for which is entirely mine.

Jenny McEwan

Table of Cases

Table of Statutes

Introduction

The purpose of this book is to examine critically the nature of English laws of evidence, asking why such laws, which are frequently exclusionary of evidence, must exist. And if there must be rules of evidence, are those operated in the Anglo-American[1] systems of trial rules which rational persons would adopt as the best possible means to achieve justice? It will be argued that many of these rules evolved to strike a balance between competing private interests which characterize the adversarial system of trial. There are, admittedly, other factors which have contributed to the content of the law of evidence, for example the function of the jury and the traditional emphasis upon the taking of evidence on oath. But it is adversarial systems which develop laws of evidence, those familiar and intricate mazes upon which books are written and students sit examinations. The complexity of the law can lead to injustice in that mistakes during trials can lead to 'technical' appeals; we find that reliable and relevant evidence may be excluded. The complicated mysteries of this area of law may be a source of fascination or dread, according to one's lights. The Gothic structure of often eccentric or obscure prohibitions, each with its accompanying set of exceptions, its rigid dichotomies between issue, fact, credibility, guilt, weight, may have for some a quaint charm of its own. Whether or not these devices have much to do with the discovery of the truth is another matter. And the way in which lay participants in criminal cases are treated gives little cause for pride.

[1] Many Commonwealth countries still retain exclusionary rules of evidence very close to the English ones; the United States and, surprisingly, Scotland, have not departed significantly from the traditional common law structure.

1

The Adversarial Trial

Some in their Discourse, desire rather than commendation of Wit, being able to hold all Arguments, than of Judgement in discerning what is true.
'Of discourse', *Essays* 32, Bacon

THE ADVERSARIAL TRADITION

A litigation is in essence a trial of skill between opposing parties, conducted under recognized rules, and the prize is the judge's decision. We have rejected inquisitorial methods and prefer to regard our judges as entirely independent.
Lord Justice-Clerk Thompson, *Thomson v Glasgow Corporation* [1961] SLT 237, 246

The traditional distinctions drawn between adversarial and inquisitorial procedures of trial are frequently described as trite, simplistic or as a cliché. Certainly it is difficult to find any legal system which adheres strictly to all the features of the classic models. The English legal system,[1] often regarded as the paradigm of the adversarial tradition, is not a perfect example by any means; on close examination it is found even in criminal courts to allow deviations from the proper adversarial structure, more significantly in recent times. And some tribunals dealing with some kinds of case have very little in common with it at all.[2]

Damaska, in a highly regarded critique, defined the adversarial trial as

---

[1] Although I throughout refer to 'England' and 'the English' legal system, I am referring to the system that operates in England and Wales – unless the context clearly suggests otherwise. The systems in Scotland and Ireland differ.

[2] See later, e.g. family cases such as wardship, coroners' inquiries, etc.

follows: the proceedings should be structured as a dispute between the two sides in a position of theoretical equality before a court which must decide the outcome of the contest. The model depends upon the parties to establish the existence of a contest and to delineate its borders through pleadings and stipulations drafted by them. Evidence is adduced by the parties and is exclusive to the party bringing it. The balance of advantages depends on the parties' own use of informational sources.[3] The adjudicator is an umpire whose role is to ensure that the parties abide by the rules, but is passive even in that regard; he or she intervenes only if there is an objection from one side against the conduct of the other. On this analysis, the procedures themselves are merely a facility provided by the state for persons in dispute. Only the parties themselves have any interest in the initiation of proceedings, in their subject-matter or in the outcome.

The Anglo-American criminal trial is not a pure example of this form since the state *is* interested in the bringing of proceedings[4] and in the outcome. The person aggrieved by a crime has no direct interest in such proceedings, or in the outcome, apart from the possibility of compensation (more effectively dealt with in civil proceedings brought by him or her). He or she certainly has no control over the conduct of the case for the prosecution.[5] Clearly the criminal justice system is in place today not to right private wrongs, but to protect the public as a whole. Yet many features of the adversarial model are retained. Acknowledged departures include the provision of information by the prosecution to the defence.[6] The key characteristics which remain are sufficient to make the Anglo-American criminal trial the most adversarial of all judicial proceedings.

1   The role of the judge as umpire. Not only must judges be impartial, but they are not involved with the preparation of the case or the content of the evidence. The verdict is not their concern as long as the trial is conducted fairly. They are there to keep the parties to the rules. Although Damaska points out that in the pure model it is for the parties to object to the manner in which the other side conducts its case, it is not clear that in

---

[3] Damaska, 'Evidentiary barriers to conviction and two models of criminal procedure: a comparative study' (1973) 121 U Penn LR 506.

[4] Although, incredibly, England introduced a public prosecutions system only as recently as 1985, when the Prosecution of Offences Act set up the Crown Prosecution Service.

[5] This was the case in England even before the Crown Prosecution Service was set up, since the state, through the police service, was making the initial decision and footing the bill.

[6] *Post.* Even the right of the parties to determine the issues in the case have to be controlled to prevent abuse; A. Zuckerman, *The Principles of Criminal Evidence* (OUP, Oxford, 1989), p. 15.

reality judges regard themselves as so constrained. For example, it has been said by distinguished judges that pressure for legal representation for rape complainants would not exist if trial judges (not prosecution counsel) did their jobs properly.[7] Also, many lawyers' experience is that unrepresented defendants will receive a great deal of assistance from trial judges, even though one view would be that if they have chosen not to avail themselves of the services of a lawyer, they should be assumed to be willing to accept full responsibility themselves. The theoretically limited judicial role reflects historical 'distrust of public officials and the complementary demand for safeguards against abuse'.[8] Damaska argues that, in England, we are prepared to tolerate the evidentiary barriers accompanying this model for fear of the greater horror of the abuse of power.

2   Judgment by one's peers is not an essential characteristic of adversarial trial,[9] but naturally emerges as a workable system. Rationally an independent, randomly selected jury would be the choice of a society which was afraid of its own officials. Trial by magistrates is not quite so inevitable a development, nor is that of the civil trial becoming almost exclusively the domain of the judge as the trier of fact.[10]

3   The principle of orality is again, Damaska argues, not an essential of the adversarial model, but a natural consequence of the judges' umpireal role and the evidence-gathering functions of the parties. Each party will be anxious to attack the evidence of the other, and this is easier if the emphasis is on oral testimony.

4   The role of the advocate[11] – who must present the evidence in the manner most advantageous to his or her client. 'An advocate, in the discharge of his duty, knows but one person in the world, and that person is his client.'[12] Advocates do have duties towards the court: they must not knowingly mislead it, and, in some cases, must reveal evidence in their possession even if unfavourable to the client,[13] but they have no duty to seek out unfavourable evidence. Some advocates have consequently become skilled at

[7] Lords Hailsham and Morris, HL Deb., vol. 375, col. 1773, 1785 (22 October 1976).

[8] Damaska, (1973) 121 U Penn LR 506, 583. However, the non-interventionist judge may be a myth. See below, chapter 3.

[9] Ibid., p. 564.

[10] Presumably, the risk of bias in the civil case is thought to be less probable.

[11] Usually cases are prepared by teams of lawyers rather than one. Solicitors and barristers have been synthesized into one being for the purpose of the following discussion.

[12] Lord Brougham, quoted in J. Nightingale (ed.), *Trial of Queen Caroline* (Robins, London, 1821).

[13] See below.

avoiding contact with evidence which they suspect could prejudice their client's interests. Since the judge is not entitled to demand that further evidence be produced, no participant in the courtroom process has an immediate obligation towards the truth. 'The advocate in the trial…is not engaged much more than half the time – and then only coincidentally – in the search for truth.'[14]

The essence of inquisitorial proceedings, on the other hand, is that the state *is* interested in the outcome and wishes an investigator to discover as many relevant facts as possible. Rather than a dispute, as such, there is an official inquiry triggered by the belief that a crime has been committed. Society has much less interest in the outcome of a civil dispute and therefore these proceedings remain inevitably party-dependent in terms of the gathering of evidence. Although far off the pure inquisitorial model, Continental civil proceedings are closer than the English in that judges are fully cognizant of the evidence from copious dossiers presented at the outset and therefore their questioning of witnesses at the trial is designed to supplement or test what they have already read in the paperwork. The position of the parties is weaker in this model; they cannot limit the tribunal's field of inquiry through pleadings or by consent. The court itself will pursue facts, and avail itself of any sources, including the interrogation of the defendant. The increased importance of the judicial role correspondingly diminishes the power and function of the advocate.

Since one system has its fact-finder (jury, magistrate or trial judge) operating in a factual vacuum, and the other has the tribunal of fact prepared in advance with summarized records of all the testimony taken during the preliminary investigation, evidential styles are inevitably distinct. In theory, the adversarial system gives the fact-finder the advantage of utter impartiality arising from his or her ignorance of the case. Although it is not the responsibility of a party to present the tribunal with the *truth*, only with *his or her case*, it is argued that the vigorous pursuit of evidence to serve the same interests, when added to that of the opponent, is an effective means of discovering the truth, particularly since the tribunal witnesses the attack by each side upon the evidence of the other.

> The English say that the best way of getting at the truth is to have each party dig for the facts that help it; between them they will bring all to light…Two prejudiced searchers starting from opposite ends of the field will between them be less likely to miss anything than the impartial searcher starting in the middle.[15]

[14] Frankel, 'The search for truth: an umpireal view' (1975) 123 U Penn LR 1031, 1035.

[15] P. Devlin, *The Judge*, OUP (Oxford, 1979), p. 61.

The problem is that an interested party who has dug for, and discovered, relevant facts may not feel that it would help him or her to present them before the court. The other side, of course, is entitled to make the same discovery and produce those facts, but it may be that the facts advantage neither side. Thus a key witness may be omitted altogether from an adversarial trial if both sides fear what the witness might do to their case. Supporters of this state of affairs argue that lawyers are not in a position to set themselves up as the ultimate arbiters of truth, and therefore should confine themselves to producing as effective a case as possible on behalf of the client. For the clients' interests would not be best served by finding their own representatives turning judgmental, and there is a substantial risk that citizens would be actively prejudiced if, for example, a lawyer was sufficiently convinced of his or her client's guilt to refuse to act on a plea of not guilty. It may well be that lawyers should not set themselves up as judge and jury when those bodies exist independently; but there seems no good reason that, if it appears to the independent tribunal of fact that a particular item of evidence should be produced in order to enlighten the court, the parties should be entitled to block it. That is, of course, unless the proceedings in court are seen only as an instrument for the parties to employ as they choose, rather than an important institution within society and an essential element in the enforcement and development of the law. This view of the adversarial mode of trial is to some extent tenable in the civil sphere, where the state is not directly interested in the outcome but provides the litigants with the necessary apparatus.[16] It may be that the underlying rationale of the adversarial trial is indeed an assumption that establishing the objective truth is not the purpose of the inquiry. Egglestone, for example, suggests that even when acting as the tribunal of fact, the judicial function is not to ascertain the truth in any real sense. The judge makes a decision that appears to be justifiable on the material presented in court.[17]

Jackson takes the plea of guilty as an example: 'adversary procedure is not concerned with the truth of the material facts but only the truth of facts put in issue by the accused. As a result pleas of guilty, if considered voluntary, are not investigated.'[18] Yet in criminal cases the state is a party; the defend-

[16] But this image of the civil case, born of the traditional common law actions, is no longer representative of every kind of civil case. There are cases involving individual welfare rights against the state, cases concerning the welfare of children, where the two-handed contest is not in fact involved, causing considerable problems to courts who have to proceed as if it were. See chapter 7.

[17] R. Egglestone, *Evidence, Proof and Probability*, 2nd edn (Weidenfeld & Nicolson, London, 1983), p. 32.

[18] Jackson, 'Two methods of proof in criminal procedure' (1988) 51 MLR 249; compare the position in some Eastern European countries such as the Soviet Union,

ant is far less able to influence matters than the defendant in a civil case – a fact recognized by the rules of evidence in many ways. Witnesses for the prosecution are not in the position of the plaintiff; they may not choose whether or not to proceed, and they cannot select the charge. However, since the prosecution carries the burden of proof and the accused is presumed innocent until proved otherwise, they are 'fair game' to the defence, and may emerge from court with their reputations in shreds or private lives the subject of public debate. Why should the court behave as if the 'parties' are on equal terms and the State only an interested bystander, despite initiating, organizing and funding the criminal trial, and, where appropriate, exacting punishment upon the defendant?

THE ALTERNATIVE: THE INQUISITORIAL TRADITION

In contrast to the umpireal British judge, Continental judges are expected to arrive at the truth by their own exertions.[19] The Criminal Law Revision Committee seems to regard it as the hallmark of the inquisitorial system that there is full judicial investigation of the whole case, including that for the defence, before the trial.[20] In France this is done by the *juge d'instruction*, half magistrate, half policeman. He can demand that more evidence be produced; it is not within the power of the parties to prevent him from seeing it. It is his decision whether or not the case should proceed to full trial. At the trial, which is seen as an investigation rather than a dispute, the President questions the defendant and the other witnesses from the report he has been given. It has been argued that the preparatory stage is inquisitorial and the procedure at trial accusatorial,[21] but in any event the proceedings are very different from English trials, where, in theory, the judge has a passive role. In France the President allows witnesses to tell their own story; the Code insists that they should not be interrupted.[22] Since all the evidence has

where relevant evidence may be heard despite any admission of guilt by the defendant. 'The principle of material truth…means that evidence-taking proceedings at the trial can never be entirely given up, although there was not the least doubt about the accused having pleaded guilty': Stanislaw Waltos, 'Introduction', *Code of Criminal Procedure of the Polish People's Republic* (Wydawnictwo Prawnicze, Warsaw, 1979).

[19] G. Williams, *The Proof of Guilt* (Stevens, London, 1968), p. 28.

[20] *Evidence (General)*, Eleventh Report of the Criminal Law Revision Committee, Cmnd 4991 (1972).

[21] Vouin, 'The protection of the accused in French criminal procedure' (1956) 5 ICLQ 1 and 157 (two parts).

[22] Wright, 'French criminal procedure' (1929) 45 LQR 98.

been presented at the *instruction* stage, they have had time to prepare their stories, which they should relate in the most spontaneously natural way possible, without prompting, and free from objections to hearsay. Questions may then be put by the President, and the parties may then question only through him.[23] A formal, structured cross-examination by counsel for either side is therefore out of the question: 'We are not unaware of the advantages of the English "cross-examination", but in our opinion it does not ensure free and frank testimony from the witness.'[24] However, the questioning by the President can be fairly aggressive, and, in some cases, the defendant may appear to be receiving considerably harsher treatment than the other witnesses.

The role of counsel is necessarily very different in France, tending to concentrate on objecting to questions rather than devising lines of questioning, as in England. The more active the court itself, the less important the role of legal counsel. The inactivity of the prosecutor, compared with the judge's interventionist role, may avoid jury hostility towards the prosecution case. But the unstructured process of taking evidence does not appeal to British advocates. A. C. Wright was appalled. He wrote of French trials:[25]

> The art of cross-examination has but a spark of life...No one seems to know how to dissect a statement into its component parts, find out hidden contradictions, and cut through equivocations, generalizations or hearsay to the essence of facts within the witness's own knowledge. Nor does the national temperament seem to envisage counsel quietly pressing a point, asking for precise answers, demanding explanations or particulars – in short, testing his evidence.[26]

[23] Art. 319 of the Criminal Code provides that after a witness has ~~spontaneous~~ statement the accused or counsel may question him o~~r~~ *du président.*

[24] Vouin (1956) 5 ICLQ 157, 168. See also Glanville Williams's description of French horror at the manner of cross-examination by the British at Nuremberg, where defendants were required to interpret and explain detailed items in documents selected from crateloads of papers: *Proof of Guilt*, pp. 79–80.

[25] Wright (1929) 45 LQR 98, 99.

[26] One must wonder how many examples of such cross-examinations are found nowadays in English courts, and one has only to look at the cross-examination of the subnormal Derek Bentley in the 1950s to wonder whether the description given by Wright in the 1920s would have been somewhat romantic even then. See D. Yallop, *To Encourage the Others*, 2nd edn (Corgi, London, 1990) and discussion of cross-examination below.

Honoré[27] doubts whether any system, including the French criminal procedure, is a perfect example of the inquisitorial process. It may be that many of the identified shortcomings of that system result from its hybrid nature.[28] However, one marked contrast between the English system of trial and the French depends on their view that documentary evidence is intrinsically more reliable than oral. Honoré quotes Dalloz, noting 'the primacy of written proof and the mistrust which is prima facie inspired by oral testimony'. The reasoning is that oral evidence can be tailored to fit the witness's purpose at the trial whereas what was said and done at the time is far more revealing.[29] The reliability of contemporary oral statements is taken to depend on their nature and circumstances.[30] Jury trial exists within some inquisitorial systems, although Continental juries may be composed very differently from English ones. Despite the apparent imperfections of the French version of jury trial, many French lawyers feel that considerable safeguards are provided by the *instruction* stage, not being of the view that 'the guilt or innocence of the accused should be allowed finally to depend on what may seem to the French to be, and what in France might be, the extremely fortuitous outcome of that markedly gladiatorial, and in any event highly peculiar, enterprise which in England we call a trial'.[31] The concentration in England on the trial itself is regarded as an overemphasis on the tip of the iceberg. In contrast, during *instruction*, questions may be asked and there may even be a confrontation between the victim and the accused, the outcome of which will be in the documentation available before the trial President. Clearly, such a system of justice is heavily dependent upon true impartiality from the officials able to influence it – here the investigating judge and the police. But justice will not be achieved in the adversarial model, given the enormous influence of the parties through their lawyers, without strictly ethical behaviour by those lawyers. Frankel has

---

[27] Honoré, 'The primacy of oral evidence', in *Crime, Proof and Punishment: Essays in Memory of Sir Rupert Cross*, ed. C. Tapper (Butterworths, London, 1981), p. 172; see also chapter 7.

[28] Hamson, 'The prosecution of the accused – English and French legal methods' [1955] Crim LR 272.

[29] Previous inconsistent statements in criminal trials, if admitted at all are relevant only to credibility, and we shall see below both the destructive effects of the blinkered opposition of the English legal establishment to reform of the hearsay rule, and the doubtful methods of assessing the credibility of witnesses giving oral evidence.

[30] Honoré, in Tapper (ed.), p. 191.

[31] Hamson [1955] Crim LR 272, 280.

suggested that it works better in England, with a small and specialist Bar, than it does in the United States, where trials are four times as long.[32]

The emphasis in Anglo-American systems on the outcome on the 'day in court' may seem curious to foreign observers; pre-trial inquiry allows more elements of evidence to be considered, and avoids the catastrophe, common in England, of cases collapsing at trial because witnesses fail to 'come up to proof'.[33]

> Surprise is not felt to be a substantial danger. Accordingly the lawyer's initial preparation can be less than vigorous, and no pressure is created for out-of-court discovery. As the lawyer's out-of-court investigation is narrow in scope, and what is known to the lawyer is passed on to the court in detailed writings, there is little awkwardness in having the judge take over the chief burden of interrogating witnesses – especially so, as the judge need not conclude the matter in one session but can inform himself step by step over a period of time.[34]

The Italians have a 'mixed' system, which has been criticized for excessive restrictiveness, limiting the admissibility of evidence and the power of the court to require further evidence to be adduced.[35] The Scandinavian 'mixed' version of trial has few rules of evidence; there is no hearsay rule. The parties produce their own evidence, as in England, but the judge has a responsibility to see to it that the case is satisfactorily clarified. Judges may ask for supplementary evidence. The Codes of Procedure state that a witness shall have the opportunity to give a coherent account before more specific questions are asked.[36]

[32] Frankel (1975) 123 U Penn LR 1031. This matter of professional standards has unfortunately been substantially misunderstood in the debate on the monopoly of the Bar preceding the Lord Chancellor's reforms.

[33] It is dangerous to use acquittal rates as evidence of this. It is possible that the higher acquittal rates since the advent of the Crown Prosecution Service is the result of greater efficiency rather than the reverse; it may be that defence lawyers recommend more guilty pleas than before, anticipating a well-organized opponent. This would result in a smaller number of convictions following contested cases. But one of the difficulties facing the CPS is that the likelihood of a successful prosecution has to be evaluated without sight of the prosecution witnesses, entirely on the strength of the papers.

[34] Von Mehren and Schaefer, 'Phases of German civil procedure' (1958) 71 Harv LR 1193.

[35] M. Cappalletti, J. H. Merryman and J. M. Pernillo, *The Italian Legal System* (Stanford University Press, 1967).

[36] Andenaes, 'The Scandinavian countries', in *Children's Evidence in Legal Pro-*

REALITY OF THE ADVERSARIAL TRIAL

Scientific inquiry or theatrical spectacle?

A dialectic system of proof, consisting of two sides conducting a dispute, could conceivably be an effective way of discovering the truth. But in the English system, the risk remains that the most effective advocate, rather than the truth, will win the day. Jackson[37] has argued that a more effective model would involve *more* dialectic, that is, more disclosure before trial, with defendants in criminal cases being asked to account for themselves early on. This would bring the English system closer to the Continental ones; in France it is regarded as essential that defendants should be involved in the pre-trial inquiry. It is seen as their right, rather than as an imposition. Both systems follow, inevitably, an inductive method of proof. The weakness of inductive reasoning is that there are possible explanations of events other than the one selected by the trial process. Yet no alternative appears to be available, as syllogistic reasoning depends on the correctness of those initial premises which logically proceed to the conclusion. Jackson argues that all systems of proof are based on classic scientific method, but the French particularly so. After the French Revolution the increased powers of examining magistrates allowed them to collect what evidence they could, and to evaluate it according to their experience. The Anglo-American procedure is more schizophrenic, with the exclusionary rules sometimes embodying and sometimes rejecting scientific principles. For, even if the hearsay rule can be regarded as designed to exclude evidence which cannot properly be tested for reliability, other rules acknowledged to prevent the admission of evidence which is relevant but excessively prejudicial[38] limit the amount of valuable information available to the court, detracting from the principle of completeness. Also, the parties control what facts are to be determined.

Bennett and Feldman[39] point out that the jury are not presented with a scientifically organized collection of facts to each of which they can attach statistical links to various variables and possibilities directing the proper verdict. Instead, an incoherent mass of data must be organized by the jurors themselves into a story which they can understand, and the cognitive techniques they employ are those they would use in reading a detective story or

---

ceedings, eds J. R. Spencer, G. Nicholson, R. Flin and R. Bull (Spencer, Faculty of Law, University of Cambridge, 1990).

[37] Jackson (1988) 51 MLR 249.

[38] E.g. similar fact evidence; see chapter 2.

[39] W. L. Bennett and M. Feldman, *Reconstructing Reality in the Courtroom* (Tavistock, London, 1981).

watching a thriller – identifying the central action and relating other evidence to it. For individual witnesses can testify only to matters of which they have direct knowledge, and therefore can rarely describe the event(s) in issue from start to finish. Thus, the more complex the facts in the case, the more organizational work the jury have to do.

Advocates in adversarial trials, unless the witness is given the right to speak uninterrupted as in the Scandinavian 'mixed' system, not only control what the issues are to be and what witnesses and other evidence are to be produced, but also limit what is said by those witnesses, over whom they have strict editorial control. Thus the material available to the tribunal of fact is selected by the advocates, who can then in court control the narration. Witnesses are not entitled to add to their account material which has not been asked for, and so counsel can manipulate them to obtain the (for counsel) most favourable or least damaging version of the facts. The authors observe that a common tactic is to ask questions that require precise and concrete answers; this produces the account that fits counsel's version best.[40] Once the narrow version has been achieved, counsel will interrupt the witness with another question, to prevent any damaging elaboration or explanation. Expert witnesses are regarded in the United States as being especially good at playing this game with counsel and are frequently hired for that particular skill.[41] Both sides, therefore, may miss or choose to ignore a potentially important aspect of the incident in question, leading Bennett and Feldman to conclude that trials are probably little more than highly stylized dramatizations of reality. Clearly, some theatrical gestures by advocates and even some brilliant lines of questioning have little to do with the development of a coherent story. The authors describe some fairly indefensible practices in the Washington court they studied: the use of objections to make the jury think the evidence must be suspect in some way; 'fishing' cross-examinations to make witnesses explain how they know what they know, hoping something might emerge which will discredit the witness. Techniques to make fools of the jury are described, and the authors quote instances of lawyers' admiration for 'gladiator-style' advocates. There is no reason for England to feel superior; all young lawyers are brought up on tales of Marshall Hall and his tricks. There seems to be a large measure of agreement that lawyers are there to present highly selective versions of the case.[42]

The theatricality of the English criminal trial might be regarded as one

[40] Defended by M. Stone, *Proof of Fact in Criminal Trials* (W. Green & Sons, Edinburgh, 1984).

[41] Bennett and Feldman, *Reconstructing Reality*, p. 124.

[42] M. J. Saks and R. Hastie, *Social Psychology in Court* (Van Nostrand Reinhold, New York, 1978).

of its most attractive features by those who do not find themselves unwilling participants in it. The traditional dress of the advocates is designed to impress witnesses with the solemnity of the occasion, on the assumption that they are more likely to be truthful in such a setting. There is, however, no evidence that different settings affect the reliability of witnesses,[43] and from a lay point of view it might be difficult to see how witnesses can do themselves justice if utterly intimidated. They are required to stand in a special witness-box and asked to speak up so that the jury can hear them. The accused is placed dramatically in a separate cage, the dock, whereas in some jurisdictions, such as Sweden, he or she sits at a desk. The ordeal of particularly vulnerable witnesses is discussed in chapter 4, but the experience is harrowing for most. Even practised expert witnesses find the ability of counsel to control, interrupt and ridicule their testimony difficult to handle. Experience over some years of court appearances does not make it significantly easier, since the basically subordinate position of witnesses is constant. The lack of courtesy and, in some cases, the bitter attacks on distinguished experts may make them reluctant to participate in the trial process at all.[44] Even Sheriff Stone, a well-known defender of the adversarial trial, concedes that expert witnesses can be shoddily treated.[45]

Impartial umpire?

The passive, disinterested role of the judge in the trial process is a *sine qua non* of the adversarial theory. Yet it is doubtful that this is a reality. In the civil case and the magistrates' courts we find this 'umpire' entering the arena as the trier of fact. This causes obvious problems when issues of the admissibility of evidence are discussed, since, if evidence is excluded, it must be disregarded. It is frequently difficult for an adjudication on admissibility to proceed without the nature of the disputed evidence becoming obvious. These problems are especially acute in the magistrates' courts, where a *voir dire* has to be held in certain circumstances, for instance where the admissibility of a confession is challenged.[46] Prosecutors are still struggling to devise a system where this procedure can meaningfully be employed.

The passive umpire is a creature of theory rather than practice, although American judges appear to be closer to the ideal than their English counter-

---

[43] Marquis, 'Testamentary validity as a function of form, atmosphere and item difficulty', *Journal of Applied Social Psychology*, 2 (1972) p. 167. See also Saks and Hastie, ibid.

[44] See chapter 4.

[45] Stone, *Proof of Fact*, p. 273.

[46] *Liverpool Juvenile Court, ex p R* [1987] Crim LR 572.

parts, in that they interrupt less. In the average English criminal trial you will be interrupted far more often by the judge than by your opponent.

> It has become the rule, now, for the English judge to come down into the arena and to take part to quite a surprising degree. The licence that he thinks entitles him to do this is to be found in the principle that all evidence should be relevant, and it is now the rule rather than the exception to hear judges breaking in on counsel with the question, 'What is the relevance of that?'[47]

Judges may thus protect witnesses against some of the worst abuses of cross-examination discussed above, and are often especially sympathetic with expert witnesses. But Evans points out that explaining in advance the relevance of questions put in cross-examination gives witnesses early warning that may defeat the object. He also accuses judges of pro-prosecution bias to an extent that acting for the defence is like riding a bicycle uphill. Given that the exclusive dominion of counsel over the evidence in the case means that the judge, who has no file of evidence, is completely in the dark, his or her interventions are frequently unhelpful[48] except in so far as he or she (quite properly) asks for clarification for the benefit of the jury. Judicial neutrality is the cornerstone of the adversarial system; without that, there seems to be little to be said for it.[49]

Examination and cross-examination

Strict rules govern the nature of the trial itself in terms of both the order of events and questions of admissibility. In a criminal trial the prosecution must open its case and then call its witnesses. Each witness is taken through his or her evidence-in-chief, the purpose of which is to draw out those facts which support the prosecution case. A witness may not be asked leading questions (suggesting the desired answer or putting contentious matters in a form requiring only the answer Yes or No). The defence has the right to cross-examine all the witnesses for the prosecution and may in fact be obliged to do so given the nature of the defence case. For in any civil

[47] K. Evans, *Advocacy at the Bar: A Beginner's Guide* (Blackstones, London, 1983), p. 91.
[48] Frankel (1975) 123 U Penn LR 1031, whose experience of the Bench leads him to conclude that the judges ought to have sight of the evidence before the trial begins, as a Continental judge would. He would also introduce an obligation on counsel to disclose adverse facts as well as law (see 'Disclosure of evidence', below).
[49] For further discussion of the opportunity for trial judges to comment on matters such as the failure of the accused to give evidence, the strength of the case, see chapters 3 and 5.

or criminal trial, any statement of fact made by a witness during evidence-in-chief which is not contradicted through cross-examination is taken to be accepted. In *Bircham*[50] it was in defence counsel's closing speech that he first suggested that the crime was committed by a prosecution witness and a co-defendant. He was stopped from doing this since neither allegation had been put during their cross-examinations.[51] The technique is called 'putting your case'; it is regarded as unfair not to challenge a witness on his or her statement if it is to be contradicted later. Thus in many trials counsel is obliged to ask questions knowing that the witness will not be shaken, and mystifying the jury.

A complex statement from a witness containing numerous allegations all of which need to be challenged by the defence therefore requires an elaborate cross-examination dealing with each point. But, in any event, cross-examination is a necessary counterbalance to the way evidence-in-chief is elicited. Given the way witnesses are guided through their evidence-in-chief (albeit without leading questions as such) the right to cross-examine is essential to the other party. For the questions put in chief may omit, consciously or unconsciously, significant matters, the answers to which could be to the advantage of the other side. There may have been qualifications or explanations which the witness did not have the opportunity to add to his or her in-chief testimony, and which subsequently can be uncovered only by cross-examination.

Cross-examination of witnesses is regarded by many Commonwealth lawyers as the perfect method of establishing the truth, hence the reluctance to abolish the hearsay rule. But it is frequently used to confuse witnesses, to get them to contradict themselves, showing their unreliability. Where there are many documents in a case this is easily done, as a witness is taken through the papers and asked to explain entries in them about which he or she can remember nothing. It is clear from Adler's research[52] that cross-examination of rape complainants is often used simply to humiliate them and therefore undermine the confidence with which they describe the alleged events.[53] Yet the goodwill of witnesses is necessary for the protection

---

[50] [1972] Crim LR 430. For exceptions, see Phipson, *Evidence*, 14th edn (Sweet & Maxwell, London, 1990), para. 12.13. This is not the rule in Scotland although failure to question in relation to a disputed fact may be made the subject of comment: A. G. Walker and N. M. L. Walker, *The Law of Evidence in Scotland* (Hodge, Edinburgh, 1964), pp. 31–2.

[51] This rule does not apply in the magistrates' court: *O'Connell v Adams* [1973] Crim LR 113.

[52] See chapter 4.

[53] Cf. Newby's research in Western Australia, identifying tactics designed to

of society. Fear of humiliation in cross-examination could affect their willingness to come forward or to report crimes. If a genuine victim suffers a stinging attack from the defence during a trial, it looks as if he or she is being punished for objecting to the crime against him or her, and that is surely not the object of the exercise. We have seen cases where, in the traditional obsessive pursuit of and concern for the interests of the client, valuable witnesses have been relentlessly grilled on matters which by no stretch of the imagination had any useful part to play in the proceedings.[54]

The extensive use of leading questions in cross-examination is assumed by lawyers to provide them with a scalpel with which they can clinically and remorselessly lay bare the truth. Egglestone, however, is not convinced;[55] the assumption underlying lawyers' faith in cross-examination is that all honest witnesses are equally capable of holding their own against this barrage. But people are not uniformly articulate, confident and emotionally balanced. Defendants in criminal cases, however, are unlikely to score highly in these departments:

> I have known a number of defendants who have really been quite psychologically disturbed and have been quite wrongly put into the witness box...against advice, and it has really been cutting up salami as far as the cross-examination is concerned and served up for the jury to eat. Sometimes, thankfully, juries, without any sort of caution, can see what is going on.[56]

Questions apparently designed to undermine a witness's credibility move so far from the matter to which he or she has deposed[57] that observers find the result highly inconclusive. McBarnett,[58] however, concedes that, given the nature of examination-in-chief, cross-examination is indispensable, but this is a major problem for the unrepresented defendant who has not the technique to undertake it.

demoralize rather than clarify: 'Rape victims in court: the Western Australian example', in *Rape Law Reform*, ed. J. A. Scutt (Australian Institute of Criminology, Canberra, 1980).

[54] E.g. *Hutchinson* (1986) 82 Cr App R 51 where the highly unconvincing defence of consent was run by a known Broadmoor escapee, who accused a journalist in court during the trial; consent was put at interminable length to the chief prosecution witness, who was required by the state to testify not only to her own rape, but to the murders of several of her family on the same occasion.

[55] Egglestone, 'What is wrong with the adversarial system?' (1975) 49 ALJ 428.

[56] Dr Silverman, in discussion following Gudjonsson, 'The psychology of false confessions', *Medico-Legal Journal*, 57 (1989), p. 93.

[57] D. McBarnett, *Conviction* (Macmillan, London, 1983).

[58] Ibid.

Research by psychologists casts considerable doubt on the value of leading questions. Lawyers appear to regard it as significant if a witness is led to contradict him- or herself, but work on suggestibility shows how ready witnesses are to adopt 'planted' information contained in the question.[59] Yuille tested witnesses who already had an accurate memory of the event, and they were harder to mislead.[60] But if the questioner demonstrates an apparent level of knowledge, the suggestibility of the witness increases.[61] The language used by the questioner can be enough to affect the memory, as in Loftus and Palmer's famous question, 'About how fast were the cars going when they smashed into/collided with/bumped into/hit each other?' The choice of verb had a dramatic effect on the witness's estimation of the speed of cars in an accident he had been shown on film.[62] Gudjonsson's research into acquiescent, suggestible and compliant personalities' tendency to be misled by leading questions[63] suggests even more grounds for anxiety. The personality of the subject, combined with the circumstances in which he or she is questioned, dramatically affects suggestibility. People may not declare their actual uncertainty because they believe that they must provide an answer, or that it is expected of them that they know the answer and are capable of giving it.[64] Courts of law, by accident or design, are ideally suited to effect such an interpretation by a witness. It should be noted at this point that the doubts engendered by such research must be carried over into the controversy surrounding techniques used in 'disclosure' interviews with children suspected of having suffered abuse. The context and purpose of these interviews are very different from cross-examinations in court, but, clearly, research into the reliability of answers obtained in both circumstances must be compared with caution.[65] The same anxiety should also affect the extent to which confession evidence can be considered reliable. If counsel succeeds in shaking the confidence of a witness, who begins to look nervous and

---

[59] Loftus, 'Leading questions and the eyewitness report', *Cognitive Psychology*, 7 (1975), p. 560.

[60] Yuille, 'A critical examination of the psychology and practical implications of eyewitness research', *Law and Human Behaviour*, 4 (1980), p. 335.

[61] Smith and Ellsworth, 'The social psychology of eyewitness accuracy: misleading questions and communicator expertise', *Journal of Applied Psychology*, 72 (1987), p. 294.

[62] Loftus and Palmer, 'Reconstruction of automobile destruction: an example of the interaction between language and memory', *Journal of Verbal Learning and Verbal Behaviour*, 13 (1974), p. 585.

[63] Gudjonnson and Clark, 'Suggestibility in police interrogation; a social psychological model', *Social Behaviour*, 1 (1986), p. 83; see chapter 6.

[64] Ibid., p. 92.

[65] See chapter 4.

unsure, is this an indicator of unreliability? Köhnken,[66] who found lawyers to be just another group of people who overestimate their ability to recognize dishonesty, shows that skilful liars respond well to tough questions, indicative of suspicion. They are capable of adjusting their behaviour to conform to stereotypes of honesty, whereas an honest witness may, when nervous, appear decidedly unconvincing. Confident witnesses are more likely to be believed,[67] but research finds no consistent relationship between eyewitness confidence and accuracy.[68]

Damaska argues[69] that the Continental trial is more attuned to the fact that individuals have different cognitive needs. All lay assessors exercise the right to ask questions of their own, although not as frequently as one might expect.[70] Jurors in English criminal courts are extraordinarily passive, given the importance of their decision, which the adversarial system seems designed to make it difficult to reach with any degree of confidence. If two versions of the story are presented, each in the most favourable light possible, it is difficult to be sure that one of them is the accurate account (remembering that to lawyers, it may be that the object of the exercise is *not* to arrive at the truth, only to achieve a 'just settlement of the dispute').[71] And, as we shall see, the rules of evidence may be seen to suppose that the object of a criminal trial is not to ascertain the objectively accurate picture of the facts, but to adjudge how effectively or otherwise the prosecution has proved its case.[72]

Disclosure of evidence

If the trial were an entirely adversarial proceeding, it would be the responsibility of the parties to furnish their own evidence in support of their case. Yet we find that in criminal cases defendants may expect help from the prosecution in supplying some information which otherwise they might find it difficult or impossible to uncover. There seems no reason in theory why one

[66] Köhnken, 'Psychological approaches to the assessment of the credibility of child witness statements', in Spencer, Nicholson, Flin and Bull (eds).

[67] Daffebaker and Loftus, 'Do jurors share a common understanding concerning eyewitness behaviour?', *Law and Human Behaviour*, 6 (1982), p. 15.

[68] Yarmey and Jones, 'Is the study of eyewitness identification a matter of common sense?', in *Evaluating Witness Evidence*, eds S. Lloyd-Bostock and B. Clifford (Wiley, Chichester, 1983).

[69] Damaska (1973) 121 U Penn LR 506, 545.

[70] Casper and Zeisel, 'Lay judges in the German courts' (1972) 1 JL Stud 143.

[71] Damaska (1973) 121 U Penn LR 506, 580.

[72] See chapter 2.

adversary should be required to do this; the principle that the prosecutor should supply information to the defence would appear to have more to do with obligation to the truth or with the presumption of innocence than with the idea of opponents researching for and adducing material for themselves. Merely exchanging details as to what evidence a party proposes to call is not, prima facie, inconsistent with the adversarial ideal. The task of investigation remains the party's own. But, as we shall see below, such a practice establishes a foundation for a shift towards more inquisitorial procedures involving less emphasis on oral evidence and argument. Emphasis on the trial itself is reduced; advanced notice of the evidence to be presented by the other side together with details of the legal basis of its case enables each party to adjust his or her case in advance of the proceedings. This reduces the surprise element which can result in some unmeritorious triumphs. At present, in the criminal case, the prosecution must supply witness statements in the committal bundle for offences triable either way or on indictment,[73] so that the accused will know precisely the nature of the case against him or her. This does not apply in summary cases, so the defence advocate has to persuade a prosecutor who is unwilling to show the statements.[74] The only defence duties to inform the prosecution are to give advance notice of any alibi witness to be called[75] and, like the prosecution, to give advance notice of any expert evidence to be relied upon in the Crown Court.[76] There is an exception to this in the case of serious fraud trials: under section 9 of the Criminal Justice Act 1987, the judge may at a preparatory hearing order both prosecution and defence to disclose their case. This provision represents a somewhat belated recognition that the traditional right to take the prosecution completely by surprise is entirely inappropriate, at least to complicated cases. The imbalance of the disclosure obligation as between prosecution and defence in most cases is explicable only in part by reference to the presumption of innocence; forcing the prosecution to prove its case beyond all reasonable doubt does not necessarily involve revealing its nature in advance. The fact that this occurs enables a defendant to be ready with evidence in rebuttal, if he or she has it. This leaves less to chance, as far as the defence is concerned, and thus brings the court nearer to the truth. But some police officers and prosecutors query the wisdom of not allowing the situation in reverse, although one reply would be that knowing the defence case in advance would allow prosecution witnesses to tailor their evidence

---

[73] Magistrates' Courts (Advance Information) Rules 1985 (S.I. 1985 No. 601).

[74] See P. Murphy and D. Barnard, *Evidence and Advocacy* (Financial Training, London, 1984), p. 61.

[75] Criminal Justice Act 1967, s. 11.

[76] Police and Criminal Evidence Act 1984, s. 81; Crown Court (Advance Notice of Expert Evidence) Rules 1987 (S.I. 1987 No. 716).

accordingly. Since the accused is at risk of conviction, unlike any other participant in the trial, that situation must be avoided.

Much harder to reconcile with adversarial theory is the duty[77] of the prosecutor to disclose 'unused material' to the defence. The defence must be given the unedited version of any statement by any witness upon whom the prosecution proposes to rely, and, if the prosecution elects not to call a witness who could give material evidence, his or her name and address must be supplied to the defence. Although it has been said that there is no duty to hand over any statement made by the witness,[78] the Court of Appeal recently advised that it would be wrong, and in some cases reprehensible, to conceal from the court the evidence such a witness could give.[79] The defence should also be advised of any material inconsistency between the evidence given by a prosecution witness and a previous statement in the possession of the prosecution,[80] any known previous convictions of prosecution witnesses,[81] and, if asked for, any previous convictions of the defendant, since the defence must know about these before deciding whether to put his or her character in issue.[82]

In civil cases, again, there are obligations on the parties to assist each other in their search for relevant material. At the close of pleadings, both parties must present a list of documents in their possession, whether adverse to their case or not.[83] The pleadings have not provided a list of witnesses, or proofs of their evidence, but in the Commercial Court the practice has developed of providing these. Although in no civil case has a party a duty to point out the existence of non-documentary evidence which may assist the other side, professional ethics demand that counsel does not mislead the court. This means not pleading a case inconsistent with evidence of which counsel is aware, without drawing it to the attention of the judge.[84] These procedures

---

[77] *Attorney-General's Guidelines* [1982] 1 All ER 734.

[78] *Bryant and Dickson* (1946) 31 Cr App R 146; but doubted, *Dallison v Caffery* [1965] 1 QB 348.

[79] *Lawson, The Times*, 21 June 1989.

[80] *Howe*, 27 March 1950, CCA, unreported. See J. F. Archbold, *Criminal Pleading, Evidence, and Practice*, 43rd edn (Sweet & Maxwell, London, 1988), para. 4.179.

[81] *Collister and Warhurst* (1955) 39 Cr App R 100.

[82] *Practice Direction* [1966] 2 All ER 929, para. 1.

[83] RSC Ord. 24.

[84] The interpretation of these ethical standards is not without difficulty, and one reason for opposition from the Bar to a general right of audience for all solicitors in the High Court is a fear that solicitors, who are frequently closely involved with their clients over years, may be more tempted than counsel would be to allow or even suggest non-disclosure of inconvenient documents. Introducing contingency fee payment for litigation would obviously exacerbate the problem, if it is a real one, by giving lawyers a direct financial interest in the outcome of the case.

may at first sight appear to be inconsistent with the adversarial tradition, which suggests that the parties should be turning up information entirely by their own efforts, but they acknowledge reality in that otherwise it would be impossible to predict what, if any, relevant documentary material the other side might have in their hands. The duty not to mislead the court shows that although some rules create the impression that all that it represents is a neutral facility, it is recognized that courts must never be associated in the public consciousness with underhandedness or injustice.

In the civil jurisdiction in England and Wales, recent years have seen a striking and radical departure in the procedural approach to litigation. The Commercial Court practice of exchanging written witness statements prior to the trial, which since 1986 has been an optional direction by the master in the Chancery Division,[85] has been the subject of considerable expansion. First the validity of the rule itself was challenged as an *ultra vires* attempt to alter the substantive law of evidence concerning privilege against disclosure of communications with legal advisers. In *Comfort Hotels v Wembley Stadium*[86] Hoffman J rejected that argument and found that RSC Order 38, rule 2A was entirely procedural and did not purport to change the rules of evidence. He held that it was not concerned with the proof of particular facts but with the general procedure for adducing evidence at the trial. The judge embodied in his judgment the remarks of Master Jacob,[87] which are reproduced in the *Supreme Court Practice*:[88]

> This significant rule constitutes an outstanding and far-reaching change in the machinery of civil justice. It extends the bounds of pre-trial discovery to the area of the evidence of facts, and it does so not by way of taking the depositions of the witnesses by their oral examination as in America, nor by way of 'examination for discovery' by the oral examination of the parties as in Canada, but by way of the direct written statement of the witnesses of their evidence of the facts which they can prove of their own knowledge. It embodies a fundamental innovation in the law and practice relating to the identity of the intended trial witnesses of the parties and relating to the confidentiality of their statements or 'proofs' of evidence. It provides a radical alteration to the manner of elucidating the evidence in chief of witnesses at the trial by their oral examination in open court…It removes some of the defective factors and the more confrontational aspects of the adversary system of civil procedure. Above all it greatly improves the pre-trial process by provid-

---

[85] RSC Ord. 38, r. 2A.

[86] [1988] 1 WLR 872.

[87] Ibid., p. 875.

[88] *Supreme Court Practice* (Sweet & Maxwell, London, 1988), vol. 1, para. 38/2A/2, p. 595.

ing the machinery for enabling parties to know before the trial precisely what facts are intended to be proved at the trial, and by whom, and thereby it reduces delay, costs and the opportunity for procedural technicalities and obstruction towards the trial.

Having received this judicial seal of approval this rule, described as making 'an enormous and notable advance towards the open system of pre-trial procedure',[89] has recently been extended to *all* areas of the civil jurisdiction of the High Court.[90] Perhaps most significantly of all, the Chancery Division has now by Practice Direction adopted the rule for exchange of witness statements as the ordinary practice, directing that 'henceforward on the hearing of the summons for directions the master will normally make an order for the exchange of witness statements of all oral evidence which any party intends to lead at the trial'.[91] From being merely an available direction in a particular case the practice is now, in the Chancery Division, to be adopted as a matter of course. Encouraging mutual exchange in advance of information between the parties is seen as desirable to curtail the duration and expense of the trial and to encourage earlier settlements. Taken with the growing practice of requiring written 'skeleton' arguments, written submissions and the traditional exchange of authorities, however, it can be seen that the entire framework of the modern civil trial is becoming more 'paper-oriented', and with pre-trial exchange of witness proofs the significance and impact of the trial itself – even with its adversarial features intact – become greatly reduced. In this way, the English and European models are moving closer together.

Recently, the House of Lords has encouraged further progress towards inquisitorial procedures, emphasizing that costly court time could be saved if judges were to make themselves familiar with the case in advance. In *Banque Keyser Ullmann SA v Skandia (UK) Insurance Co*[92] Lord Templeman condemned the opportunities for time wasting which reliance on the 'day in court' affords:

> Proceedings in which all or some of the litigants indulge in over-elaboration cause difficulties to judges at all levels in the achievement of a just result. Such proceedings obstruct the hearing of other litigation…The costs must be formidable…The present practice is to allow every litigant unlimited time and unlimited scope so that the litigant and his advisers are able to conduct their

---

[89] Ibid., para. 38/2A/1.

[90] RSC (Amendments) 1988 (S.I. 1988 No. 40).

[91] *Practice Direction (Chancery: Summons for Directions)* [1989] 1 WLR 133.

[92] [1990] 3 WLR 364, 380; cf. *Spiliada Maritime Corp v Cansulex Ltd* [1987] AC 460.

case in all respects in the way which seems best to them. The results not infrequently are torrents of words, written and oral, which are oppressive and which the judge must examine in an attempt to eliminate everything which is not relevant, helpful and persuasive. The remedy lies in the judge taking time to read in advance pleadings, documents certified by counsel to be necessary, and short skeleton arguments of counsel, and for the judge then, after a short discussion in open court, to limit the time and scope of oral evidence and the time and scope of oral argument. The appellate courts should be unwilling to entertain complaints concerning the results of this practice.

Barring the appearance of an advocate-general, this description is highly reminiscent of proceedings in the European Court at Luxembourg. Whether or not it is entirely feasible within the existing English commercial framework may be doubted,[93] but the same will be true of the new care proceedings to be instituted under the Children Act 1989; there will be disclosure of witness statements to the parties and to the court, and pre-trial hearings to identify both the most appropriate court in which to hear the application and further evidence which may assist.

Development of exclusionary rules

It has long been thought that the British tradition of trial by jury has played a substantial part in the evolution of the rules of evidence. Phipson argues that the law of evidence assumes jury trial: 'It is of importance that they should not have before them matters which it is not proper for them to take into account when arriving at a verdict.'[94] Thus, it is supposed that in civil trials the rules are considerably less rigid; the Civil Evidence Act 1968 is thought to have relaxed many restrictions on admissibility, particularly those connected with the hearsay rule. But this is now a myth; in reality, civil cases would collapse under the weight of time and expense if the hearsay provisions of the Civil Evidence Act were actually complied with. It is now considerably more straightforward to admit documentary hearsay evidence in criminal trials under the Criminal Justice Act 1988. Civil cases depend heavily on the willingness of the parties to dispense with the formalities, accepting technically inadmissible evidence by consent.[95] It is very rare for that consent to be withheld, since the disadvantage to both sides in cases involving large quantities of 'paper' (as most commercial cases do), were

---

[93] For example Harmon J in *Re Harrods (Buenos Aires) Ltd* [1990] BCC 481, 486; see chapter 8.

[94] Phipson, *Evidence*, para. 1.02.

[95] See chapter 7.

such evidence to be unavailable, would be considerable, and in some cases insuperable.

Thayer and Wigmore[96] regarded the survival of the jury as highly important to the historical origin and continuance of the exclusionary rules, although the latter also attributed some of these to the limitations imposed by the trial having to be held at a fixed time and place (which applies equally to civil cases). Yet the exclusionary rules are retained in Singapore despite the abolition of trial by jury in non-capital criminal cases.[97] Professor Morgan[98] is more sceptical of the claim that so much turns on the presence of the jury at a criminal trial. The first juries were expected to inquire locally into the disputed events, and therefore were likely to rely heavily on second-hand information. Doubts as to the capacity of jurors realistically to assess the proper weight of hearsay evidence were first expressed (comparatively recently) in *Wright v Tatham*,[99] by which time the hearsay rule had been operating for a hundred years at least. Earlier cases had reflected concern about the inability to cross-examine the maker of the original statement. Cross acknowledges that the presence of lay jurors does not entirely account for the development of exclusionary rules, suggesting that a second factor is the common law adversarial system of procedure.[100]

There are examples within the English jurisdiction of non-adversarial proceedings, both with and without juries. Coroners' courts, which, although juries are used less than before, must have a jury for inquests into deaths in prison, deaths from notifiable accidents or diseases, and cases where there is a risk of prejudice to public health or safety,[101] are non-accusatorial proceedings which are not circumscribed by the usual procedural and evidential restrictions: an inquest 'is an inquisitorial process, a process of investigation, quite unlike a trial where the prosecutor accuses and the accused defends, the judge holding the balance'.[102] Consequently, it is for the coroner to decide which witnesses are to be summoned to attend.[103] Yet, it is interesting to note, the leading textbook on inquests, while acknowledging

---

[96] See W. Twining, *Theories of Evidence: Bentham and Wigmore* (Weidenfeld & Nicolson, London, 1985).

[97] Criminal Procedure Code (Amendment) Act 1969.

[98] E. M. Morgan, *Some Problems of Proof under the Anglo-American System of Litigation* (University of North Carolina, New York, 1956).

[99] (1837) 7 Ad & E 313.

[100] C. Tapper and R. Cross, *Evidence*, 6th edn (Butterworths, London, 1985), p. 1. A third factor is said to be the importance attached to the oath.

[101] Coroners (Amendment) Act 1926, s. 13(2).

[102] *R v South London Coroner, ex p Thompson* (1982) 126 SJ 625.

[103] *McKerr v Armagh Coroner* [1990] 1 All ER 865.

that they are not bound by the rules of evidence, nevertheless reproduces a basic outline of them 'to reduce as far as possible the number of occasions upon which it is necessary to depart from them'.[104] The General and Special Commissioners of Income Tax are also given rather more freedom than the conventional court; they can summon a witness at any stage of proceedings before them if those called by the parties appear to them to be unlikely to supply all the relevant evidence.[105]

There has recently been considerable confusion about the nature of proceedings concerned with child welfare. It had been supposed that care proceedings were 'essentially non-adversarial',[106] and that therefore the strict rules of evidence did not apply. This belief was weakened by the Court of Appeal decision in *Re H and Re K*,[107] where the privilege of exemption from those restrictions was held to be solely that of the High Court exercising the wardship jurisdiction; however much other courts might feel that the purpose of the proceedings is simply to protect the welfare of the child in question, the normal rules, including the hearsay rule, apply.[108] The absurdity of attempting to force this kind of case into the stereotypical model of civil adversaries battling it out was the reason that Lord Widgery distinguished care proceedings in *Humberside*,[109] where he reasoned that it would be entirely inappropriate for the admissibility of an admission of misconduct in a care case to depend on whether or not it came from a party (in the strict sense) to the proceedings. Yet in *Bradford City Metropolitan Council v K*[110] the doubts expressed in *Re H and Re K* were resolved in a categorical assertion that the hearsay rule applied in care proceedings. The chaos resulting from this dichotomy between wardship and other kinds of case dealing with child abuse is under review.[111] It is obvious that resolution of the question whether or not such rules should apply will have nothing to do with the fact that no juries are involved.

A further, closely related and still highly influential factor in the development and dominance of exclusionary rules, it is submitted, is that of the presumption of innocence.[112] It governs the order of events in criminal trials,

---

[104] P. Matthews and J. C. Foreman, *Jervis on Coroners* (Sweet & Maxwell, London, 1986), paras. 15.24–5.
[105] Taxes Management Act 1970, s. 52.
[106] Lord Widgery CJ in *Humberside County Council v DPR (an Infant)* [1977] 3 All ER 964.
[107] [1989] FCR 356.
[108] *In Re W (Minors)*, The Times, 10 November 1989.
[109] [1977] 3 All ER 964, 966.
[110] *The Times*, 18 August 1989.
[111] See chapter 7.
[112] Under attack, see chapter 5.

the exclusion, in general, of the accused's bad character although that of all other witnesses is admissible,[113] and the operation of the right to silence.[114] Furthermore, although the inability to cross-examine absent witnesses is one of the objections to hearsay evidence, we find that since 1988 the disadvantage is regarded as significant, and therefore a justification for excluding the evidence, only where it affects the defence.[115] Many defenders of the adversarial trial in fact argue that it is the most effective means of preserving the right of the unconvicted to be presumed innocent until proved guilty.[116]

A common criticism of the structure of the Anglo-American trial is that it is a device to protect the interests of lawyers; the minefield of technical requirements in evidence and procedure is a fertile source of appeals, many of which have no intrinsic merit. But it is not central to the theory of adversarial trial that these rules should be rigid. The same object could be achieved by leaving it to the discretion of the trial judges whether particular items of evidence should be admitted; appeals would then succeed only where the discretion has been improperly exercised. The idea that judicial discretion should replace the current law of evidence is highly controversial. In Canada, for example, the legal profession mounted strong resistance to the suggestions of the Law Reform Commission of Canada, whose Draft Evidence Code would provide a more flexible system with a greater role for judicial discretion. An unrepentant advocate of the proposals, Professor Delisle, has pointed out that the rules of evidence themselves were originally merely illustrations of the exercise of judicial common sense; but guidance which was developed to help judges use their discretion wisely has ossified into unhelpful and sometimes lunatic rigidity.[117] At the same time, in reality considerable discretion already exists behind the technical distinctions, and leading writers have identified the advantages of this.[118] For instance, Pattenden lists these as being that it may be impossible to formulate a rule in some contexts, it avoids bad results in hard cases, and enables the court to

---

[113] See chapter 5.

[114] See chapter 5.

[115] Criminal Justice Act 1988, ss. 25, 26; see chapter 7.

[116] E.g. Wright (1929) 45 LQR 98, whose observations of French criminal trials led him to conclude that the defendant appeared to be presumed guilty from the start. However, he gave insufficient weight to the preparatory stage, *instruction*, which, the French believe, ensures that there is a strong case for the prosecution which the defendant should be required to answer. This explains the admittedly hostile attacks by some presidents in the opening examination of the accused.

[117] Delisle, 'Judicial discretion and the law of evidence', paper presented to Conference of Society for the Reform of the Criminal Law (London, July 1987).

[118] E.g. Zuckerman, *Principles*, p. 12; R. Pattenden, *The Judge, Discretion and the Criminal Trial* (OUP, Oxford, 1982).

strike the right balance between conflicting interests.[119] There is a certain amount of intellectual dishonesty in objecting to discretion determining the admissibility of evidence and at the same time defending the current system, where so much has been shown already to exist.[120] And we find the judges being given more discretion still, as with the new provisions on documentary hearsay in criminal trials,[121] precisely because it is impossible to formulate rules in advance and preserve fairness and workability. Yet the Pigot Committee on child witnesses in criminal trials[122] appears far more reluctant than the Scottish Law Commission to give judges a general discretion as to the means by which vulnerable witnesses give evidence.[123] It is time to abandon ambivalence, and specifically address the issue of judicial discretion in the law of evidence. As Zuckerman points out, there is little guidance as to its proper exercise developed in a climate where the prevailing fiction is that it does not exist; and the reality is that the more familiar with the current rules judges are, the more they can manipulate them to achieve the result they want. It is quite clear that in practice many judges and advocates virtually ignore such matters as the exceptions to the hearsay rule because they do not understand them. If all participants in the trial are of the same mind, these unwelcome complications effectively cease to exist.

It is difficult, therefore, to be convinced by those who say that to extend judicial discretion would create great uncertainty since it would be impossible to predict in advance what evidence will be used. Yet the legal profession, whether in Canada or in other common law systems, is highly resistant to moves substantially to reform the law of evidence, whether by extending discretion, altering procedure, or, as was seen in the House of Lords when the Criminal Justice Bill was being discussed, introducing new exceptions to existing rules. The scope of the Bill's original provisions on documentary hearsay produced a reaction little short of horror.[124] Is the hostility to change a manifestation of pure self-interest? A cynic might say that the rules are there to enable lawyers to pull technical tricks and manipulate the participants. They can score points or whole victories which are nothing to do with the real merits of the case. But it is probably more realistic to accept that many lawyers are deeply committed to the adversarial trial and the presumption of innocence. The fact that from these foundations springs an eccentric Gothic edifice composed of extraordinary rules, pre-

---

[119] Pattenden, ibid., pp. 35–9.
[120] Delisle, 'Judicial discretion'; Pattenden, ibid.; Zuckerman, *Principles*.
[121] See chapter 7.
[122] *Report of the Advisory Group on Video Evidence* (Home Office 1980).
[123] See chapter 4.
[124] See chapter 7.

sumptions, exceptions and confusion has its own charm. The seductive appeal of this structure in itself breeds a sentimental attachment, so that one might feel that preservation of the traditional form of trial, with all its historic characteristics, is indeed worthwhile to protect England's heritage, just as we conserve ancient monuments.

2

Proving Facts in Court

RELEVANCE

In *R v Blastland*[1] B was charged with the murder of a boy, K. He suggested that the murderer was another man, M, who had been in the vicinity while B was with the boy. M was investigated by the police but not charged. There was evidence that M had arrived home mudstained and told certain witnesses that a boy had been killed in the woods. This was correct, but he said it before K's body had officially been found. In his defence at his trial, B wished to call these witnesses in order to suggest that M's knowledge had not been innocently come by, and could be explained by the conclusion that M had committed the murder himself. The House of Lords upheld the trial judge's decision to disallow this evidence; apart from possible conflict with the rule against hearsay,[2] the evidence of these witnesses should be excluded on the ground that it was irrelevant.

What, then, is the legal perception of relevance? Clearly, evidence which is not relevant is not admissible. There are numerous definitions of relevance, but it is doubtful whether they express its meaning any more clearly than rule 401 of the Federal Rules of Evidence of the United States, which defines relevant evidence as: 'Evidence having any tendency to make the existence of any fact that is of consequence to the determination of the action more probable or less probable than it would be without the evidence.' Unfortunately, the effect of disputed evidence, in terms of whether it does indeed make the fact in issue more probable, is frequently the subject of heated arguments which it may be difficult to resolve. And relevance as an instrument of logical reasoning is not the same thing as relevance as judges

[1] [1985] 2 All ER 1095.
[2] See chapter 7.

see it.[3] Logical relevance is a *sine qua non* of admissibility; but it cannot guarantee that the evidence will be admitted; in fact, on its own it is far from sufficient.[4] Case law has developed a legal refinement upon the concept of relevance, and, whether or not one adopts the complicated distinctions in leading textbooks between relevance (in the judicial sense), materiality and admissibility, it seems that the ultimate fate of evidence which can be seen to be *logically* relevant depends upon the nature and purpose of the trial.

Since it is for the parties to determine which are the issues to be decided in any case, we can see that the relevance of an evidential fact to the matter in dispute depends upon which issues each party chooses to introduce. For instance, if A is accused of murder, is it relevant to his guilt that his wife was having an affair? If the allegation is that he stabbed a supporter of a rival football team in a public house, that fact appears to be irrelevant. But if A pleads that as a result of his wife's affair he suffered severe depressive illness to an extent affecting his responsibility for his action and seeks therefore to rely on the defence of diminished responsibility,[5] the affair is a material fact. A more obvious example is where the wife was herself the victim of the killing, in which case her affair would suggest that he might rely on the defence of provocation,[6] but it is entirely up to A to decide upon what defence (if any) he will rely. That decision can then make a fact which hitherto appeared to be irrelevant an important matter in the case. Some lawyers use the word 'materiality' here, by which they mean the relationship between the evidential fact and the issues in the trial. Whether or not a particular item of evidence is material depends upon whether the party who seeks to adduce it has successfully raised the issue on which it depends, and also on the substantive law. In the example just given, A would not be able to raise the defences of either provocation or diminished responsibility if he were charged with any offence other than murder. In a grievous bodily harm case his wife's affair would be irrelevant on the issue of guilt, although it might have some bearing at the sentencing stage.

Zuckerman has argued that 'materiality' is an unnecessary concept; whether or not a certain fact can affect a legal result is not a question of evidence but of interpreting the substantive law.[7] Zuckerman is right to point

---

[3] E.g. Coleridge J, referring to the 'fallacy that whatever is morally convincing and whatever reasonable beings will form their judgments and act upon, may be submitted to the jury': *Wright v Tatham* (1837) 7 Ad & E 313.

[4] R. W. Baker, *The Hearsay Rule* (Pitman, London, 1950).

[5] Homicide Act 1957, s. 2.

[6] Ibid., s. 3.

[7] Zuckerman, 'Relevance in legal proceedings', in *Facts in Law*, (ed. W. Twining) (Steiner, Wiesbaden, 1983).

out that the trier of fact is concerned only with those facts which the substantive law allows to have legal effect.[8] But it is still within the power of the parties to exclude elements of the substantive law altogether by choosing not to rely on them. It is for the parties to decide upon which planks (depending on the evidence and the law) to rest their case. They may find that they lose the opportunity to introduce an item of evidence if they fail to raise the issue which would render it material, either because they have not satisfied the required procedures[9] or because the evidential burden has not been discharged.[10] Thus the concept of materiality does exist independent of the effect of the substantive law; it is a creature of adversarial theory. Objective facts and operation of law are far from being the only influences on the conduct and outcome of trials; choices made by individuals have an important part to play too.

Remoteness: credibility a collateral issue?

The law imposes artificial limits on evidence which may be both relevant and material, by demanding that other conditions are met. For there are limits to the amount of time and energy which courts are prepared to expend on cases in court. If the inquiry is not to go on for ever, there have to be limits on its scope. To this end, the law has developed a distinction between matters of central importance to the case, and those which are only peripheral (or collateral or subordinate) to the main issue. Also, judges talk of 'probative force' as opposed to relevance; some writers consider that relevance is absolute (either the fact is a relevant fact or it is not) whereas facts can have varying degrees of probative significance.[11] For instance, if a rape is committed by a man who throughout sang 'Land of Hope and Glory', is it relevant that the man charged with the rape has in his flat a copy of the sheet music of that patriotic song? It is relevant in that he would find it difficult to deny that he knows it. If it were the only music in the flat it might have some probative value in suggesting that it is a particular favourite. But if he has

---

[8] A. Zuckerman, *The Principles of Criminal Evidence* (OUP, Oxford, 1989), p. 52.

[9] E.g. in civil cases pleadings must contain the necessary particulars of any claim, defence or matter pleaded: RSC Ord. 18, r. 12. This limits the generality of issues at the subsequent trial.

[10] If A's defence above had been automatism, for example, he must raise it by introducing evidence of involuntariness. If he does not do this, the evidence of medical experts on the likely effect of epilepsy or diabetes is immaterial. A must make the issue 'live' by adducing evidence of his own condition. See below.

[11] J. Michael and M. Adler, *The Nature of Judicial Proof* (privately printed, 1931); Trautman, 'Logical or legal relevancy – a conflict in theory' (1952) 5 Vand LR 385; *contra* Cross, who states that 'Relevance is a matter of degree': C. Tapper and R. Cross, *Evidence*, 7th edn (Butterworths, London, 1990), p. 56.

many shelves of sheet music the probative value diminishes, and may reach the point where it has insufficient significance and is inadmissible. To say that it is irrelevant overstates the situation – he *does* know 'Land of Hope and Glory'. But, since many other people also know it, his knowledge on its own may not be of sufficient probative value to interest the court. If relevance is a variable quality, then it is not sufficiently relevant to be admissible.

The exigencies of time and place inevitably restrict courts of law in their assessment of the relevance of evidence. They cannot afford the sort of thoroughness which a scientist would employ before reaching a conclusion. Hence Phipson's assessment: 'Evidence is not a matter of mere logic. It is a question of ascertaining the truth as to facts that are in dispute. Such an inquiry must be reasonable, practical and fair.'[12] The problem is that although restricting the scope of the inquiry may be necessary for practical reasons, it may impede the establishing of the truth. If this is the case, then it is not fair. One example of legal recognition of this is the number of exceptions to the rule that witnesses may not be challenged by contradictory evidence on answers given in cross-examination to questions relating to their credibility.[13] The rule assumes that the credibility of a witness is a collateral, not a central, issue, and therefore answers to questions put in cross-examination on that collateral issue are final. Although the rule keeps the scope of the inquiry within reasonable practical limits, it would be wrong to apply it uncompromisingly. In fact the recognized exceptions are an implied acknowledgement that some facts affecting credibility are of central importance – such as a witness's criminal record,[14] or an interest in the case which could lead to him or her being biased.[15] Yet the law of evidence, in its frequent attempt to draw a distinction between facts relating to guilt and those relating to credit, assumes that there is a clear logical distinction between the two.

Zuckerman, on the other hand, argues most powerfully that the credibility of witnesses is always relevant to the issue in the proceedings, and therefore the distinction between collateral questions and those going to the issue is unsound. He suggests that for this reason the principle is often ignored. He gives as an example an eyewitness, W, who says that he saw a stabbing from 50 yards and identifies the accused as the attacker. The defence has evidence that W cannot see beyond 10 yards. In strict law, they cannot use this evidence if W insists in cross-examination that he can see perfectly well. Yet, argues Zuckerman, the court could not properly convict in such a case.[16]

---

[12] Phipson, *Evidence*, 13th edn (Sweet & Maxwell, London, 1982), para. 6. 04.

[13] *Harris v Tippett* (1811) 2 Camp 637.

[14] The witness's denial can be disproved; Criminal Procedure Act 1865, s. 6.

[15] *A-G v Hitchcock* (1847) 1 Exch 91.

[16] Zuckerman, *Principles*, p. 95.

Presumably for this reason, many judges would disregard the restriction and allow the evidence to be called. The problem appears to arise because the distinction between evidence which goes to the issue and evidence which goes to credibility does not exist in logic, only in the minds of lawyers. In other contexts we recognize that probative value can vary according to the issues and the other available evidence – hence the rather haphazard set of exceptions to the general rule that a witness cannot be contradicted by evidence on answers given while being cross-examined on credibility.[17] In *Busby*[18] police officers were cross-examined to the effect that they invented alleged admissions by D, and had threatened a potential witness. The Court of Appeal held that it went beyond establishing credibility, and related to an issue, which was whether police officers would go so far to secure a conviction. Effectively, here the credibility of a particular witness *was* the issue. The reality is that credibility, or, more particularly, specific facts connected with the credibility of a witness, may or may not be important, given the other evidence before the court in the light of the arguments relied on. Hence the exceptions relating to particular *kinds* of credibility evidence, which all involve recognition that in some cases the witness's credibility is crucial; but the exceptions are too narrow.

In an Australian case, *Piddington v Bennett and Wood*,[19] P sought damages from D, alleging that he had been injured by a motor car as a result of D's negligence. One of P's witnesses claimed to have seen the accident, and was asked in cross-examination to account for his presence at the scene. He replied that he had gone to the bank to deposit or withdraw money in relation to a certain account. There had in fact been no transactions in respect of that account that day, and D was allowed to call the bank manager to say so, despite P's objection. The High Court of Australia was divided on the correctness of the trial judge's decision. The three judges in the majority held that the evidence was wrongly admitted, since the credibility of the witness was only collateral. According to the test in *Hitchcock*,[20] the court was right, as Egglestone explains: 'Evidence about [the] bank account could not have been relevant in any sense if that particular witness had not given that answer in cross-examination. But the case demonstrates the difficulty of drawing the line.'[21]

[17] See *Hitchcock* (1847) 1 Exch 91.

[18] [1982] Crim LR 232.

[19] (1940) 63 CLR 533.

[20] The matter is central if the party seeking to adduce the evidence would have been allowed to do so as part of his or her case in chief, irrespective of what a witness may or may not say: (1847) 1 Exch 91, 99, *per* Pollock CB.

[21] R. Egglestone, *Evidence, Proof and Probability*, 2nd edn (Weidenfeld & Nicolson, London, 1983), pp. 76–7.

The question remains whether the line is worth drawing at all. Facts do not fall neatly into two categories relating to issues which are either collateral (including credit) or central. Sometimes the matter of the state of an identifying witness's eyesight is of crucial importance, and should be investigated with just as much vigour as his or her criminal record, bias or previous inconsistent statements.[22] But if we have to conclude from Zuckerman's argument that the kind of general character evidence such as employment record, which is commonly put to witnesses on the assumption that any disagreeable characteristics go to credibility, is central, we are putting the case too strongly. The apparent inability of judges to protect rape complainants from cross-examination on previous sexual relationships, despite statutory reform,[23] indicates the blurred line between questions going to an issue in the trial and questions going to credit. Zuckerman should not be taken to propose the gratuitous humiliation of even more of such witnesses. The point is that previous sexual history is of little evidential value, as it has no bearing on whether or not the witness would invent a rape. An untrue explanation of why the witness was allegedly at the scene, as in *Piddington*, is of much more interest. The problem in that case resulted entirely from the formal structure of the adversarial trial, with its rigid division between the case in chief and cross-examination, and its insistence that everything be proved 'on the day'. A pre-trial inquiry might have elucidated the matter of the bank account; in any event, it seems unfair to D that what might be an important (or trivial) inconsistency in the witness's story should not be brought out at all, just because he could not have shown the relevance of the bank account evidence to his case in chief since its significance depended entirely on the explanation given by the plaintiff's witness during the trial. Abandoning the inflexible dichotomy between credit and issue, relying instead on the actual probative value of the evidence in the case, would be far more helpful. But it is probably impossible to achieve this while we still require the parties to produce a case in chief setting out the evidence on which their case rests.

Remoteness and probability

Courts have tried to invent devices to draw a line so that the inquiry does not become too bogged down with detail and peripheral facts, but not all solutions appear to be entirely successful. For instance, in *Stephenson*[24] D

---

[22] Criminal Procedure Act 1865, ss. 4, 5.

[23] See chapter 4.

[24] [1976] VR 376.

was accused of causing an accident which killed three people and injured a fourth in another car. Defence counsel wished to introduce evidence of blood tests for the alcohol level of the three dead, but there was no evidence as to who was driving, and it appeared that at least one of them was not over the legal limit. It was held that if all the occupants of that car had been over the limit, that evidence would have been admissible even without evidence as to who was the driver, since logically the driver must have exceeded the limit. But in this case the evidence was so vague that it was inadmissible on the ground of remoteness. Egglestone[25] criticizes this reasoning. If only one of the occupants of the car had been drunk, that would increase the probability of D's claim that the other car was to blame being true, even though the chance of that man being the driver was only one in four. Here the probability was higher than that, and D's chances of conviction were greatly increased by the exclusion of the evidence. Evidence is relevant if it increases or decreases the probability of the existence of a fact in issue. The maxim *res inter alios acta alteria nocere non debet* (nobody should be harmed by a transaction between strangers) sometimes seems to be used as a test, but is not consistently so treated, nor should it be. In *Manchester Brewery v Coombs*[26] the question was whether a brewer had sold bad beer to a publican. The fact that the brewer sold good beer to other publicans was regarded as relevant, since the beer was all from the same brewing. But in *Holcombe v Hewson*,[27] with a similar question, Lord Ellenborough dismissed it as *res inter alios acta*. 'We cannot inquire into the quality of different beer sold to different persons. The party might deal well with one and not with others. I cannot admit evidence of his general character and habits as a brewer.' Here the beer was from various brewings. So the relevance of evidence depends not on a general principle expressed in a maxim, but on the usefulness in probative terms of the facts in question. The probability of bad beer being supplied in the first case, if the brewing was shown to be good, was only slight. In the second, the possibility of one brewing going badly was sufficient for evidence of the quality of other brewings not to take the court much further. It has been argued that some evidence which is highly probative can be excluded under this maxim; if 95 per cent of all motorists at an intersection cut the corner, that fact must have bearing on whether or not the defendant did. His denial asks us to accept that he is exceptional. Yet such evidence would not be admitted. Judges do not wish to involve themselves in sociological inquiries about the probabilities of human beings behaving in a particular way. In *Metropolitan Asylum District v Hill*[28] the

---

[25] Egglestone, *Evidence*, p. 83.
[26] (1900) 82 LT 347.
[27] (1810) 2 Camp 391.
[28] (1882) 47 LT 29.

issue was the effect of a smallpox hospital on the health of the inhabitants of the neighbourhood. A majority of the House of Lords held that evidence of the effect of similar institutions on other localities was inadmissible. There is a general dislike of the style of argument that A caused (or did not cause) B, therefore wherever A occurs B will (or will not) follow and therefore did so here.[29]

It is far from clear, however, that courts can entirely escape this kind of statistical argument. For example, where fingerprint or DNA evidence is adduced, its reliability is assessed in statistical terms; the chances of the wrong person being identified by DNA evidence is said to be one in 30,000 million,[30] or less.[31] Data are available on the significance of sexual play by young children with anatomically correct dolls,[32] evidence which is frequently used in child abuse cases. This kind of statistical evidence does not trouble judges, nor should it. In industrial tribunals, where the issue is whether a condition of employment is such that fewer women than men can comply, statistical evidence has been allowed[33] although in some matters 'general knowledge and expertise' are to be preferred.[34] In cases such as this the statistical evidence is used indirectly, in that it goes to the reliability of other evidence which is used directly in the case. It does not seek to implicate persons on the basis of probability alone, as would have been the case if the general effect of having smallpox hospitals in an area had been allowed as evidence in *Metropolitan Asylum v Hill*. Judith Thompson has explained the difference between 'individualized' and 'non-individualized' evidence. If Mrs Smith was hit by a cab, and if more Red Cabs are operated in town than

[29] Judges are right to be cautious. Egglestone could perhaps himself face the objection frequently levelled at statisticians that they assume a continuity of circumstances. In his example from *Stephenson*, if it were the case that one occupant of the car was sober and the rest drunk, that does not necessarily make it 75 per cent probable that the driver was drunk. The people concerned could have agreed that three would drink and the other drive – a common agreement among party-goers, and, given that the other three were drunk, highly likely.

[30] Kelly, Rankine and Wink, 'Methods and application of DNA fingerprinting: a guide for the non-scientist' [1987] Crim LR 105.

[31] Possibly only tens of millions to one: Hall, 'DNA fingerprints – black box or black hole?' [1990] NLJ 203. Sometimes apparent discrepancies are the result of understanding the expert to be describing the likelihood of finding a duplicate anywhere in the world, when he or she is actually talking about the probability of coincidence between the two samples occurring in a random selection of people.

[32] Glaser and Collins, 'The response of young, non-sexually abused children to anatomically correct dolls', *Journal of Child Psychology and Psychiatry*, 30(4) (1989), p. 547.

[33] *Meeks v NUUAW* [1976] IRLR 198.

[34] *Home Office v Holmes* [1984] IRLR 299.

Green Cabs so that the probability that the cab which caused the accident was a Red Cab is 0.6, why should we be reluctant to impose civil liability on Red Cabs on the basis of that evidence alone? We are equally reluctant to convict of a crime in the following example: T and S both hate Y and independently but simultaneously shoot all the pellets in their shotguns at him. Only one pellet hits Y and kills him. T had 95 pellets, S only 5; if the prosecution can show that T shot 95 pellets out of 100, why have they not proved murder by T beyond reasonable doubt? The objection is that the evidence is not individualized against the defendant in either instance. Thompson, in accepting that weakness, warns against assuming that individualized evidence must therefore be 'uniquely highly probabilifying'; categories of 'real' evidence such as eyewitness identification or confessions have alarming shortcomings of their own,[35] so the explanation cannot be that direct or individualized evidence is more probative than statistical probabilities. She argues that the answer is that it is unjust to act on a probability to someone's disadvantage. To find against a defendant and therefore impose liabilities upon him, to cause him loss, one must feel (rightly or wrongly) that one knows the truth. Knowing that there is a 95 per cent probability of D's guilt is not the same as feeling 95 per cent sure that D is guilty. In her example X has a lottery ticket and Y explains to him that his chance of winning is statistically so slender that he may as well tear it up. His knowledge of the probabilities involved does not entitle him to advise X to act to his own detriment. (If he has knowledge of causally relevant facts, such as a 'fix' in the way the lottery is run, or if he knows that the ticket seller has destroyed X's stubs, he has better grounds.) If Y should tear up X's ticket without his consent, simply because of the low probability of X winning the lottery, X would justifiably feel aggrieved; and if Y should turn out to be right, X would complain that this was only by way of luck, rather than judgment.[36]

A further objection to non-individualized mathematical probabilities being used as items of evidence is shown by the famous American case of *People v Collins*.[37] Witnesses to a robbery said that the culprits were a couple, a male negro with a beard and moustache, and a caucasian woman with her blonde hair in a ponytail. They escaped in a yellow car. Collins, his wife and their car answered this description, and the prosecution called a mathematician to give evidence that there was only a one in 12 million chance that 'a couple' would possess all these features. They were convicted, but the Supreme

[35] See chapter 3.
[36] J. J. Thompson, 'Probabilities as relevant facts', in Thompson, *Rights, Restitution and Risk* (Harvard University Press, Cambridge, Mass., 1986).
[37] 438 P 2d 33 (1968).

Court of California set aside the verdict on appeal. The rival mathematical arguments offered by the court have themselves been challenged;[38] in fact, the extent of disagreement among specialists coupled with the impenetrability of the debate for lay persons[39] suggests that judges have been well advised not to be drawn into the field of probability. But it is obvious to anyone that the evidence in *Collins* suffered from the number of imponderables in the 'population of interest',[40] that is, whether the search for the couple was random over the whole country, and if not, how was it limited? Also, the idea that people occupy an item known as a 'couple' on a permanent basis is unconvincing. Certainly, Collins and his wife are a couple for some purposes, but there is no particular reason to assume that the robbers were a couple in any context apart from committing a robbery, and none whatever to conclude that they were married to each other!

Relevance and Blastland

Judges appear determined to turn the (to others) logical concept of relevance into a creature of their own making. This policy is further illustrated in the case of *Blastland* mentioned at the beginning of the chapter. How should we explain the view of the House of Lords that M's knowledge of the boy's death before it was officially known was irrelevant? Lord Bridge explained that it might have been relevant if the prosecution could show that M came by this knowledge by committing the crime himself, but the evidence did not amount to that. M could have acquired it in various other ways, for instance by witnessing the murder. Given that B would not have been able to use a confession by M if he had made one,[41] the evidence here had an even weaker case for admissibility. It is difficult to follow Lord Bridge's reasoning. An out-of-court confession by a third person is certainly inadmissible under the hearsay rule, but that does not affect the potential relevance of the behaviour of M. The significance of that was the justifiable inference from it that he knew a boy had been killed because he had killed him himself. Lord Bridge suggested that if an eyewitness had seen M do it, that would have been relevant because it would have been direct evidence against M, rather than a possible interpretation of the evidence, as here. Thus it seems that a defendant may not make out a circumstantial case against another person, but may

---

[38] Finkelstein and Fairley, 'A Bayesian approach to identification evidence' (1970) 83 Harv LR 489; Kreith, 'Mathematics, social decisions and the law', *International Journal of Mathematical Education in Science and Technology*, 7(3) (1976), p. 315.
[39] Egglestone, *Evidence*, pp. 159–76.
[40] See ibid.
[41] Because it would be hearsay; *Turner* (1975) 61 Cr App R 67.

accuse another of the crime if he has direct evidence against him – and then not if it is a confession, since that is hearsay.

The Court of Appeal in an earlier case, however, seems to have gone even further than the House of Lords. In *Steel*[42] the defence wished to put to a police witness during cross-examination questions concerning the interrogation by police of one R. R had given the police an alibi which Steel wished to contradict. The trial judge refused to allow such questions on the ground that R's statements to the officer were hearsay. In the Court of Appeal Lord Lane CJ agreed that it probably was hearsay, but added that it 'is absolutely certain that what Mr R may or may not have been doing as related by the police or anyone else at this particular time was an irrelevance, and on that basis the evidence was rightly rejected'. This view of the Court of Appeal is not limited to the narrower ground given in *Blastland* (that what M knew or did not know had nothing to do with the case) since here the claim is that what R *did* was nothing to do with the case. The allegation that someone other than the accused was responsible for the crime is most frequently made where several persons are jointly charged, but is seen often enough in other cases to show the remarks in *Steel* to be a misleading exaggeration. In his judgment Milmo J referred to a case cited by the defence in which the out-of-court confession of a third person was admitted, but dismissed it on the grounds that the hearsay rule was never mentioned. This case, *Cooper*,[43] is of some interest. A group of youths were harassing a girl whose friend walked off in embarrassment. The friend realized help was needed and turned back, only to be punched in the face by one the youths. The others she did not see. She selected C at an identification parade, but other evidence undermined the significance of this. A member of the gang accused another member, B, of being the assailant. A friend, D, gave evidence that B admitted to him that he had hit the girl. From photographs, which the jury saw, the physical resemblance between C and B was 'really quite striking'. Lord Widgery CJ was not in the least disturbed by all this evidence going before the jury; on the contrary, he commented that they had 'every advantage' and that 'every issue was before' them.[44] Despite the natural reluctance of the court to interfere with the verdict of a jury which was aware of the risk of wrongful identification, and which had had the opportunity (not available in the Court of Appeal) to observe the demeanour of the witnesses, the court was sufficiently worried about the reliability of the conviction to overturn it. Granted, Lord Widgery CJ did not refer to the hearsay rule once throughout his judgment on behalf of the court, which

[42] (1981) 73 Cr App R 173.
[43] [1969] 1 QB 267.
[44] Ibid., p. 270.

may be regarded as a triumph for common sense. It should also be noted that not only did he not dismiss all the evidence against B as irrelevant, he clearly thought it so important that his only concern was whether the jury had underestimated its significance.

It is impossible to reconcile the remarks in *Blastland*, indicating that it was the wholly circumstantial nature of the evidence against M which made it objectionable, with those in *Steel*. But it is not difficult to identify some areas of concern which may underlie these judgments. There are three candidates: the first is that judges fear that trials would be too time-consuming if they examined the likelihood of persons other than the accused having committed the crime. This could not seriously be maintained as a proper principle. Innocent men cannot justifiably be convicted because we will not go to the trouble and expense of listening to their defence. However, there must be limits to the probative value of the evidence against the third party; the court is not to be involved in chasing hares. The judgment in *Blastland* seemed concerned to draw that line, but *Steel* is a much less convincing example of this. The second concern may be that it is unfair to persons not present in court to accuse them. But this would not explain the assertion in *Blastland* that the defence could have called an eyewitness (had there been one) to establish M's guilt. Are the judges worried that any defendant could escape justice by establishing a vague circumstantial case against someone else, who, if charged, would promptly rely on the evidence incriminating the other to cast doubt on the evidence against him? There is a short answer to that, which is that in any case the prosecution must have sufficient evidence to prove guilt beyond a reasonable doubt. Third, and this seems to be the only remaining possible rationale of *Steel*, is that judges may be thinking that the purpose of the trial is to test the strength of the prosecution case, and that if the disputed evidence is nothing to do with that case as pleaded, it has nothing to do with the trial. In other words, the prosecution must be met on its own terms. Thus the jury are not there to determine what actually happened. They are there to decide who won.

Exclusion for reasons of policy

The fact that in criminal cases the defence may, in general, conceal its case from the prosecution until the trial creates some difficulties in establishing the probable relevance of evidence. How can the prosecutor tell in advance whether particular items of evidence are material or not? The cases on 'similar fact' evidence[45] demonstrate the difficulty involved in hanging relevance on to the nature of particular defences raised by the accused; if the pro-

---

[45] See below.

secution evidence is not to be included at the last minute, then the defence must be anticipated before it is actually raised. It may, at first sight, look simple enough to tell which evidence establishes *actus reus* and *mens rea*, which, generally, must be proved in all criminal cases. But the accused may bring other matters into play, which complicate that question. In *Harrison-Owen*[46] the accused was charged with burglary, having been found in a house at night in possession of keys taken from a car outside. He had a history of burglary, which, prima facie, was irrelevant. But he raised a defence of automatism, that he had at the time been unaware of what he was doing, and so the judge put the criminal record into evidence at the trial. The Court of Appeal overturned the conviction; Lord Goddard CJ held that the defendant's criminal record had insufficient probative value. However, in *Mortimer*[47] a different line was taken. A man was accused of the murder of a female cyclist by driving a car at her, and he pleaded that he had no memory of the event. Evidence was admitted of his having driven at three other women cyclists at around the same time. *Mortimer* is the better decision. Harrison-Owen's presence in a private house in possession of someone else's car key gave rise to an obvious inference of deliberateness and dishonesty, all helpful to the prosecution. Since the defence raised the question of automatism, or involuntariness, it was relevant to consider his story in the light of a long record for housebreaking and burglary. How likely was it that, by coincidence, someone with such a history had wandered involuntarily into a private house?

These problems arise from the insistence of the common law that the bad character of the defendant *per se*, although relevant, is not admissible simply to show general unsavoury propensities. The mere fact that the evidence adduced tends to show the commission of other crimes does not render it inadmissible if it be relevant to an issue before the jury, but the courts will not allow prejudicial evidence to be heard if its probative value is slight. As we shall see below, that involves judges in a balancing exercise, seeking to measure the amount of prejudice caused against the probative force of the evidence. The 'similar fact' cases which require this feat of the judiciary are criticized on many grounds, but here Zuckerman's is the most forceful; he has shown[48] that it is entirely inappropriate to compare relevance or probative force (which are matters relating to the proof of fact) with prejudice, which is not solely concerned with the discovery of the truth, or the avoidance of mistakes by the jury, but includes matters of policy and moral choice:[49]

---

[46] [1951] 2 All ER 726.
[47] (1936) 25 Cr App R 150.
[48] Zuckerman, 'Similar fact evidence – the unobservable rule' (1987) 103 LQR 187.
[49] Ibid., p. 195.

Similar fact evidence threatens two central principles of our criminal justice. The first is that in any criminal trial the accused stands to be tried, acquitted or convicted, only in respect of the offence with which he is charged. The second is that convictions must take place only if the jury are persuaded of the accused's guilt beyond all reasonable doubt.

There is a risk that the jury's moral reaction to the accused's proclivity would affect their judgment, and that knowledge of his criminal past would reduce the standard of proof.[50] This argument derives some support from the civil cases on disposition evidence, which seem less concerned about the possible prejudicial effect,[51] and so could be explained as an attempt precisely to measure the probative force of the similar facts.

There are many exclusionary rules affecting the admissibility of what at first sight appears to be relevant evidence. These rules provide meat and drink to lawyers, whether they write books, teach students or participate in trials. Laymen have heard of some of them, like the hearsay rule (which appears even in Dickens),[52] and have a vague idea that the criminal record is excluded. Judges have shown a new vigour in excluding relevant evidence if they disapprove of police conduct. These matters have been said to be instances of judicial concern with the reliability of evidence, but will be dealt with in more detail in later chapters.

Relevance and logic: similar facts

The courts rely heavily on inductive or empirical reasoning: 'The law furnishes no test of relevancy. For this, it tacitly refers to logic and experience.'[53] Thayer was quite clear that he meant here the inductive logic of knowledge or science.[54] Attempting to construct a logical syllogism to illustrate the way findings of fact are made, as Stephen did,[55] is frustrated by the impossibility of identifying the contents of the initial premise without adopting everyday assumptions about human behaviour or commonplace experiences. Inevitably, there are divergent views on these matters, whether the supposition is 'Those who have a motive to kill are more likely to do so

---

[50] Ibid.

[51] E.g. *Mood Music v De Wolfe* [1976] 1 All ER 763.

[52] As Sam Weller gives evidence in *Bardell v Pickwick*: 'You must not tell us what the soldier said, sir,' interposed the judge; 'it's not evidence': Dickens, *The Pickwick Papers*.

[53] J. B. Thayer, *Preliminary Treatise on Evidence at the Common Law* (Sweet & Maxwell, London, 1898), p. 265.

[54] Thayer, 'Law and logic' (1900) 14 Harv LR 139.

[55] J. F. Stephen, *General View of the Criminal Law*, 1st edn (Sweet & Maxwell, London, 1898), p. 236.

than those with none' or 'A man with an elegant and intelligent wife is unlikely to seek the services of a prostitute, or to hand over large sums of money to a prostitute he has never met'.[56] Findings of fact, say Binder and Bergman, are based upon conventional wisdom about how people and objects function in everyday life. All of us, through our own personal experience, through hearing about the personal experience of others, and through knowledge gained from books, films, newspapers and television, have accumulated vast storehouses of commonly held notions about how people and objects generally behave in our society. From this storehouse one formulates a generalization about typical behaviour. This generalization, in turn, becomes the premise which enables specific evidence to be linked with an element to be proven.[57] The development of presumptions illustrates how the law itself attempts to save time and argument by adopting some of these commonsense assumptions, processing them into conveniently snappy formulations. Circumstantial evidence also relies on such inferences. The law has got itself into difficulty whenever it insisted on proof in the strict logical sense, failure to admit the inductive nature of its own reasoning having led to unrealistic restrictions being imposed. Bentham asked what were the realistic possibilities of documents produced being forgeries – yet rules to eliminate this insubstantial risk prevented vast numbers of perfectly genuine documents being used. How likely is it that someone will set out deliberately to manufacture evidence, for instance by making remarks that will be overheard by bystanders, and then disappearing, all to incriminate someone else? Yet the hearsay rule strives to protect us from these remarkable possibilities. Thus the baby is thrown out with the bathwater; it may be that the odd forgery or concoction is preferable to the loss of so much valuable evidence.

It has been known from David Hume's time that inductive reasoning has logical weaknesses. But one of the law's strengths is that it reflects the common experience and embodies the layman's understanding of common sense. How then, to understand the cases on similar fact, or disposition evidence? Zuckerman has pointed out[58] that the rules of inductive logic have nothing to say about what standard of proof is desirable in criminal trials, or whether there is a moral objection to punishing the accused twice for the same offence, but these are major concerns throughout the case law on disposition evidence. Hence these judicial decisions cannot be seen entirely as an application of inductive reasoning, the objective being to minimize the risk of unreliable evidence being given too much weight. As Zuckerman has

---

[56] *Archer v Daily Star*, July 1987.

[57] D. Binder and P. Bergman, *Fact Investigation* (West, St Paul, Minn., 1984), p. 274.

[58] Zuckerman (1987) 103 LQR 187.

shown, the common law attempts to place inductive notions of relevance in the balance against what is actually a concept redolent of moral issues. The width of the considerable discretion left to trial judges as a consequence has been defended on the basis that by this means justice is given due attention.[59] Generally, judicial discretion is acceptable where it is operated on a rational basis which can be perceived. Unfortunately, here it seems that judges are condemned to an exercise in irrationality; it is therefore entirely to be expected that the Court of Appeal, in reviewing the exercise of this discretion, has produced surprising results from time to time.

The nature of this reasoning process still appears to be[60] best explained in the famous passage from Lord Hershell's judgment in *Makin v A-G for New South Wales*:[61]

> It is undoubtedly not competent for the prosecution to adduce evidence tending to show that the accused has been guilty of criminal acts other than those covered by the indictment, for the purpose of leading to the conclusion that the accused is a person likely from his criminal conduct or character to have committed the offence for which he is being tried. On the other hand, the mere fact that the evidence tends to show the commission of other crimes does not render it inadmissible if it bears upon the issue whether the acts alleged to constitute the crime are designed or accidental, or to rebut a defence which would otherwise be open to the accused.

But the key question is begged here; when does the allegedly 'disposition' evidence bear upon the issue? A common mistake since the House of Lords case *DPP v Boardman*[62] is to assume that evidence of previous misconduct by the accused is sufficiently probative only when the other incidents were 'strikingly similar', and that one must reason by analogy with Lord Hailsham's example of the homosexual in the Red Indian head-dress:[63]

> Whilst it would certainly not be enough to identify the culprit in a series of burglaries that he climbed in through a ground floor window, the fact that he

---

[59] *R v Davis* [1980] 1 NZLR 257: 'The price...is some uncertainty in borderline cases, but some uncertainty is inevitable with the questions of relevance or degrees of relevance. In criminal law it is more important to have a just and fair trial than a certain one.'

[60] Although Hoffman thought that *Boardman* entirely replaced this judgment, 'Similar facts after *Boardman*' (1975) 91 LQR 193, subsequent case law demonstrates that the House of Lords made no great innovation. See Zuckerman (1987) 103 LQR 187.

[61] [1894] AC 57, 65.

[62] [1975] AC 421.

[63] Ibid., p. 454.

left the same humorous limerick on the walls of the sitting room, or an esoteric symbol written in lipstick on the mirror, might well be enough. In a sex case...whilst a repeated homosexual act by itself might be quite insufficient to admit the evidence as confirmatory of identity or design, the fact that it was alleged to have been performed wearing the ceremonial head-dress of a Red Indian chief or other eccentric garb might well in appropriate circumstances suffice.

Any lawyer who concludes from this that such exotic circumstances are always necessary before the evidence is admissible will soon come to grief; many students are puzzled by the contrast between these vivid illustrations and the far less dramatic cases where courts have found the instances to be sufficiently similar. More prosaic cases include *R v Mustafa*.[64] A was seen putting meat into a trolley at a supermarket. A store detective thought A realized he was being watched.[65] He left the meat in the trolley and left the shop. A few months later he allegedly bought the same amount of meat from the same shop using a stolen Barclaycard and forged signature. The sole issue was whether it was A. There was also evidence that on arrest he was in possession of a stolen Access card, and that he was identified as the man who purchased meat on the same day from another shop using a forged Barclaycard signature. The forgeries were all of poor quality, and when the police found him he was trying to copy the signature on the Access card. The admission of all these incidents into evidence at the trial was upheld by the Court of Appeal. Similarly unremarkable was the case of *R v Seaman*,[66] where A brought a bag of empty beer bottles into a supermarket, which he exchanged at the wine counter for new ones. He also pocketed some bacon, which first he had carried in the wire basket provided, without paying for it. He said he forgot. The prosecution sought to admit evidence of two previous occasions where he had placed bacon into a wire basket in the same supermarket. On the first, the bacon disappeared, and the store was unsure where it went to. On the second, he saw that he was being watched,[67] and put the bacon back on the counter. The Court of Appeal held that the evidence was rightly admitted at trial.

The contrast between these cases and Lord Hailsham's colourful language has caused some confusion, even in the Court of Appeal itself; in *Mustafa* Scarman LJ said that there must be a striking similarity between the

---

[64] (1976) 65 Cr App R 26.

[65] This apparently inadmissible opinion evidence was not commented on in the Court of Appeal.

[66] (1978) 67 Cr App R 234.

[67] See note 65.

incidents (it might be thought that the case before him was a curious example of this), but in *Mansfield*[68] Lawton LJ urged lawyers not to attach too much importance to phrases such as 'uniquely and strikingly similar' in House of Lords judgments. The test is whether the evidence can be explained away as coincidence. Misunderstandings arise from an urge to over-simplify the principle at work here. Unfortunately, it is not susceptible to simplification, and the cases are impossible to categorize, which is why in *Boardman* the House of Lords gave up the struggle to do so. Lord Hailsham gives specific examples of the nature of evidence required in particular circumstances, and it is entirely wrong to generalize from his remarks to every kind of case. Any disputed item of similar fact or disposition evidence must be examined in the light of the issue to be decided and the other evidence available to the court. Zuckerman has attempted to show the importance of the context in which the evidence is to be used; it is in fact central to the *Boardman* decision, but many lawyers seem nevertheless unaware of the importance of this.

> It is…very important that due regard should be paid to the other evidence adduced or about to be adduced by the prosecution, for….evidence which incidentally shows bad disposition must be substantially relevant for some other purpose, and the degree of relevancy of such other evidence may be greatly affected by the other evidence.[69]

An example of this is the case of *Bond*,[70] in which a medical practitioner was accused of unlawfully procuring an abortion on J; one T gave evidence that Bond had done the same thing for her, saying that he 'had put dozens of girls right'. Both women had become pregnant by the accused. The defence pleaded that there was no intent; the result of the medical examination was accidental. The Court for Crown Cases Reserved approved the admission of all T's evidence, given the defence. Although *Boardman* has removed the traditional need to place the case within a known category, it is still not clear at first sight why the evidence is admissible, given that there is apparently no striking similarity between the 'dozens' of unlawful abortions performed by Bond. (There is a similarity between the cases of J and T by virtue of their relationships with him.) There is no suggestion that Bond performed these operations wearing eccentric headgear or by using extraordinary utensils. But despite this, the evidence was significant; it is hard to swallow the defence of

[68] [1978] 1 All ER 134.
[69] R. Cross, *Evidence*, 3rd edn (Butterworths, London, 1967), pp. 303-4, approved by O'Connor J in *Horwood* [1970] 1 QB 133, 139.
[70] [1906] 2 KB 389.

accident from a man with apparent expertise in abortion, particularly when he benefits from it. That point can be made with no 'striking similarity' between the incidents. The principle as expressed by Lord Cross does not insist upon it:[71]

> The question must always be whether the similar fact evidence taken together with the other evidence would do no more than raise or strengthen a suspicion that the accused committed the offence with which he is charged or would point so strongly to his guilt that only an ultra-cautious jury would acquit in the face of it.

The issue in *Boardman* was not identification. There was no question but that two students accused their headmaster of homosexual offences against them. Since he denied this, the implication of the not guilty plea was that they were lying. The 'similar fact' issue is merely the likelihood of two young men independently constructing the same lie. The similarity between their accounts was hardly striking, but the fact that both alleged that D wished to take the passive role was arresting enough to suggest that the resemblances between the incidents went beyond coincidence. In contrast, even striking similarities may not justify the admission of previous offences in some cases, as when the defence alleges that the police fabricated or planted evidence for the prosecution.[72]

The passage so often quoted from Lord Hailsham does not require for every case the kind of Gothic situation he describes. The humorous limerick is necessary to identify the burglar, because burglary is such a common crime. Homosexual tendencies are no longer enough to identify a homosexual offender (if they ever were) because such a tendency is not sufficiently unusual. But (one hopes) paedophilia is still unusual enough for us to think that *Thompson*[73] was decided correctly on its facts: it was not disputed that sexual offences had been committed on some boys by a man who arranged to meet them at a particular time and place. A arrived at that time and place, and gave the boys money. On him at the time of arrest were some powder puffs, and later, in his room, indecent photographs were found. The chance that the boys had seized upon the wrong man by mistake was fairly remote. Of course, it was possible that A had been wrongly identified; but the evidence was undoubtedly material to the issue of identity, given the other evidence in the case. Nevertheless, the judgment of Lord Sumner is frequently resurrected as an example of the narrow-mindedness of judges:

---

[71] *Boardman* [1975] AC 421, 457.
[72] See *Jeffrey Wells* [1989] Crim LR 67, and Birch's note thereon, ibid.
[73] [1918] AC 221.

'Persons...who commit the offences now under consideration seek the habitual gratification of a particular perverted lust, which not only takes them out of the class of ordinary men gone wrong, but stamps them with the hall-mark of a specialized and extraordinary class as much as if they carried on their bodies some physical peculiarity.'[74]

But he would appear to be referring to Thompson in particular and not homosexuals in general. This interpretation is reinforced by his next sentence, in which he says that the photographs show Thompson to have the propensity under discussion − a propensity to which Lord Sumner seems unable or unwilling to put a name.

The misleading version of *Thompson* comes in fact from the judgment of Lord Goddard CJ in *Sims*[75] and is repeated in *DPP v Kilbourne*,[76] where it was disapproved on that point. In *Boardman*, Lord Cross said that in a climate where 'the attitude of the ordinary man towards homosexuality has changed very much' Lord Sumner 'sounds nowadays like a voice from another world'.[77] But more particular homosexual proclivities can be relevant; for instance *Twomey*,[78] in which previous offences of homosexual acts accompanied by violence were held to have been rightly admitted where a murder victim had been subjected to a violent homosexual attack, and where there was evidence that D had been in the vicinity at the time. In *Sims* itself the question was whether the four accusers were concocting the allegations of homosexual acts by Sims, which, if there were no evidence of conspiracy between them, seemed unlikely given the similarity of the accounts. In *Boardman* Lord Cross stresses the importance of context, contrasting cases such as *Sims* and the instant case, where the issue was effectively the veracity of the complainants, from *Smith*[79] and *Straffen*,[80] where the victim was dead and therefore the issue was the defendant's responsibility:[81]

If collaboration is out of the way it remains possible that the charge made by the complainant is false and that it is simply a coincidence that others should be making or should have made independently allegations of a similar character against the accused. The likelihood of such a coincidence obviously

[74] Ibid., p. 235.
[75] [1946] KB 531, 540.
[76] [1973] AC 729.
[77] [1975] AC 421, 458.
[78] [1971] Crim LR 277.
[79] (1915) 11 Cr App R 229.
[80] [1952] 2 QB 911.
[81] [1975] AC 421, 457.

becomes less and less the more people there are who make the similar allegations and the more striking are the similarities in the various stories. In the end...it is a question of degree.

The courts, in their hurry to show awareness of social and moral developments, may have dismissed Lord Sumner's opinions to their own cost. Earlier in his judgment, he distinguishes the sexual proclivities of Thompson (paedophilia) from other kinds of criminality:[82]

> The evidence tends to attach to the accused a peculiarity which, though not purely physical...may be recognized as properly bearing that name. Experience tends to show that these offences against nature connote an inversion of normal characteristics which, while demanding punishment as offending against social morality, also partake of the nature of an abnormal physical propensity. A thief, a cheat, a coiner, or housebreaker is only a particular specimen of the genus rogue, and, though no doubt each tends to keep to his own line of business, they all alike possess the by no means extraordinary characteristic that they propose somehow to get their living dishonestly. So common a characteristic is not a recognizable mark of the individual.

The familiar attempts in textbooks to classify similar fact cases tend to do so either in terms of the defence raised (usually pre-*Boardman*) or in terms of the issue in the trial. Insufficient attention has been paid to this passage, which shows the importance of the nature of the disposition itself.

An example of the over-generalized approach which results from this is *R v Beggs*.[83] D was accused of having murdered O. D claimed that he put up O for the night and awoke to find him indecently assaulting him. D, a student, had met O, a practising homosexual, in a club. D said he lashed out with a razor blade in self-defence. O died mainly from throat wounds. The police carried out extensive inquiries which resulted in D being charged with five counts of unlawful wounding. The incidents all took place before the alleged murder, and were rather unusual. The first related to a fellow student, S, living in the same house as D, who had gone to bed and awoke to find D attending to a wound on his (S's) leg. D told him that he had heard him call out in his sleep and had gone to assist. He noticed a protruding bedspring. Under the bed was S's penknife. S told his doctor he had been injured by a bedspring. A few weeks later, while S and D were sharing a bed-sitting room, S awoke to find superficial lacerations on his leg and a razor blade lying on the sheet of his bed. (In evidence, D said he might have cut S's leg when, as a joke, he decided in the night to shave his friend's legs and his

---

[82] [1918] AC 221, 235.
[83] [1989] Crim LR 898.

own.) A further count concerned R, another occupier of the same students'
house, who awoke to find a four-inch laceration in his calf, about five months
afterwards. R told his doctor it might have been a bedspring. Three months
later, L, another occupier of the house, went to bed after drinking with D
and awoke with a large gash in his leg. The Court of Appeal held that the
judge was wrong to refuse an application to sever the indictment so that the
murder could be heard separately, and consequently quashed Beggs's conviction for murder. The striking aspect of this case, it was said, was not so
much the similarities between the woundings and the fatal incident, but the
differences. O was not a student, he did not live in the house, his wound was
to the neck rather than the leg and the death was caused by a razor, of which
there was no sign in relation to the woundings.

Reasoning from *Boardman*, how likely is the story put forward by Beggs to
be true, given (if the prosecution evidence is believed) a propensity to gore
the legs of young men who are asleep, whatever the implement used? It is
certainly a remarkable coincidence that someone with such a habit, which
has strong homosexual overtones, and who brings home a practising homosexual whom he meets at a club, should be forced to defend himself with a
razor, with fatal effect, from an indecent overture during the night. There
is an inference of emotional instability from the earlier incidents which
diminishes the credibility of the self-defence story. As Lord Sumner, albeit
in highly coloured language less appropriate these days, appreciated, sexual
offenders are different from 'career' or 'professional' criminals. Their history
frequently shows a progression from less serious to downright dangerous
behaviour, as one might expect from the mentally or emotionally sick. The
reasoning appropriate to cases of burglary or shoplifting will not fit crimes
which demonstrate a disturbed personality which the jury ought to know
about. The decision in *Beggs* is a denial of the common sense and application
of experience which are thought to characterize the similar fact cases. Why
insist upon similarities of an entirely superficial nature, such as D attacking
the same part of the body, or using the same kind of implement, when the
point is that here is someone who appears to enjoy causing injury to men
who are asleep? Treating sexual offences in the same way as other crimes
belies their peculiar nature, as Lord Sumner attempted to point out.

Suppose a woman alleges rape and D pleads consent; there follows a
credibility battle which she is likely to lose, given the standard of proof in
criminal cases. How would the jury react if they were told that the same man
had been accused of rape before? Even if he were acquitted, a plea of consent
on that occasion may cause us to pause. For to fall out with two ex-lovers to
such an extent that they both falsely accuse him of rape would seem very bad
luck. And more than one previous instance would be still more significant.
Yet we find that previous rape *convictions* are treated as inadmissible unless

the circumstances are strikingly similar.[84] This makes a nonsense of the basic test from *Boardman*; given the nature of the defence and the other evidence in the case, these previous events do indeed deepen suspicion about the accused; there is a point at which it goes beyond the realms of coincidence that a person previously accused of rapes, whether convicted of them or acquitted on a plea of consent, should be accused by an erstwhile willing partner out of spite, bearing in mind that the argument is only for admitting the evidence, not for an automatic conviction. There are moral, not rational, objections to admitting evidence of trials which led to acquittal; but in relation to previous convictions for rape, the courts have not derived from *Boardman* the flexibility that is certainly there.

The speciousness of the judicial claim that the accused's disposition can never be used against him[85] has been noted.[86] *Ball*[87] and *Straffen*[88] have often been cited as cases where the similar fact evidence was relevant *because* of the accused's disposition. In *Ball* the previous sexual relationship of a brother and sister was admitted against them on charges of incest; it was highly probative given the circumstances in which they were now cohabiting. In *Straffen* Slade J argued that an abnormal propensity was itself a means of identification in this case. There was no direct evidence that he had murdered the little girl, Linda Bowyer, although he admitted meeting her. The child had been manually strangled, but not sexually assaulted. Straffen had escaped from Broadmoor at the time, having been sent there after being found unfit to plead to charges of murdering two other little girls, found strangled in similar circumstances. The unlikelihood of another man with Straffen's propensities being in the same place at the time meant that the jury should hear of it. The same probably would apply even if the circumstances had been less similar, because the personality involved is so unusual. But an abnormal propensity does not have to be a sexual one, nor does it

---

[84] A supposition not appreciated by the judge who explained to a jury who had just acquitted of rape a man who pleaded consent, that they had been prevented by the law from hearing his previous conviction for that offence, and told the defendant, who had not given evidence, to 'keep his hands off young girls'. Judge Wilson Mellor also castigated a system which 'allows allegations of shameful sexual conduct to be laid against a witness and to be persisted in without any evidence at all being offered in support of it': *Daily Telegraph*, 7 March 1987. There have been other examples of judges reading out an acquitted rape defendant's record for sexual offences after a successful defence of consent. This is clearly upsetting for the jury, but only because of the commonsense inference that D's defence was probably not true.

[85] See *Seaman* (1978) 67 Cr App R 234.

[86] Hoffman (1975) 91 LQR 193.

[87] [1911] AC 47.

[88] [1952] 2 QB 911.

have to serve only as identification evidence. *Armstrong*[89] is now regarded as a weak authority[90] on its own facts, but a variation gives an example of a propensity which could be highly probative. If more visitors to the solicitor's house for tea than the one produced had suffered arsenic poisoning, the death of one from arsenic poisoning would look very like murder. The disposition evidence would establish both *actus reus* and *mens rea*.

The post-*Boardman* cases require us to apply a coincidence test. Disputed evidence must be considered in its context, and this opens the way for unusual propensities and/or evidence which is not, prima facie, strikingly similar. There is, therefore, a sliding scale of necessary similarity. In cases such as *Makin* and *Smith* the similar fact or dispostition evidence is required to fulfil a large part of the prosecution's task; without it, there was little to suggest that the defendants were responsible for the deaths of their victims.[91] In cases of this nature a high degree of similarity would be required between the incidents before a sufficient link could be established. In *Boardman* there was other evidence to perform that function, requiring correspondingly less of the similar fact evidence. The degree of similarity required in cases of this sort is much lower. But the courts are failing to grasp this, and have become caught in the margin between this line of cases and those dealing with evidence of the character of witnesses in the proceedings.[92]

Douglass[93] is an example of the overlap. The Court of Appeal, in attempting to explain why the bad character of a non-witness was relevant, such evidence being generally understood to go to credibility on oath, ended up having to say that here character went to guilt because it was a case of 'cut-throat' defences. But if a cut-throat case is of the nature that if X is not guilty Y is, and vice versa, it is hard to see how the court managed to find that the evidence of bad character went to guilt and should have been admitted, at the same time as upholding Douglass's conviction by applying the proviso.[94] D was convicted of causing death by reckless driving. It was the

---

[89] [1922] 2 KB 555.

[90] See e.g. P. Carter, *Cases and Statutes on Evidence*, 2nd edn (Sweet & Maxwell, London, 1990), p. 453.

[91] The dead baby found at the Makins' house could not be shown to have been murdered by them but for the numerous corpses of other dead babies found at three houses in which they had lived. Similarly in *Smith*, the death of his 'wife' in the bath appeared innocent even though Smith stood to gain financially, until compared with the deaths of his other brides in similar circumstances soon after their weddings.

[92] See chapter 5.

[93] [1989] Crim LR 569.

[94] See Birch's note [1989] Crim LR 67; the court appeared to assume that if the jury had heard about S's appalling drinking and driving record, D would have been convicted anyway.

prosecution case that he and his co-accused (S) had been vying with each other and that they were responsible for a collision between S's van and an oncoming vehicle as S sought to overtake D. A passenger in the oncoming vehicle was killed. S was acquitted. The prosecution alleged that D had been drinking before the accident. He gave evidence denying having been drinking, denying responsibility for the accident, and blaming S. S did not give evidence but during interview had blamed D for the collision. S's girlfriend, a passenger in the van, gave evidence for the prosecution to the effect that D had pulled out, apparently deliberately, as S tried to overtake. She went on to give evidence that S had not drunk alcohol in the two years she had known him. The Court of Appeal held that the trial judge should not have refused to allow a police witness to give evidence of S's previous convictions (including offences of violence, dishonesty, dangerous and careless driving and driving with excess alcohol), for here the co-accused's character was relevant to the issue of guilt, rebutting the misleading evidence of good character (which S was lucky to get in).[95] It is difficult to see why this is a case of cut-throat defences, which the court regarded as a justification for its decision, since it is conceivable that both caused death by reckless driving. Could the case have been better dealt with by the similar fact principle? It is a remarkable coincidence that S, who has such a dreadful driving record, should find himself targeted for harassment by a drunken driver. It is possible, but perhaps the jury should be told what kind of man is making that claim. The difficulty of *Douglass* is that it was the defence who sought to have the evidence adduced, whereas similar fact evidence forms part of the prosecution's case in chief.

The assumption behind these cases appears to be that where the disposition evidence is not highly probative, the jury would attach excessive weight to it and therefore the defendant would not get a fair trial. The Criminal Law Revision Committee[96] points out that such fears do not exist in France, where the defendant's criminal record is read out at the beginning of the trial. The Committee also suspects that the system in England, where the record is frequently suppressed until, for instance, the accused loses his or her shield,[97] maximizes the damage done, since the jury is suddenly alerted to the existence of a 'past' in dramatic circumstances, fairly late in the day. The Committee rightly doubted whether English jurors were congenitally less able than French to take a balanced view of such information about the accused. And the fact that he or she can 'lose his shield' through the nature

---

[95] See below.
[96] *Evidence (General)*, Eleventh Report of the Criminal Law Revision Committee, Cmnd 4991 (1972).
[97] See chapter 5.

of his or her defence discloses considerable inconsistency in the English approach.

The fact that these rules peculiarly characterize the Anglo–American method of trial suggests that there is a relationship between the adversarial system and the desire to exclude the defendant's previous criminality. Why this should be is not self-evident. There is an obvious link between such a desire and the presumption of innocence – but other countries operate the same presumption without following a similar practice. The distinction may be influenced by the extra significance of the trial itself in adversarial structures; the evidence must be marshalled on the day by the party seeking judgment, and the constraints of the time available limit the party to evidence directly related to the issue he or she has raised. As we saw earlier in this chapter, courts are not prepared to deviate from the most direct of routes towards resolution of this issue. The (slight) materiality of the accused's record to the prosecution's case does not warrant its introduction into evidence unless the prosecution can show that of its nature it directly implicates the accused in the offence. Again, the adversarial trial is forced into its demarcation between evidence which goes to credibility and evidence which goes to guilt. The impossibility of drawing a clear line between the two ensures that the cases on similar fact will never be coherent, despite the best efforts of the judiciary. And a further problem arises from the adversarial structure; since the relevance of the disposition evidence may be established only after the nature of the defence is known, the prosecutor has to hope that it will become clear before closing his or her case. If not, he or she will have to seek the judge's leave to reopen it, and become involved in a procedural argument that has no bearing on guilt. This problem could be averted either by allowing for more disclosure by the defence, or by admitting evidence of the accused's disposition as a matter of course.[98]

PROOF

Despite patriotic declarations to the contrary,[99] it is not only in the Anglo-Saxon system of trial that we find a presumption of innocence in relation to allegations of criminality.[100] But in inquisitorial systems this may be at its most evident during pre-trial procedures, where there is a greater possibility of discontinuance than in the English system. Also, the burden of proof on

---

[98] See chapter 5.
[99] E.g. Wright, 'French criminal procedure' (1929) 45 LQR 98.
[100] E.g. Polish Code of Criminal Procedure (1969), Art. 3(2).

prosecutors in such systems operates rather differently where the court itself has an obligation to elucidate the truth.[101] Rather than castigate the Continental trial for indifference to the plight of those accused, we might do better to consider the fact that the much-vaunted burden of proof is reversed, that is, imposed upon the accused, in a considerable number of cases in England; in Poland the accused never carries a legal burden in any circumstances. So, since the complicated exchange of evidential burdens does not take place in an inquisitorial trial, the accused's only problem is tactical: 'if you do not try to prove your own assertions you will heighten the chances of adopting the opposite one.'[102] As we go on to examine the curious ping-pong effect of evidential burdens springing from side to side, and the erosion of the presumption of innocence in criminal trials, the simplicity and naturalness of the Continental trial have some appeal.

Legal burden of proof

The closing speech of that renowned criminal advocate, Horace Rumpole, typically emphasizes in the most moving and poetical terms that there is a 'golden thread which runs through British justice';[103] that is, that the prosecution bears the ultimate responsibility of proving its case. It is not for the accused to prove his or her innocence. But how true is this? The principle that the prosecution must prove the case against derives not only from paternalistic concern as to the fate of accused persons, but is an application of the basic theory of the trial, that parties who wish the machinery of the law to assist them should have the obligation of proving their case. If there are several issues in the trial, and both parties find themselves carrying legal burdens on individual points, it may appear to shift from one to the other, but in fact it remains fixed on that particular issue.[104] The principle that the party seeking judgment bears the legal burden applies to the state itself if it seeks to accuse someone of a crime. In *Woolmington v DPP*[105] the accusation was that the defendant had murdered his wife, while the defendant pleaded a

---

[101] Stanislaw Waltos, *Code of Criminal Procedure of the Polish People's Republic* (Wydawnictwo Prawnicze, Warsaw, 1979).

[102] M. Cieslak, *Polish Criminal Procedure* (Nawkowe, Warsaw, 1973).

[103] E.g. J. Mortimer, *Rumpole's Last Case* (Penguin, Harmondsworth, 1987).

[104] E.g. *Medawar v Grand Hotel* [1891] 2 QB 11. The plaintiff had to show that the defendants' negligence led to the loss of his property, and on that point he had the burden of proof. To escape liability altogether, the defendants needed to show that the loss resulted from the plaintiff's negligence, and on that issue they had the burden of proof.

[105] [1935] AC 462.

shooting accident. The following passage from the judgment of Viscount Sankey is regarded as a cornerstone of the criminal justice system:[106]

> Throughout the web of the English Criminal Law one golden thread is always to be seen, that it is the duty of the prosecution to prove the prisoner's guilt... If at the end of and on the whole of the case, there is a reasonable doubt, created by the evidence given by either the prosecution or the prisoner, as to whether the prisoner killed the deceased with a malicious intent, the prosecution has not made out the case and the prisoner is entitled to an acquittal. No matter what the charge or where the trial, the principle that the prosecution must prove the guilt of the prisoner is part of the common law of England and no attempt to whittle it down can be entertained.

The ringing clarity of these words is somewhat misleading; the omitted section of the passage refers to exceptions to the principle, and in recent decisions it appears that attempts to whittle it down *are* being entertained. Unfortunately, there is now a tendency, both in the courts and in the legislature, to impose upon defendants in criminal trials legal burdens of proof where evidential ones are all that is necessary.

The nature of the evidential burden should be explained before taking the *Woolmington* debate futher. In criminal trials, as will be seen in chapter 3, the trial judge must remove an issue from the consideration of the jury if there is no evidence on which they could decide in its favour. The party raising that issue bears an evidential burden of proof – the obligation to adduce sufficient evidence to raise the issue given the standard of proof required in that context. The party bearing the legal burden therefore has an additional obligation, of 'passing the judge', so that an evidential burden lies under the legal one. In simple terms, the court will not even consider the defence relied on unless there is some evidence to support it. The prosecution bears the initial evidential burden, which is to show there is a prima facie case, a 'case to answer',[107] and this means passing the judge on all the constituent elements of the crime charged. This obligation exists in trials other than trials by jury, so all litigants must raise sufficient evidence to entitle them to consideration by the tribunal of fact on any issue. The reasons for the requirement are that the other side should not be forced to the trouble, expense and stress of defending themselves against an allegation which there is no evidence whatever to support, and that the tribunal is entitled to know what the range of the inquiry is. An evidential burden may be imposed on a party who does not bear the legal burden. In *Woolmington*, for example, the

[106] Ibid., p. 481.
[107] See chapter 3.

defence of accident would not have been put to the jury if no evidence were raised in support of it; on that issue he bore the evidential burden. It would be sufficient for the purpose if the accused person during his own testimony claimed that the shooting was accidental. Whether the claim were sufficient to raise a reasonable doubt, preventing the prosecution from satisfying its legal burden of proof, would then be for the jury to decide. In *Gill*[108] the plea was duress, although the accused never mentioned the alleged threats to himself and his wife when questioned by police. The trial judge told the jury that they must be satisfied that the defendant had lost all will of his own, bearing in mind that his earlier statements suggested that he acted freely. On appeal it was held that the legal burden remains with the prosecution, although the accused must raise his defence by sufficient evidence to go to the jury. He must make duress a 'live issue'. This can be done through cross-examination of prosecution witnesses, or by evidence called on his behalf, or a combination of the two. Once he has succeeded in doing this, it is then for the Crown to destroy that defence in such a manner as to leave in the jury's minds no reasonable doubt that the accused cannot be absolved on the grounds of the alleged compulsion.[109] The court felt that the direction on the whole made it clear that the prosecution had the burden of proving that the appellant had not acted out of duress, and upheld the conviction.

The *Woolmington* principle that the prosecution bears the burden of proof in respect of all elements of the crime alleged is subject to three exceptions. The first, specifically referred to in the judgment, is that the burden is upon a defendant who pleads insanity.[110] This exception may have been derived from the common law presumption of sanity;[111] however, the standard of proof required of the defence is only on the balance of probabilities.[112] In any other case where the accused denies *mens rea*, the burden of proof remains with the prosecution, who must show that it was present.[113]

The second exception exists in relation to statutes which specifically place the legal burden on the accused.[114] There appears to be an increasing readi-

---

[108] [1963] 1 WLR 841.
[109] Edmund Davies J, ibid., p. 846.
[110] *Woolmington* [1935] AC 462, *Hill v Baxter* [1958] 1 QB 277.
[111] *Imperial Loan Co. v Stone* [1892] 1 QB 599; *Sutton v Sadler* (1857) 3 CB (NS) 87.
[112] *Hill v Baxter* [1958] 1 QB 277.
[113] Non-insane automatism, *Hill v Baxter*, ibid., *Moses v Winder* [1981] RTR 37; drunkenness, *Kennedy v HM Advocate* [1944] SC (J) 171, *Foote* [1964] Crim LR 405.
[114] E.g. Bills of Exchange Act 1882, s. 30(2); Prevention of Corruption Act 1916, s. 2; Prevention of Crime Act 1953, s. 1; Homicide Act 1957, s. 2; Theft Act 1968, s. 25; Misuse of Drugs Act 1971, s. 28(2); Criminal Damage Act 1971, s. 1.

ness in the legislature to add to the list: the Public Order Act 1986 is a recent example of this tendency.[115] Although the standard of proof is never as great where the legal burden is imposed upon the defendant rather than the prosecution, being proof on the balance of probability,[116] it is not clear why protection of the community cannot be achieved by imposing merely an evidential burden. It is interesting to note in this context that section 74 of the Police and Criminal Evidence Act 1984 has had unexpected consequences. The problem which Parliament had in mind was that caused by the operation of the rule in *Hollington v Hewthorn*[117] in criminal cases, which prevented the court from using a court record of conviction as evidence that an offence had been committed. This meant that, for example in a trial for handling stolen goods, the conviction of the thief was inadmissible, and the prosecution had to start from scratch to show the goods were indeed stolen. Section 73 of the 1984 Act allows evidence of the certificate of conviction to be admitted as evidence of the fact of conviction, and section 74 provides that where the certificate is admitted as evidence of the conviction of a person other than the accused, that person shall be taken to have committed the offence unless the contrary is proved. This provision has caused considerable difficulty in cases where one or more co-defendants plead guilty, if the prosecution seeks to use section 74 to bring in the conviction in the trial of those accused who deny their guilt. The situation is worst in conspiracy cases, since section 75 provides that all the details contained in the relevant count on the indictment should be included. The effect on the jury of hearing that one party to the alleged conspiracy has admitted it could be very damaging as far as the other is concerned.[118] The effect of the provision is to shift the burden of proof in some cases where accomplice convictions are admitted under section 74; the judges have attempted to mitigate its effects by using their discretion under section 78 of the 1984 Act, in cases which are discussed in detail in chapter 5.

The third exception springs from the principle that if facts are peculiarly within the knowledge of the defendant, this imposes a burden of proof on him or her, since it is easier for the defendant to produce the relevant evidence. In *Turner*[119] there were ten possible justifications in the relevant statute for the defendant's possession of pheasants or hares. Since only Turner could know which, if any, applied to him, he should have the burden of proof despite the prosecution allegation that he lacked the necessary

---

[115] E.g. ss. 5(3), 23(3).

[116] *Sodeman* [1936] 2 All ER 1138; *Carr-Briant* [1943] KB 607.

[117] [1943] KB 587; see chapter 5.

[118] *O'Connor* [1987] Crim LR 260.

[119] (1816) 5 M & S 206.

qualification. In *Edwards*[120] the court went much further, arguing that the common law rule did not relate solely to cases where the defendant has peculiar knowledge; it is a burden which applies generally if an offence carries with it exceptions and provisos. Then the accused must show that he or she is within one of the excepted categories. This meant that section 81 of the Magistrates' Courts Act 1952 (now Magistrates' Courts Act 1980, section 101) merely enacted for summary trials the existing common law on the point. The provision states:[121]

> Where the defendant to an action, information or complaint relies for his defence on any exception, exemption, proviso, excuse or qualification, whether or not it accompanies the description of the offence or matter of complaint in the enactment creating the offence or on which the complaint is founded, the burden of proving the exception...[etc.] shall be on him; and this notwithstanding that the information or complaint contains an allegation negativing the exception.

Edwards applies the same rule to trials on indictment; this is controversial,[122] particularly as the Court of Appeal rejected the argument that the difficulty presented by such cases would be adequately dealt with by construing the defence burden as an evidential one only: 'What rests upon [the defendant] is a legal, or as it is sometimes called, the persuasive burden of proof. It is not the evidential burden.'[123] This categorical statement seems unnecessarily harsh to the defence and has provoked a storm of criticism.[124]

Despite the hostility to this approach, which was noted by the Court of Appeal in *Hunt*,[125] that court attempted to extend the *Edwards* principle in an inexcusable fashion. The defendant was charged with unlawful possession of morphine, contrary to section 5(2) of the Misuse of Drugs Act 1971. Regulations issued under the statute provided that section 5 had no effect in relation to preparations containing no more than 0.2 per cent morphine. The

---

[120] (1974) 59 Cr App R 213.
[121] This section governs summary trials, which include trials of indictable offences in the magistrates' courts.
[122] See Zuckerman, 'The third exception to the rule in *Woolmington*' (1976) 92 LQR 402.
[123] (1974) 59 Cr App R 213, 271.
[124] See C. Tapper and R. Cross, *Evidence*, 7th edn (Butterworths, London, 1990), pp. 140–1; G. Williams, *Criminal Law, the General Part* (Stevens, London, 1953), p. 905; Phipson, *Evidence*, 14th edn (Sweet & Maxwell, London, 1990), para. 4.18. Cf. Eleventh Report, paras. 137–42, which argued that all burdens on the accused should be evidential only.
[125] [1986] 1 All ER 184.

defence was that the morphine content in the substance in the possession of the accused was too low to amount to a prohibited drug. The Court of Appeal held that he was attempting to bring himself within an exception created by the regulations and the legal burden therefore rested on him. The court conceded that there was a difference from *Edwards*, in that there the defendant was not in a special position with regard to the regulations, as a pharmacist would have been, for example. In *Edwards* the accused was a publican, and the question was whether or not he had been granted a justices' licence. Here it could not be said that the regulations in question had created a special category of person who could claim a particular excuse or justification. The Court of Appeal considered it significant that its interpretation of the statute meant that the prosecution need not produce an analyst in every case to show the proportion of morphine present. But to require citizens to prove that substances in their possession are not prohibited drugs – in other words, to create a presumption that they are – is absurd and oppressive. Of course it is for the prosecution to show that the substance in question was the substance prohibited in the statute and defined in the regulations. This was the opinion of the House of Lords,[126] which felt that no excessive burden was placed on the prosecution thereby. The House of Lords confirmed the *Edwards* decision that statutes can by implication cast the legal burden of proof on the accused. Which statutes do this is a matter of construction in every case. The House conceded that the task of construction is not straightforward. Lord Griffiths suggested that generally the court should consider the seriousness of the offence and the fact that any doubt should be resolved in favour of the accused. Lord Ackner added the practical consequences of placing the burden on the defendant to the list.

Although it was a relief to all that the Court of Appeal's decision was overturned, commentators vary in their reaction to the House of Lords judgment in *Hunt*. Zuckerman argues that it stops the rot which began in *Edwards*;[127] Di Birch has valiantly attempted to extract comprehensible guidelines from it;[128] Mirfield is far more sceptical,[129] and Bennion thinks the courts may disregard the whole thing.[130] Certainly, a cynic might feel that the Court of Appeal decision in *Hunt* was merely a wrong-headed effort to save a

---

[126] [1987] 1 All ER 1.

[127] Zuckerman, 'No third exception to the *Woolmington* rule' (1987) 103 LQR 170.

[128] Di Birch, 'Hunting the snark; the elusive statutory exception' [1988] Crim LR 221.

[129] Mirfield, 'The legacy of Hunt' [1988] Crim LR 19; 'An ungrateful reply' [1988] Crim LR 233.

[130] Bennion, 'Statutory exceptions: a third knot in the golden thread' [1988] Crim LR 31.

conviction despite a serious error by the prosecution, who for some reason had no analytical evidence on the day of the trial. No great advance of principle is necessary in such circumstances, and it may be that *Hunt* will be forgotten in due course.

Standard of proof (civil cases)

Although the standard required is frequently given as 'proved on the balance of probabilities', the phrase is slightly misleading in so far as it suggests an even balance or 50/50. This is not the case: 'If the evidence is such that the tribunal can say that we think it more probable than not the burden is discharged, but if the evidence is equal it is not.'[131] This is a low standard of proof, and yet, according to Egglestone, in a case which could be decided on a likelihood of 51 per cent, a judge who thinks the plaintiff's account more believable than the defendant's will say that he believes the plaintiff.[132] Egglestone suggests that in arithmetical terms the plaintiff is entitled to judgment if his or her case is proved only to a probability of 0.501 – resulting in the defendant losing his or her case and probably costs where his or her own case has been proved to a probability of 0.499.[133] But such an outcome is extremely unlikely. Trial judges are aware of the consequences of their own decisions, and inevitably will bear in mind what would be the effect upon the defendant of accepting the plaintiff's version of events where that is barely proven. In fact, there is authority (apart from the dictates of common sense) for the proposition that the greater the impact on the defendant of a decision for the plaintiff, the more evidence the latter will have to find. For example, although if a crime is alleged during civil proceedings the standard of proof remains the civil one, there have been suggestions that the degree of proof required in civil cases may vary according to the seriousness of the allegation.[134]

A civil court, when considering a charge of fraud, will naturally require a higher degree of probability than that which it would require when asking if negligence is established. Likewise a divorce court should require a degree of

---

[131] *Miller v Minister of Pensions* [1947] 2 All ER 372, 373–4, *per* Denning J.

[132] Egglestone, *Evidence*, p. 129.

[133] See reply by R. J. Cohen, *The Probable and the Provable* (OUP, Oxford, 1977), also his debate with Professor Williams: [1979] Crim LR 297, 340; [1980] Crim LR 91, 103. This kind of mathematical debate will probably stiffen judicial resolve not to become involved in mathematical arguments – see *People v Collins* 438 P 2d 33 (1968).

[134] *Hornal v Neuberger Products* [1957] 1 QB 247.

probability which is proportionate to the subject-matter.[135] Recently, judges hearing cases involving accusations against parents of sexual abuse of their children have operated a varying standard of proof according to the nature of the allegation.[136] There have been criticisms of this approach; Carter argues that shifting standards lead to confusion, and that it is hardly fair to impose a higher standard on a party merely because he or she has suffered a grievous wrong.[137] But surely that is the point: the more grievous the wrong, the more the plaintiff is asking the court to demand of the defendant by way of redress. A defendant may lose his or her job, home, company or family. What judge would go so far on a probability of 0.501?

Standard of proof (criminal cases)

R v Winsor[138] settled that criminal cases must be proved beyond a reasonable doubt. Society in the present day is so much stronger than individuals, and is capable of inflicting so much more harm on them than they as a rule can inflict on society, that it can afford to be generous. Other countries also demand a high standard before a finding of guilt, but may express it rather differently. For example, the Polish Criminal Code states that the accused shall not be considered guilty before his or her guilt has been proven as provided by the Code,[139] and that 'Unresolvable doubts shall not be resolved to the prejudice of the accused.'[140] This last does not mean that all doubts have to be resolved in the accused's favour, but that they shall not be resolved to his or her detriment – allowing a neutral resolution.[141] The Supreme Court takes the view that the agency conducting the proceedings should try to exhaust every possibility and only when the remaining doubts prove immune to elucidation, should the final decision be made, and that without prejudicing the accused's interests.[142] The reasoning process involved in the Polish proceedings is rather clearer, then, than it is in English ones. There is great mystery to the idea of beyond reasonable doubt, both in

[135] *Bater v Bater* [1906] P 209.
[136] *Re H and Re K* [1989] 2 FLR 313; See Yates, 'Burden of proof past and future: *Re H and Re K* revisited' (1989) 2 JCL 109.
[137] Carter, *Cases and Statutes*, p. 61.
[138] (1865) 4 F & F 363; confirmed by the House of Lords in *Woolmington* [1935] AC 462.
[139] Art. 3(2).
[140] Art. 3(3).
[141] Waltos, *Code of Criminal Procedure*.
[142] Ibid.

conceptual terms and in terms of how jurors reach an agreement. There is some suggestion in the case law that judges feel that the best course is to leave the matter as vaguely described as possible. Ultimately a verdict in a criminal case is a reflection of the judgment of the people on the action of this particular defendant, and if that is a moral, rather than a rational reaction, that may not be altogether indefensible.

There have been attempts to define what is meant by reasonable doubt for the benefit of the jury, but these have proved to be at least as confusing as the expression itself. Generally, a definition should be avoided,[143] but a judge who is specifically requested by the jury to explain it may be forced to attempt one.

> If the judge feels that any of [the jurors]…are in danger of thinking that they are engaged in some task more esoteric than applying to the evidence adduced at the trial the common sense with which they approach matters of importance to them in their ordinary lives, then the use of such analogies as that used by Small J in the present case, whether in the words in which he expressed it or in those used in any of the cases to which reference has been made, may be helpful.[144]

The approach of Small J was as follows:[145]

> But surely, upon reflection, you remember that in dealing with matters of importance in your own business affairs you do not allow slight, whimsical doubts to deter you from going along; you brush them aside and go ahead. But surely, then comes a time when, in dealing with matters of your own affairs, you stop to think, and by reason of that doubt you decide what to do in your business of importance. Well, this is the quality and kind of doubt of which the law speaks when it speaks of reasonable doubt.

It is no criticism of Small J that there is little enlightenment in the business analogy. That has been employed in other cases.[146] But the attempt to equate commercial decision-making with fact-finding in courts is misconceived for two reasons. In the first place, the factors involved are very different. Business decisions involve an assessment of the degree of commercial risk involved, taking account of the consequences of failure against the potential gain. Jurors trying cases are not themselves at risk, and therefore

---

[143] *Walters v The Queen* [1969] 2 AC 26.

[144] Lord Diplock in ibid., p. 30.

[145] Ibid., p. 28.

[146] E.g. *Manning* (1849) 30 CCC Sess Pap 654, *per* Pollock CB; *Ching* (1976) 63 Cr App R 7.

need take no note of consequences, except in so far as their sympathies have been engaged by the accused or the complainant in the case before them. It is doubtful, too, whether all business people employ the same standards in their business affairs,[147] and, even if they did, whether the jury would recognize them.

The other, and more profound reason that this is a doomed exercise is that jurors are required to determine the truth, as far as they can from the evidence before them, whereas a business executive's decision-making is rarely an exercise in *adjudication*, it is a conclusion based upon *prediction* (whether as to market forces, labour relations, or other variables). Judith Thompson's example of the lottery illustrates this difference. If A knows that B bought five lottery tickets and that 100 were sold altogether, A is entitled to conclude that there is a 0.95 probability that B will lose. But A does not *know* that B will lose, and would be wrong to tell B to tear up the tickets. Knowing that there is a high degree of probability is not the same as a belief in a fact beyond reasonable doubt. A business executive might well operate on the basis of the former, but would hardly ever be able to make a decision if he or she waited until achieving the latter.

Is the meaning of 'beyond reasonable doubt' obvious to juries, so that elaboration is unnecessary, as indicated by the Privy Council in *Walters*?[148] Or is the reality that judges are themselves so unsure of what it means that they are best advised to conceal the fact by avoiding definition? Some points are clear; there cannot be an obligation to prove the case beyond *all* doubt, as that would mean that entirely improbable possibilities, which would exist in every case, would entitle the accused to an acquittal. It is possible, although not at all likely, that Martians land secretly on Earth, commit murders, and leave behind fingerprints identical to those of certain unlucky human beings, but no jury would acquit on that basis. In *Miller v Minister of Pensions*[149] Denning J explained that 'beyond reasonable doubt' does not mean beyond the shadow of a doubt, since the law would not protect the community if fanciful possibilities could 'deflect the course of justice'. He concluded that therefore if the evidence against an individual is so strong that there is only a remote possibility in his or her favour, such that a juror could dismiss it as possible but not in the least probable, then the case is proved beyond a reasonable doubt.

Although these remarks may look like a step on the way towards understanding, a trial judge who attempts to define a reasonable doubt for the benefit of the jury increases the risk of the conviction being quashed on

---

[147] *Hepworth and Fearnley* [1955] 2 QB 600, *per* Lord Goddard CJ.
[148] [1969] 2 AC 26.
[149] [1947] 2 All ER 372.

appeal.[150] Lord Goddard CJ said: 'Once a judge begins to use the words "reasonable doubt" and try to explain what is a reasonable doubt and what is not, he is much more likely to confuse the jury than if he tells them in plain language, "It is the duty of the prosecution to satisfy you of the prisoner's guilt."'[151] However, a direction which does no more than urge the jury to be satisfied of guilt is not sufficient.[152] It should be stressed that the jury should be so satisfied that they feel sure,[153] or the judge should tell them to satisfy themselves beyond all reasonable doubt.[154] In sum, although judges must stress the incidence and standard of proof in criminal cases, they are best leaving the jury to interpret that standard for themselves rather than attempting to define what it is impossible to define.[155] Instead, a more contextual approach is preferred; the judge should give a proper direction when going through the facts, explaining what inferences may be drawn from particular items of evidence. However, it may be that variations in language at this juncture affect the readiness of juries to convict. Mock trials staged for the London Jury Project of the London School of Economics resulted in a significantly lower conviction rate where the jury were told that they 'must feel sure and certain on the evidence that the accused is guilty',[156] than where they were told: 'You should be sure beyond a reasonable doubt and by a reasonable doubt I mean not a fanciful doubt that anyone might use to avoid an unpleasant decision, but a doubt for which reasons can be given.'[157]

There is some evidence that juries adopt a sliding scale according to the seriousness of the offence.[158] Such an approach has some limited judicial approval; apart from the observations in relation to civil cases discussed above, there is authority in an elderly criminal case. Holroyd J in *Sarah Hobson*[159] said: 'The greater the crime, the stronger the proof required for the purpose of conviction.' The introduction of causing death by driving offences as an alternative to gross negligence manslaughter was an acknow-

---

[150] *Summers* [1952] 1 All ER 1059; *Walters*, ibid.; *Ching* (1976) 63 Cr App R 7; *Gray* (1973) 58 Cr App R 177.

[151] *Kritz* [1950] 1 KB 82, 90.

[152] *Blackburn* (1955) 39 Cr App R 84n; *Hepworth and Fearnley* [1955] 2 QB 600.

[153] *Kritz* [1950] 1 KB 82; *Walters* [1969] 2 AC 26.

[154] *Hepworth and Fearnley* [1955] 2 QB 600.

[155] *Ching* (1976) 63 Cr App R 7.

[156] As *per* Lord Goddard CJ in *Kritz* [1950] 1 KB 82, 90.

[157] Cornish and Sealy, 'Juries and the rule of evidence' [1973] Crim LR 208.

[158] Simon and Mahan, 'Quantifying burdens of proof' (1971) 5 L & Soc Rev 319.

[159] (1823) 1 Lewin 261; cf. *Bater v Bater* [1951] P 35, 36–7: 'In criminal cases the charge must be proved beyond reasonable doubt, but where may be degrees of proof within that standard', *per* Lord Denning, quoted with approval by Lord Pearce in *Blyth v Blyth* [1966] AC 643, 673.

ledgement of jurors' reluctance to convict of the latter more serious offence.[160] Carter, while conceding that the commission of a serious crime is 'intrinsically less likely than is the commission of a petty crime', objects to the idea of a varying scale. 'The policy of the law is that a man ought not to be convicted of even a minor crime except on proof beyond reasonable doubt.' He argues that the gravity of the consequences of the verdict has no rational bearing on a fact-finding process concerned only with probabilities.[161] It is hoped that it has emerged from this chapter that trials are far removed from this description, and are certainly not dedicated first and foremost to discovery of actual facts. There is no real cause for alarm for those who share Carter's views, however, since there is no evidence that judges are suggesting to juries that the more serious the crime, the more they must be sure. But there is nothing to prevent jurors from forming such an opinion independently, and applying their own standards based on their conception of fairness – surely a well-known argument for trial by one's peers.

---

[160] Originally in Road Traffic Act 1956, s. 8.
[161] Carter, *Cases and Statutes*, p. 61.

3

Telling the Truth:
Witnesses and the Court

There's no art
To find the mind's construction in the face

Shakespeare, *Macbeth*, I, iv

The evidence before the court consists of more than sworn testimony. The tribunal of fact may be presented with such evidence as a live dog for inspection on the question of its alleged viciousness,[1] may be expected to travel to view a site[2] or may even be required to scrutinize the very bath in which one of the 'Brides in the Bath' was drowned.[3] On some matters no evidence is necessary; a presumption may take effect, such as the conclusive presumption of law that a boy aged under fourteen is incapable of the sexual act,[4] or the rebuttable presumption that someone who, despite due inquiries, has not been heard of for seven years by those who normally would hear of him, is dead.[5] On some issues a judge trying a civil case is entitled to take judicial notice of a notorious fact.[6] Similarly, where facts are within the everyday knowledge of the members of the jury they, like the judge, may take judicial notice of them.[7] But, generally in cases where facts are in dispute, the court will rely heavily on its assessment of the veracity or reliability of witnesses,

---

[1] *Line v Taylor* (1862) 3 F & F 731.
[2] *Buckingham v Daily News* [1956] 2 QB 534.
[3] *Smith* (1915) 11 Cr App R 229; the bath had in fact already been purchased with a view to exhibition in the Chamber of Horrors at Mme Tussaud's.
[4] *Groombridge* (1836) 7 Car & P 582.
[5] *Chard v Chard* [1956] P 259.
[6] *Brandao v Barnett* (1846) 12 Cl & Fin 282; *Taylor v Barclay* (1828) 2 Sim 213.
[7] *Hoare v Silverlock* (1848) 12 QB 624.

particularly in the adversarial trial, where the emphasis is on orality. In the adversarial system the opportunity to see and hear witnesses being examined is considered essential. Therefore, in addition to considering the content of the witness's evidence, the tribunal will consider the appearance and demeanour of witnesses. It might be relevant that a witness is tall, heavily built or deformed. How wisely these observations are used is discussed below.

INFLUENCE OF THE JUDGE

The judicial function in the adversarial trial is in theory, severely curtailed. In civil cases the role of impartial referee is strictly separated from that of tribunal of fact. In criminal cases the judge is supposed to have no opinion of the facts; the special function of the jury in deciding facts is carefully protected from intrusions, as will appear below with regard to opinion evidence. But, as we saw in chapter 1, it has been doubted whether the judge in modern criminal trials in England bears much resemblance to the passive referee of the adversarial model. He or she is in any event expected to adjudicate on issues of law such as the admissibility of evidence, and also on facts which affect admissibility; this must be done in the absence of the jury in a trial within a trial, or *voir dire*. The judge's decision therefore may deprive the jury of the opportunity of hearing certain items of evidence or may have the effect of altogether preventing a particular witness from giving evidence if the entire contents of his or her testimony are found to be inadmissible. Although the subject of admissibility appears to be closely bounded by exclusionary rules, it can be argued that a considerable amount of personal discretion is involved. This factor is most apparent when judges rule on the relevance of particular evidence, but may also underlie the application of exceptions to particular exclusionary rules. An obvious example is the operation of the doctrine of *res gestae*; the concept affords a convenient cloak for discretion and frequently provides a useful escape route from the rigours of exclusionary rules such as the hearsay rule. Many of the rules themselves, such as that requiring a corroboration warning where an accomplice incriminates the co-accused, appear to have developed from the 'good common sense of trial judges' over the years.[8] Just as judges responded to the risk of self-interested testimony carrying too much weight in accomplice cases, the intrinsic defects of hearsay evidence were also noted, and rules designed to deal with it were developed. Professor Delisle argues that rules which evolved gradually from the operation of judicial discretion

---

[8] Delisle, 'Judicial discretion and the law of evidence', paper presented to Conference of Society for the Reform of the Criminal Law (London, July 1987).

have ossified into utter rigidity: 'the so-called exclusionary rules are not meant to be mechanically applied like some calculus, but rather need to be used with discretion'.[9] He has made a strong case for the expansion of judicial discretion at the expense of a code of exclusionary rules; to attempt to exclude it altogether is in any case a hopeless exercise. In some contexts the existence of discretion in relation to admissibility is acknowledged; for example, if questions about the accused's previous misconduct are prima facie permissible under section 1(f)(ii) of the Criminal Evidence Act 1898, the trial judge may nevertheless refuse to allow them if he or she considers that justice requires that they should not be put. The balancing of probative value against prejudicial effect required of trial judges by the similar facts rule is another area where discretion is inevitably involved. However, in *Viola*[10] Lord Lane CJ held that it was wrong to speak of discretion in the context of section 2 of the Sexual Offences Act 1976, which directs trial judges to exclude certain evidence or questions unless it would be unfair to the defendant to do so. The sole question here is relevance, and Lord Lane CJ thought that if a matter is relevant the judge has no discretion to exclude. This opinion ignores the considerable degree of flexibility involved in decisions about relevance. In identifying the borderline between those facts which are too remote from the issue and those which are not, the judge is inevitably involved in evaluation of evidence and therefore is close to trespassing into the jury's territory in the criminal case.

It is not entirely true to say that judges do not descend into 'the dust of the arena'. In civil cases witnesses can be called only with the consent of one of the parties,[11] but in criminal cases the judge may call and cross-examine witnesses in the interests of justice and particularly if the jury request it,[12] although this power should be exercised sparingly and with great care.[13] Cross argues that together with the power to recall witnesses, this 'serves as a reminder that the English judge is more than an umpire in the strict sense of the word',[14] quoting Denning LJ:[15]

> In the system of trial we have evolved in this country, the judge sits to hear and determine the issues raised by the parties, not to conduct an investigation or examination on behalf of society at large, as happens, we believe, in some

[9] Ibid.

[10] [1982] 3 All ER 73; and see chapter 4.

[11] *Re Enoch and Zaretsky, Bock and Co.'s Arbitration* [1910] 1 KB 327.

[12] *Chapman* (1838) 8 Car & P 558; *Holden* (1838) 8 Car & P 606.

[13] *Edwards* (1848) 3 Cox CC 82.

[14] C. Tapper and R. Cross, *Evidence*, 7th edn (Butterworths, London, 1990), pp. 268–7.

[15] *Jones v National Coal Board* [1957] 2 QB 55, 63.

foreign countries. Even in England, however, a judge is not a mere umpire to answer the question 'How's that?' His object, above all, is to find out the truth and to do justice according to law.

Quite how judges are expected to achieve this aim from their lofty and disinterested perch is not clear; certainly, their position is an uneasy one in its ambiguous stance somewhere between detachment and involvement.

It is true that, contrary to adversarial theory, trial judges in criminal cases have considerable influence on the way in which evidence is presented. They may question any witness at any stage,[16] although they should not do so in a way indicating that they believe the accused to be guilty.[17] They may cross-examine the accused if he or she gives evidence, but not in a manner suggesting that they wish to help the prosecution rather than the defence.[18] If a judge's intervention indicates that he or she thinks that the witness is not to be believed, the judge must remind the jury that the question of credibility is for them.[19] But if the judge goes so far as to invite the jury to disbelieve the defence evidence the conviction must be quashed.[20] A judge's interruptions must not prevent counsel from presenting his or her case. In *Perks*[21] the defendant was giving his evidence-in-chief. Out of a total of 700 questions put to him, 147 were asked by the judge, who also interrupted defence counsel's final address. The Court of Appeal held that the point was not the number of interruptions so much as their hostile nature, which hindered the development of the defendant's evidence-in-chief. Such interventions should be kept to a minimum. However, discourtesy to counsel as such is not a sufficient reason to overturn a conviction;[22] there must be positive interference with counsel in pursuit of his or her task.[23] Even a lord chief justice has been known to cause concern on this ground; Lord Hewart CJ was criticized more than once in the Court of Appeal for failing to keep an open mind;[24] more recently, the Court of Appeal expressed disapproval of a judge who during the defence address to the jury made gestures of impatience, sighed and several times 'observed in a loud voice "Oh God"

---

[16] *Hopper* [1915] 2 KB 431; *Cain* (1936) 25 Cr App R 204; 'a judge may put such questions as the interests of justice require'.

[17] *Rabbitt* (1931) 23 Cr App R 112.

[18] *Cain* (1936) 25 Cr App R 204.

[19] *Gilson and Cohen* (1944) 29 Cr App R 174.

[20] Ibid.

[21] [1973] Crim LR 388.

[22] *Ptohopoulos* [1968] Crim LR 52.

[23] *Hircock and others* [1970] 1 QB 67; *Wilson* [1979] RTR 57.

[24] See C. P. Harvey, *The Advocate's Devil* (Stevens, London, 1958); *Hobbs v Tinling* [1929] 2 KB 1.

and then laid his head across his arms and made groaning noises'. Despite this behaviour, the court did not feel it necessary to quash the conviction.[25]

Judge and jury

A judge may withdraw an issue from the jury altogether. Generally if the defendant does not raise a particular defence, the trial judge should put it to the jury only when there is evidence from which they could reasonably infer that the defendant acted in a way which provided a defence at law. There is no duty to leave to the jury defences which are fanciful or speculative.[26] So the trial judge must decide whether as a matter of law any evidence has been raised which, if believed, would establish the facts in issue. His or her duty to assist the defendant in a criminal trial in this way departs from the normal adversarial principle that it is for the parties to select the issues to be tried. Thus although the jury are the tribunal of fact and decide which evidence is to be believed, their ability to do this is circumscribed by the judge's power (and duty) to withdraw an issue from them altogether. Here the judge is deciding whether or not the defence has discharged its evidential burden of proof. In *Metropolitan Railway v Jackson*[27] P sued the defendant company for negligence, alleging that his thumb had been trapped in a slamming door because the carriage of their train was overcrowded. He had evidence to show the overcrowding arose from the defendants' negligence, but none to show that his thumb had been in the path of the door because of the overcrowding. The House of Lords therefore held that the judge should have withdrawn the case from the jury. A single judge hearing a negligence case nowadays in the county or High Court would, in theory, go through two stages of reasoning. First, he or she should consider whether there is a case made which demands subsequent adjudication on the facts by him- or herself as tribunal of fact. How is the initial decision to be made? In *Ryder v Wombwell* Willes J observed that whereas previously judges would leave an issue to the jury if there was only the slightest evidence to support it, 'it is now settled that the question for the judge is...not whether there is literally no evidence, but whether there is none that ought reasonably to satisfy the jury that the fact sought to be proved is established'.[28] This can be a difficult question, for instance with circumstantial evidence. A judge will similarly withdraw an issue from consideration if a witness asserting the contrary was not challenged on it by way of cross-examination. This is because of the

[25] *Hircock and others* [1970] 1 QB 67.
[26] *Critchley* [1982] Crim LR 524.
[27] (1877) 3 App Cas 193.
[28] (1868) LR 4 Exch 32, 39.

emphasis English courts place on the value of cross-examination as a way to the truth.

In criminal cases the defence may submit, at the close of the presentation of the evidence for the prosecution, that there is no case to answer. If successful, a verdict of not guilty is returned by the magistrates, or by the jury on direction from the trial judge. In a civil case without a jury, the judge must decline to rule on the submission unless the person making it elects not to call evidence;[29] it is thought unreasonable to ask a judge who has to decide on the facts as well as the law to make a decision before the evidence is complete. Before the case of *Galbraith*[30] there was a school of thought that a trial judge should stop a criminal case if in his or her view it would be unsafe or unsatisfactory to convict. But Lord Lane CJ decided that this is so only where the judge concludes that the prosecution evidence, taken at its highest, is such that a jury, properly directed, could not properly convict upon it; only then should the judge decide, on submission being made by the defence, that there is no case to answer. Where the strength or weakness of the prosecution evidence depends on the view to be taken of a witness's reliability or other matters which are, in Lord Lane's opinion, the province of the jury, and where on one possible view of the facts there is evidence on which a jury could properly convict, then the judge should allow the matter to be tried by the jury. Thus the judge should not make a judgment of how safe a conviction in this case would be. But it may be that a ban on any sort of qualitative judgment by the trial judge is not entirely a good thing. To be sure, Lord Lane does allow a trial judge to reject evidence which is inherently weak or vague or inconsistent with other evidence. Lord Diplock has said in *Haw Tua Tau v Public Prosecutor*[31] that evidence which was 'inherently so incredible that no reasonable person could accept it as being true' would not prevent a submission of no case from succeeding. But that is a minimal intervention by the judge. The Court of Appeal in *Galbraith* has reverted to the neutral referee position for trial judges abandoned in the kind of matters discussed above. This approach is inconsistent with *Turnbull*,[32] which requires the judge to withdraw the case from the jury if the quality of identification evidence is poor, as with the 'fleeting glimpse' cases. Pattenden observes[33] that the whole object of the no case procedure is to protect the accused from the risk of a perverse jury verdict or from a pros-

[29] *Alexander v Rayson* [1936] 1 KB 169.
[30] [1981] 2 All ER 1060.
[31] [1981] 3 All ER 14.
[32] [1976] 3 All ER 549.
[33] Pattenden, 'The submission of no case to answer: some recent developments' [1982] Crim LR 558.

ecutor who cannot establish even a prima facie case, but who hopes to make good this deficiency in his or her cross-examination of defence witnesses. The increased admissibility of hearsay evidence in criminal trials may bring the judge further into the arena of contested facts than Lord Lane anticipated. For when hearsay evidence is admitted it carries less weight than sworn testimony.[34] Under the Criminal Justice Act 1988 judges are given a discretion to exclude hearsay evidence, taking account of the interests of justice. When it is admitted in proper exercise of that discretion, given the lower probative value of hearsay, judges may be forced to consider the question of how safe a conviction based entirely on such evidence would be. Consider *Hovells*.[35] An elderly lady said that she had been raped, but died before the trial began. There was medical evidence of sexual activity and a police record of her statement describing the attack and the attacker, but the latter only in vague terms. Hovells admitted being at her flat but said that he could not remember anything about it as he had been very drunk. The judge, who had a discretion whether or not to admit the hearsay evidence under the New Zealand legislation,[36] allowed it in, which is not objectionable. The question remains, however, whether he should have let the case go to the jury on the basis of that evidence; he did so, and they convicted Hovell, whose appeal was subsequently rejected.

It seems somewhat artificial to insist on the one hand that judges vacate the fact-finding arena, scrupulously leaving the jury its task, when in the context of the judicial summing-up on the evidence at the close of the trial, considerable scope for influencing the jury remains. Fear of excessive judicial influence has led many states of the United States to restrict the summing-up to an explanation of the law, leaving the jury to untangle the facts for themselves, but in the United Kingdom the judge sums up on the facts as well as the law. That the defence does not have the last word is regarded as extraordinary in France, but there the judge retires with the jury, so his influence is considerable. The advantage of the English system is that the judge, by reviewing the facts as well as the law, can relate the one to the other in a manner avoiding complicated technical definitions. Although the judge can direct an acquittal, he or she may not usurp the jury's function by directing a conviction.[37] Yet, it is said that it is impossible for a judge to deal with doubtful points of fact unless he or she can state some of the facts confidently to the jury.[38] Although judges may not usurp the function of the

[34] See chapter 7.
[35] [1987] 1 NZLR 610.
[36] See chapter 7.
[37] *DPP v Stonehouse* [1978] AC 55.
[38] *R v Cohen and Bateman* (1909) 2 Cr App R 197.

jury,[39] they are entitled to express themselves strongly on the facts in a proper case, since they have experience on the bearing of evidence and in dealing with the relevancy of questions of fact, and it is therefore right that the jury should have the assistance of the judge:

> The judge is more than a mere referee who takes no part in the trial save to intervene when a rule of procedure or evidence is broken. He and the jury try the case together and it is his duty to give them the benefit of his knowledge of the law and to advise them in the light of his experience as to the significance of the evidence.[40]

Judges feel free therefore to tell juries that they may find the witness's account 'incredible' or 'almost beyond belief', as long as they remind the jury that ultimately it is for them to decide whether or not to believe it. Lord Goddard LCJ's direction to the jury in *Craig and Bentley* is a notorious example of this 'advice':[41]

> Can you suppose for a moment...that [Craig] would not have told his pals he was out with that he had got a revolver? Is it not almost inconceivable that Craig would not have told him and probably shown him the revolver which he had?...Can you believe it for a moment although Bentley had said he did not know Craig had the gun?

It is widely believed by practitioners that a judge who tries to influence a jury strongly in favour of the prosecution may find that the attempt back-fires and that the jury deliberately counter what they perceive as bias. The London Jury Project at the London School of Economics found that most jurors who thought the judge hostile to the defence acquitted; there was an even higher acquittal rate,[42] though, where the jury thought the judge favoured the defence, apparently being happy to follow his or her line in this. Where the judge was perceived as impartial, the acquittal rate fell to 50 per cent.[43] Despite the risk of reaction from the jury, some judges clearly do

---

[39] *West* (1910) 4 Cr App R 179; *Beeby* (1911) 6 Cr App R 138; *Frampton* (1917) 12 Cr App R 202.

[40] Lawton LJ in *Mutch* [1973] 1 All ER 178.

[41] (1952). See D. Yallop, *To Encourage the Others*, 2nd edn (Corgi, London, 1990). Bentley was hanged in January 1953.

[42] 78 per cent compared with 68 per cent. However, the jurors, all participating in a simulation, did not give the summing-up as a reason for the acquittal.

[43] Sealy, 'An analysis of jury studies', in *Psychology, Law and Legal Process*, eds D. F. Farrington, K. Hawkins and S. Lloyd-Bostock (Macmillan, London, 1979).

make their scepticism of the defence case plain, as an eminent judge has conceded:[44]

> Some judges almost tell a jury how they ought to find, and so seem to me to assume a function which is not theirs according to our constitution. I have always striven to avoid this and to leave the question really as well as formally to the jury, taking, however, great care that they should never find a man guilty whom I believed innocent.

So we find the judges given licence to comment strongly on the facts, although in strict adversarial theory they should concern themselves exclusively with the law. There is another contradiction: there seems to be an increasing tendency in the appellate courts to argue that the trial judge's direction on the law should leave the jury with considerable scope to define elements of the crime charged for themselves.[45] This avoids having to find definitions for difficult and sometimes metaphysical concepts, but may lead to different verdicts in similar cases, should different juries disagree on the meaning of intention[46] or dishonesty.[47] The reply that such concepts require no explanation to men and women of good sense is not entirely convincing, and another view might be that the jury are entitled to help in these matters; jurors may have oppressive responsibilities in serious cases, and questions of fact are difficult enough. There seems no reason to encumber them with the task of defining the offence as well. Genuine anxiety may be seen in the reaction of the jury in *Moloney*'s case,[48] but the fact that the jury were troubled by the definition of intention they were given in that case was seen by the House of Lords as an argument for giving them no definition at all.

WITNESSES

The witnesses who may be called

There are few restrictions on the parties in civil cases as to whom they may call to give evidence on their behalf. The position of child witnesses is

---

[44] Fry LJ, quoted in Agnes Fry, *Memoirs of Sir Edward Fry* (Milford, OUP, London, 1921).

[45] The leading case is *Brutus v Cozens* [1972] 2 All ER 1297, where the House of Lords held that the meaning of 'insulting behaviour' in the Public Order Act 1936 could safely be left to the jury.

[46] *Hancock and Shankland* [1986] 1 All ER 641.

[47] *Feely* [1973] 1 All ER 341.

[48] [1985] 1 All ER 1025.

complex and is discussed in chapter 4. Persons of defective intellect may not give evidence if incapable of understanding the nature of the oath, a decision for the judge.[49] If the judge allows the testimony to be introduced, it is for the tribunal of fact to adjudge how much credit to give it. Non-compellable witnesses include the Sovereign and foreign ambassadors.[50] In criminal cases there are restrictions on the competence and compellability of accused persons,[51] and in the past there were complicated rules governing the competence and compellability of their spouses. These elaborate prescriptions were a source of inspiration to the writers of detective stories; the simplification of the position under the Police and Criminal Evidence Act 1984 has therefore cost us a fascinating oddity, but even so, is to be welcomed as a step towards some coherence. Some of the traditional explanations for the limited availability of spouse witnesses were brushed aside by the Criminal Law Revision Committee: 'Objections...based on the theoretical unity of the spouses or on the interests of the accused's wife in the outcome of the proceedings,[52] and in particular on the likelihood that his wife will be biased in favour of the accused, can have no place in the decisions as to the extent of competence and compellability nowadays.'[53] However, the Committee did give serious consideration to issues such as the 'objection on social grounds to disturbing marital harmony more than is absolutely necessary', and 'what many regard as the harshness of compelling a spouse to give evidence against her husband'.[54] But the interests of marital harmony were not thought to demand restrictions on the *competence* of spouses as prosecution witnesses. For if a wife chooses to give evidence against her husband, it seems excessively paternalistic to prevent her from doing so on the grounds that the state is anxious to preserve goodwill in her marriage even if she no longer cares. Some lawyers have warned against the vindictive spouse who seizes the opportunity provided by the witness box of settling old grudges, but the fact remains that there may be other prosecution witnesses who are similarly motivated, and it is up to the defence to bring this out in cross-examination and to emphasize the point to the jury.

Reformers seem to make heavy weather of the question of whether spouses should be compellable for the prosecution. Section 80 of the 1984 Act rightly

---

[49] *Hill* (1851) 2 Den 254.

[50] See Phipson, *Evidence*, 14th edn (Sweet & Maxwell, London, 1990), para. 9.14.

[51] See chapter 4.

[52] A reference to the old common law rule that persons with an interest in the trial were inherently unreliable and should not give evidence.

[53] *Evidence (General)*, Eleventh Report of the Criminal Law Revision Committee, Cmnd 4991 (1972), para. 147.

[54] Ibid.

assumes that the spouse is potentially as damaging to the defence case if she gives evidence on behalf of the co-accused, whose interests may directly conflict with her husband's, as if she acts as a prosecution witness. Whether or not this justifies dealing with both situations in the same way is more doubtful; Zuckerman argues that if the co-defendant requires the spouse to show his innocence, he is entitled to her testimony, whatever the effect on her marriage might be.[55] Be that as it may, the Police and Criminal Evidence Act provides in section 80(3):

> In any proceedings the wife or husband of the accused shall...be compellable to give evidence for the prosecution or on behalf of any person jointly charged with the accused if and only if –
> (a) the offence charged involves an assault on, or injury or a threat of injury to, the wife or husband of the accused or a person who was at the material time under the age of sixteen; or
> (b) the offence charged is a sexual offence alleged to have been committed in respect of a person who was at the material time under that age; or
> (c) the offence charged consists of attempting or conspiring to commit, or of aiding, abetting, counselling, procuring or inciting the commission of, an offence...[in (a) or (b) above].

Before this, spouses were effectively not compellable for the prosecution except, arguably, for the common law exceptions of high treason and forcible marriage.[56] The new exception relating to offences against children is justified in the Eleventh Report in relation to the seriousness of 'some of these cases',[57] and because of the difficulty of proof where the victim is a young child. The lack of alternative evidence is a pragmatic argument which is not altogether convincing. Difficulty in securing a conviction is held to justify abandoning the erstwhile concern for the stability of the defendant's marriage; this difficulty will not exist in every case where a child has been injured, but may exist in some cases of injury to a seventeen-year-old – and there the spouse is not compellable.

A further argument is put forward by the Committee: 'She may have been a party to the violence or at least acquiesced in it, although it may not be possible to prosecute her. For similar reasons we think that the wife should be compellable on a charge of a sexual offence against a child under sixteen *belonging to the accused's household*.'[58] It is alarming to find changes in the law

---

[55] A. Zuckerman, *The Principles of Criminal Evidence* (OUP, Oxford, 1989), p. 295.

[56] Phipson, Evidence, 13th edn (Sweet & Maxwell, London, 1982), para. 31.24.

[57] Eleventh Report, para. 60.

[58] Ibid., para. 150. The qualification, italicized for convenience, does not appear in s. 80(3)(b).

being advocated on the strength of what appears to be a wild and unsupported generalization. If the wife's compellability is to serve as some sort of punishment, there ought to be a better case against her than that.

There have been suggestions in the past that to call a reluctant spouse–witness would be counterproductive, in that her distress or refusal to co-operate on the day might alienate the jury from the prosecutor or bring the trial to a complete standstill. The emotional conflict suffered by the spouse, who may face imprisonment for contempt of court if she refuses to testify, with the alternative of incriminating her husband or perjuring herself, is not unique, however. There may be others who feel equally anguished on the accused's behalf, and there is no legal bolthole for them. The possibility of an alternative approach which takes account of the emotional involvement of the accused's family never seems to have been addressed in England. In the French *Code du Procédure Pénale* the father, mother or other ascendant of the accused, his children, siblings, relatives by marriage to the same degree or wife should not take the oath.[59] In the English system there is no halfway house, but if in any case it appears to a prosecution that the spouse–witness is unlikely to further its cause, the witness will not be called.

Why, if spouses were to become compellable only in exceptional circumstances, introduce as an exception cases where they have suffered violence to themselves? For they are unlikely to place another person at risk if they refuse to give evidence voluntarily in cases of domestic violence. The Criminal Law Revision Committee said, 'On the whole we think that the public interest in the punishment of violence requires that compellability should remain.'[60] The Committee added that the fact that the wife therefore would have no choice whether to give evidence or not 'should make it easier to counter the effect of possible intimidation by her husband and to persuade her to give evidence'. The suggestion that a violent husband will participate in a rational debate upon contempt of court and accept that his wife's participation in the trial is not a betrayal is astonishing. The Committee goes on blithely to conclude, 'At any rate, there does not seem to us to be any evidence that the present rule of compellability[61] does any harm so it seems safest to preserve it.'[62]

The Report of the New South Wales Task Force on Domestic Violence[63]

---

[59] Art. 335.

[60] This view, that wives were compellable at common law in domestic violence cases, was subsequently rejected by the House of Lords in *Hoskyn v MPC* [1979] AC 474.

[61] See previous note.

[62] Eleventh Report, para. 149.

[63] 1981:55.

says that to place a choice in the hands of a woman who suffers from domestic violence is 'almost an act of legal cruelty'. A contrary view would be that forcing her to give evidence when she is afraid or does not wish to destroy her marriage is just as cruel. And it appears to be the case that in jurisdictions where victims of domestic violence can be compelled to give evidence, they are rarely forced to do so, probably for pragmatic reasons.[64] Policies of this kind reduce the cogency, if any, of arguments that women are helped by having no choice, since the ability to choose seems to survive a change in the law. On the other hand, it is difficult to imagine circumstances where the prosecutor would benefit by invoking the power to compel, although it may be that more women give evidence voluntarily precisely because the power exists. In 1987 Scotland Yard announced a new approach with an increased willingness to use compulsion in domestic violence cases.[65] Even so, in 1989 Susan Edwards writes: 'In the United Kingdom compellability has not been enforced';[66] it is impossible to tell whether the publicity on the subject made it unnecessary in that women became more co-operative, but this seems doubtful. Whatever the force of these arguments, the fact remains that the position of cohabitees who suffer domestic violence has always been that they enjoy no special protection from the general obligation to give evidence. Despite this, furore followed the decision of Judge Pickles to sentence to seven days' imprisonment for contempt an unmarried girl who declared herself too frightened to give evidence against her boyfriend.[67] This seems to demonstrate considerable public sympathy with the dilemma of battered women who seem to seek the protection of the law without being willing to participate to the extent required by the trial process, a dilemma which the English system of criminal justice has not seriously addressed. It is widely believed that battered women are prone to making complaints, perhaps summoning the police in an emergency, but withdrawing them later and refusing to take any further part in the investigation or prosecution process. The evidence for this is anecdotal,[68] but nevertheless convincing, being supported by many experienced practitioners. As a result, it is said, the police are slow to intervene in 'domestics', because they believe that the woman will change her mind and so their time would be wasted. The police may be being maligned unfairly; there is research

---

[64] Evidence to New South Wales Report on Domestic Violence (1985:31); Evidence to Law Reform Committee of Australia, (1986: Report No. 30 *Domestic Violence*); see Edwards, 'Compelling a reluctant spouse' [1989] NLJ 691.

[65] *Independent*, 24 June 1987.

[66] Edwards [1989] NLJ 691, 692.

[67] *Williams*, Leeds Crown Court, December 1989.

[68] See Edwards [1989] NLJ 691.

suggesting that there is in fact a high response rate.[69] If the allegations are true, it may be that police lack of interest stems from too narrow a view at all levels of the force as to the proper role of the police. It is wrong to assume that the police function is entirely bound up in arrest, prosecution, trial and conviction. Much may be achieved in protecting society without the consummation of a guilty verdict.[70]

The Eleventh Report pays surprisingly little attention to the issue of whether spouse compellability should be limited at all. In view of the comparative weakness of the arguments adduced in favour of the excepted cases, it might have been instructive to include a discussion of whether it would be best to make spouses compellable in all cases, given the recommendation that they should be generally competent. Instead, there is only the following, baffling, passage:[71]

> We do not think that the wife should be compellable for the prosecution in the case of offences other than those mentioned above...It might be argued that the wife should be compellable in very serious cases such as murder and spying or perhaps in all serious cases of violence; but the law has never, except perhaps in treason, made the seriousness of an offence by itself a ground for compellability, and we do not favour doing so now.

There is no apology for the earlier passage emphasizing the seriousness of violent crimes against children. Perhaps the explanation for the apparent refusal to explain precisely what, then, *is* the ground for compellability is a natural caution from a Committee which did not wish its proposals to appear so radical that they would not be implemented, which would be ironic in the light of what happened to the Eleventh Report because of the recommendations on the accused's right to silence.[72]

Questions of competence and compellability are of particular significance in an adversarial procedure which relies heavily on sworn oral testimony, preferring it to depositions and other kinds of hearsay evidence. Time and again appeal court judges emphasize that those who saw the witnesses give their evidence are far better able to form a view of the facts than anyone subsequently reading transcripts.[73] The insistence on the importance of the

---

[69] See Buzawa, 'Explaining variations in police responses to domestic violence: a case study in Detroit and New England', in *Coping with Family Violence*, eds E. T. Hotaling, D. Finkelhov and E. Kirkpatrick (Sage, Newbury Park, 1988).

[70] Smith, 'Victims who know their assailants', in ibid.

[71] Eleventh Report, para. 152.

[72] See chapter 5.

[73] *Yuill v Yuill* [1945] P 15.

opportunity to watch the witness at first hand colours the debate on video-taped depositions[74] and is the reason behind decisions such as *Dunne*;[75] in this case the trial judge questioned a seven-year-old girl in the absence of the jury to see whether she understood the nature of the oath. She was subsequently sworn and gave vital evidence for the prosecution. The Court of Appeal quashed the conviction. Lord Hewart CJ appreciated the kindly motives of the trial judge but held that witnesses should not be assessed in this way, without the jury or the defendant being present. In *Reynolds*[76] Lord Goddard CJ observed that although the decision whether the child should be sworn is for the trial judge, the jury should see her demeanour and manner of answering questions, even at that preliminary stage, in order to assess the credibility of her testimony, should she be allowed to give it.

Believing witnesses: credibility

The extent to which the credibility of witnesses in a trial may be lauded or assailed is an astonishingly obscure part of the law of evidence. The position of the accused in a criminal case, safeguarded as he or she is by the presumption of innocence, is inevitably distinct from and rather more the subject of reported decisions than that of other kinds of witness. Evidence of the defendant's good or bad character is discussed in chapter 5. As far as other witnesses are concerned, all are open to attack on such matters as powers of recall or observation, experience on which knowledge or belief is said to be based, and anything else which might render the witness less able than he or she claims to give the evidence in question. Witnesses are equally open to be cross-examined about their own bad character, unless the judge regards the questions as vexatious or irrelevant,[77] for instance if they are remote in time and character, or if there is a lack of proportion between the evidence of misdeeds in the past and the importance of the witness's evidence to the case in hand. The cross-examiner may remind the witness of his or her previous convictions, although there may not be an unfettered right to do this,[78] and, generally, 'spent' convictions under the Rehabilitation of Offenders Act 1974 would not be put without the leave of the judge.[79] If the accused has a criminal record, cross-examining prosecution witnesses on their bad character

---

[74] See chapter 4.
[75] (1929) 21 Cr App R 176.
[76] [1950] 1 KB 606.
[77] *Hobbs v Tinling* [1929] 2 KB 1.
[78] *Sweet-Escott* (1971) 55 Cr App R 316.
[79] Ss. 4(1), 7(3); *Practice Note* [1975] 2 All ER 1072. In a civil case, of course, a judge deciding to exclude the convictions would know about them anyway.

could cost the accused his or her 'shield',[80] so that his or her record could be revealed to the jury. This may inhibit the way the defence is conducted. Some judges appear to have exercised their discretion on the relevance of cross-examination as to credit rather oddly; Wolchover[81] has unearthed some surprising cases in which police officers giving evidence for the prosecution have been asked about earlier cases in which they were prosecution witnesses, but which resulted in acquittal. The defence suggestion is that the acquittal reflects the jury's distrust of that officer and that therefore the officer is not worthy of belief in the present case.[82] Courts should ensure that no general practice of this kind is allowed to develop, irrespective of the nature of the case – for example whether there is a relationship between the two prosecutions or not. An acquittal can rarely if ever be said to demonstrate that a jury disbelieved a particular prosecution witness. The jury are, after all, constantly reminded of the high standard of proof; and in any case, the opinion of one jury on a particular occasion as to the reliability of certain testimony has no bearing in logic or common sense on the case before a different panel, who are there to assess the quality of the prosecution evidence in the case before them.

In a civil case it is not generally possible to adduce evidence of the good character of the parties, as it is assumed,[83] unless character is an issue in the case, as in a libel suit. As usual, the witness may be cross-examined on the issue of credibility. Also, there is an obscure but ancient right to call a witness to say whether a witness for the opposing side can be believed on oath. The character witness must speak from personal knowledge[84] but must not refer to particular events, only his knowledge of the other's general character.[85] This little-understood rule was reaffirmed relatively recently by the House of Lords in the criminal case *Toohey v MPC*,[86] despite the

---

[80] Under Criminal Evidence Act 1898, s. 1(f)(ii); see chapter 5.

[81] Wolchover, 'Attacking confessions with past police embarrassments' [1988] Crim LR 573.

[82] *Cooke* (1987) 84 Cr App R 286; *McCann* (1987) CCC, 5 November, unreported. Clarification is unfortunately not provided by *Edwards* [1991] 2 All ER 266, where the Court of Appeal quashed a conviction and yet forbore to provide guidance, despite acknowledging that such cross-examinations run the risk of introducing any number of matters collateral. However, Lord Lane CJ expressed the view that it would be improper to suggest to an officer that he or she had committed perjury unless he or she had been found guilty of it by a court or disciplinary tribunal.

[83] *Attorney-General v Bowman* (1791) 2 Bos & P 532(n).

[84] *Trial of O'Connor* (1798) 26 How St Tr 1191.

[85] *Rudge* (1805) Peake Add Cas 232.

[86] [1965] AC 595; cf. *Richardson* [1969] 1 QB 299, where the Court of Appeal sympathized with the trial judge for his error, since cases where such witnesses are called are rare.

procedure being a 'cumbersome, anomalous and unconvincing exercise'.[87] There is little authority on the extent to which character evidence on the question of credibility can be used, probably because points of evidence are rarely taken. Cross notes that most civil cases proceed without much reference to the technical rules: 'It is certain that there are very many...examples of evidence of the character of a party being adduced without the slightest advertence to this branch of the law.'[88]

Witnesses in civil and criminal trials may have their previous inconsistent statements put to them for the purpose of undermining their credibility.[89] The witness's earlier consistent statements are said to be inadmissible because of their minimal probative value[90] unless they fall within one of the recognized exceptions to the general prohibition.[91] Where admitted, such statements are not evidence of the fact stated in a criminal case, going only to the witness's credibility on the basis of consistency. The position is different in civil cases, where they are admitted as exceptions to the hearsay rule under the Civil Evidence Act 1968.[92] The known exceptions include *res gestae*, previous identification of an accused person, complaints in sexual cases and statements on arrest or when first taxed with incriminating facts.[93] It has been suggested that there are more exceptions than generally supposed in textbooks.[94] Classification of instances into yet more categories is probably wasted effort; it may be the case, as it ought to be, that judges allow previous consistent statements to be admitted when they have a bearing on the credibility of the witness, whatever their nature. However, it is not clear how realistic it is to ask the jury in criminal cases to treat such statements solely as an indication of the consistency of the witness. That is the effect of the hearsay rule, a rule which evolved partly because of the emphasis on cross-examination of oral evidence in the adversarial tradition. Murphy has argued[95] that it is not necessary to apply the hearsay rule to these cases, since the witness who made the out-of-court statement is present in court and can

---

[87] Tapper and Cross, *Evidence*, 7th edn (Butterworths, London, 1990), p. 319.
[88] Ibid., p. 338.
[89] Criminal Procedure Act 1865, ss. 4, 5, governs both kinds of trial.
[90] *Roberts* [1942] 1 All ER 187; *Gillie v Posho* [1939] 2 All ER 196.
[91] In civil cases they are admissible either with the leave of the judge under Civil Evidence Act 1968, s. 2(2)(a) or in any event to rebut a suggestion of afterthought under s. 3(1)(b).
[92] Ss. 2, 3.
[93] See Tapper and Cross, *Evidence*, pp. 281–95.
[94] Gooderson, 'Previous inconsistent statements' [1968] CLJ 64.
[95] Murphy, 'Previous consistent and inconsistent statements: a proposal to make life easier for juries' [1985] Crim LR 270.

be cross-examined on it. He proposes reform on the lines of the United States Federal Rules, which allow some previous statements to be treated as 'non-hearsay'.

The operation of the hearsay rule in this context, confining earlier consistent statements to the issue of credibility, has caused problems beyond the not insubstantial one of juror comprehension. For example, the traditional view of a self-serving statement when applied to an accused person would be that if made when first taxed with incriminating facts, it is more significant than the usual run of self-serving statements, since here it shows that he or she has stuck to the same story from that point all the way through to trial. This would appear to present courts with no difficulty; it would be up to the defence to decide whether or not the statement is sufficiently similar to serve their purpose and whether or not to call the defendant, who must put the story again if there is to be anything for the previous statement to be consistent with. Recently, the courts have been placed in an awkward position because of an unthinking prosecution practice which has become well established over years, whereby prosecution witnesses have been reading out all statements made by the accused on arrest, whether admissions,[96] denials, or something else entirely. The cases which examine the conceptual problems arising from this are reviewed in detail in chapter 7; they are of great interest in that judges appear to think evidence of *reaction* to being accused of a crime is itself relevant, even where there is no admission and no previous consistent statement. Thus we find evidence which occupies a novel halfway house between evidence of a fact and evidence going to the credibility of a witness. The fact that it fails to find a convincing niche for itself within the accepted dichotomy between evidence on the issue and evidence of credibility indicates how impossible it is to divide all relevant evidence neatly into one or the other category. The case of *Douglass*[97] is another instance where the character of someone who was not a witness at all was clearly relevant, and the court had embarrassingly to skirt around the problem that, strictly speaking, the character evidence should relate to the credibility of someone giving evidence at the trial. The same problem arose in *Chapman*;[98] C1, C2, and J were charged with affray. None of them gave evidence. The only evidence against them was that of S, who had been involved in the riot but not charged. All the defendants made statements to the police, wholly or partly exculpatory. Witnesses gave evidence at the trial of J's good character. Counsel for C1 and C2 objected to this, arguing that it had no relevance since J gave no evidence and therefore the issue of his

---

[96] Admissible as evidence of the fact stated by way of exception to the hearsay rule.
[97] [1989] Crim LR 569; above, pp. 53–5.
[98] [1989] Crim LR 60.

credibility did not arise. J was acquitted, the Chapmans convicted. The Court of Appeal held that the evidence was rightly admitted; the credibility of J did arise, in relation to the statement he gave the police (rightly admitted in accordance with *Sharp*[99]), and how much weight to give it.

These difficulties arise from the adversarial nature of the criminal trial, with its insistence on oral testimony and consequent distrust of hearsay evidence. The result is an inflexible and frequently unworkable dichotomy between matters of credit and matters of fact, a distinction only barely understood by many lawyers. Also, the emphasis on the trial itself as opposed to any pre-trial inquiry means that issues such as the character of witnesses have to be dealt with in an abrupt fashion in order to cut down the time devoted to what are necessarily classified as collateral issues. Newark has argued[100] that the adversarial character of the proceedings, with witnesses being clearly identified as being on one side or the other, effectively means that a party is taken to guarantee the credibility of his or her own witness. If that witness subsequently lets him or her down, which is frequently a problem for prosecutors, the party may not normally impeach the witness's credit for that reason. Given the rigid, two-sided structure of the trial, the only way to attack the credibility of your own witness is to treat him or her as 'gone over' to the other side. Thus, if the witness can be regarded as a hostile witness he or she may be cross-examined by the party who called him or her and have previous inconsistent statements put to him or her. This solution is not entirely successful, as the hostile witness's relationship with the other side is not clearly defined. It is not settled whether he or she is now their witness (which may or may not suit them) and therefore whether they can cross-examine him as well.[101] And, in a criminal case, the hostile witness's previous inconsistent statements are not to be relied on as evidence of the facts stated,[102] and are only matters affecting his or her credibility.[103] The absence of a pre-trial inquiry exacerbates the risk of collapse in the prosecution case because the betrayal of the hostile witness could be a complete surprise. And when it comes, the dominance of the hearsay rule and the principle of orality ensure that the witness's previous statements, which may well be true, are almost completely useless.

How is judgment made about the veracity of witnesses? Jury studies are unanimous in showing that evidence has a far greater effect on the verdict of

---

[99] [1988] 1 All ER 65; see chapter 7.
[100] Newark, 'The hostile witness and the adversary system' [1986] Crim LR 441.
[101] Ibid.
[102] *Golder* [1960] 3 All ER 457.
[103] In a civil case such statements can be used as evidence of the facts stated.

the jury than the individual character of jurors,[104] but there is a general tendency for people to overestimate their capacity to identify persons who are telling the truth.[105] This may be because they have indeed managed to identify obvious lies they are told, but have not known when they have been successfully deceived. It may be, however, that they were relying on misleading indicators; there is a tendency to believe witnesses who have a great deal of confidence.[106] Lawyers have recently been accused of applying inappropriate criteria to witnesses, and therefore of drawing the wrong conclusions[107] in an experiment where various subjects were shown videotaped interviews with children purporting to describe sexual abuse. Lawyers were seen to stress irrelevant criteria such as spontaneity and confidence, placing little value on non-verbal behaviour and child play. They were accused of becoming irritated by hesitant or ambiguous accounts. Police officers and social workers had more success at identifying genuine cases. But Richard White, a participant in the study and a leading family lawyer, objected to the tiny scale of the research, which used only four lawyer-subjects, and argued that the lawyers' more cautious approach was connected to the anticipated use of the interviews as evidence in the trial. His defence of the lawyers involves a circular argument, however. Judicial assumptions about witness reliability are behind the difficulties of admissibility which they were trying to predict.

Are there indicators of truthfulness? It seems that confidence and fluency are misleading, and are easily copied by a clever liar.[108] Most people look for the wrong clues: 'the eyes are very efficient instruments of deception'.[109] According to Köhnken, lying behaviour is not similar from person to person, and may even vary in the same person. Rather than being fidgety and tense, habitual liars are still and calm. Non-psychologists assume that the best way to expose them is to show suspicion and ask them tough questions. This does not work; a skilful liar will notice this and adjust his or her behaviour to conform to an honest stereotype. On the other hand, an honest witness may

---

[104] M. J. Saks and R. Hastie, *Social Psychology in Court* (Van Nostrand Reinhold, New York, 1978).

[105] Köhnken, 'The evaluation of statement credibility: social judgment and expert diagnostic approaches', in *Children's Evidence in Legal Proceedings*, eds J. R. Spencer, G. Nicholson, R. Flin and R. Bull (Spencer, Faculty of Law, University of Cambridge, 1990).

[106] Daffenbacher and Loftus, 'Do jurors share a common understanding concerning eyewitness behaviour?', *Law and Human Behaviour*, 6 (1982), p. 15.

[107] Vizard, Wiseman, Leventhal and Bentovim; cited in *The Times*, 2 July 1990.

[108] Köhnken, in Spencer et al. (eds).

[109] Ibid.

become nervous if subjected to a grilling and appear less convincing. The only genuine characteristics of truthful stories pertain to their contents, and include such factors as internal consistency and accordance with other known facts. Truthful people are more likely than liars to make spontaneous corrections or to admit that they have forgotten something – but an intelligent liar knows this and imitates it.[110] Some years ago naïve faith in technological development encouraged flirtations with truth drugs and lie detector machines, but experience has since proved these guides to truthfulness to be unreliable. Courts have tended to dismiss evidence so obtained on technical grounds, as inadmissible previous consistent or hearsay statements. Lie detector or polygraph machines are not allowed in courts.[111] They are in fact simple devices which measure the level of moisture on the palms of the hands, and so may indicate nervousness, but nothing more.[112] Truth drugs such as sodium pentathol, which releases inhibitions, have been shown not to prevent people fabricating or concealing matters of which they speak.[113]

Egglestone's observations on the propensity of witnesses to lie is an example of the tendency, possibly a chronic one amidst lawyers, to assume that falsehoods can be recognized; he suggests that witnesses are more likely to lie to protect their good name or that of friends or relations where the matter does not seem to them to have any bearing on the case.[114] The old adage *falsus in uno, falsus in omnibus*[115] is, therefore, quite wrong. 'Witnesses were regarded categorically as being either truthful persons or not.'[116] According to Wigmore, the maxim was no more than a working rule, but he supported it, arguing that an individual who would lie about a collateral matter is perhaps more likely to be a determined liar than one who would lie on oath about a material fact.[117] However, Wigmore was against the principle hardening into a rule of law, and today it does not appear in the evidence textbooks at all. Egglestone thinks that in fact people will lie more readily

---

[110] Ibid.

[111] See Phipson, *Evidence*, 14th edn, para. 32.10.

[112] Saxe, Dougherty and Cross, 'Validity of polygraph testimony', in *On the Witness Stand*, eds L. S. Wrightsman, C. E. Willis and S. M. Kassim (Sage, Newbury Park, 1987).

[113] Saks and Hastie, *Social Psychology*.

[114] R. Egglestone, *Evidence, Proof and Probability*, 2nd edn (Weidenfeld & Nicolson, London, 1983), p. 195.

[115] A witness had to be treated as telling nothing but the truth, or as having lied throughout.

[116] M. Stone, *Proof of Fact in Criminal Trials* (W. Green & Sons, Edinburgh, 1984), p. 100.

[117] Wigmore, *Evidence*, 3rd edn (Little, Brown & Co., Boston, 1940), p. 676.

where they regard the suppression of the truth as more important than the issue in the case, or if they think that the question is irrelevant to the facts in issue. Withholding the truth may be seen by some as less reprehensible than actually telling lies. If Egglestone is right, the basic assumptions behind many cross-examinations as to credit are misconceived and are being allowed to mislead the court. Revealing previous convictions, shady business practice or proven lying in the past is not a reliable indicator of dishonesty in the present. Yet much may be made of these. The wide-ranging nature of cross-examination on credibility is redolent of the belief that a person who has lied about anything will have lied in everything.

Believing witnesses: corroboration

It is possible to become very confused about the law on corroboration; this is made more likely when we find academic writers using the term 'rule of practice' in completely different ways in this context.[118] Much of the confusion arises because the nature of the corroboration warning has not been clearly understood. Where a judge *must* give a corroboration warning, he or she must warn the jury of the need for caution before relying on this witness's evidence; the judge must explain (giving the reason) that it is regarded as dangerous to convict on it unless there is corroborative evidence; he or she must go on to identify any items of evidence before the jury which could, if accepted by them, serve as corroboration, or, if there is none which could so serve, explain that this is the case. A full corroboration warning is therefore a different matter from a simple reminder without more of the possible weaknesses or underlying motives of a particular witness, yet there is a tendency for writers to treat the cases as similar, or adopt confusing terminology to distinguish them. There are not a great many kinds of case where judges should give the full corroboration warning. Well-known examples are cases where accomplices give evidence for the prosecution[119] and complaints in sexual cases.[120] From *Baskerville*,[121] corroboration is evidence which is independent of that which requires corroboration and implicates the accused in a material particular. In cases where judges should merely alert the jury to possible weaknesses or hidden motives in a witness

---

[118] See Tapper and Cross, *Evidence*, p. 224; contrast Wells, 'Corroboration of evidence in criminal trials' [1990] NLJ 1031.
[119] *Davies v DPP* [1954] AC 378.
[120] *Midwinter* (1971) 55 Cr App R 523; *Marks* [1963] Crim LR 370; *Trigg* [1963] 1 WLR 305.
[121] [1916] 2 KB 658.

they are allowed to express themselves in the most appropriate way; this is not a corroboration warning. Such cases include the evidence of psychiatric patients,[122] evidence from persons who are not accomplices in the technical sense but have purposes of their own to serve,[123] and evidence of identification.[124] Statutory provisions said to require corroboration for particular cases actually vary a great deal. Some require corroboration in terms.[125] Others may insist on the evidence of more than one sworn witness.[126] Section 89(2) of the Road Traffic Regulation Act 1984 merely lays down that in relation to an offence of driving a motor vehicle at a speed greater than the maximum allowed, an accused shall not be liable to be convicted solely on the evidence of one witness to the effect that in the opinion of that witness the vehicle was being driven at a greater speed. That wording permits convictions where there is only evidence which would not be regarded as corroboration in the strict sense; an example is where a police officer's opinion of excessive speed is supported by his or her reading of the speedometer on his or her car.[127] There is no need for independence, as is required for corroboration proper – the weakness of the evidence in a speeding case derives not from doubts as to the veracity of the witness, but doubts as to the reliability of a subjective judgment of the speed of a car. Thus it can be seen that the corroboration warning in its full splendour is reserved for witnesses who are presumed by the law to be likely to be untruthful: mothers who claim that a certain man is the father of their child, those who allege that they were victims of a sexual offence, and accomplices of the accused.[128]

Defendants may not give evidence as prosecution witnesses,[129] and therefore in order for an accomplice to give evidence for the prosecution, he or she is usually either granted immunity from prosecution, or is convicted before the trial of his or her colleagues. It is only where an accomplice appears for the prosecution that a full corroboration warning is required,[130] although he or she is equally capable of damaging the prospects of his or her co-defendants and is just as likely to lie if giving evidence in his or her own defence during a joint trial. If co-defendants cast the blame on one another, however, the judge has a discretion as to the nature of the direction to the

---

[122] *Spencer* [1987] AC 128.

[123] *Beck* [1982] 1 All ER 807.

[124] See below.

[125] Sexual Offences Act 1956, ss. 2–4, 22, 23; Affiliation Proceedings Act 1957, s. 4.

[126] Such as Treason Act 1795, s. 1; Perjury Act 1911, s. 13.

[127] *Nicholas v Penny* [1950] 2 All ER 89.

[128] And, formerly, children; see chapter 4.

[129] *Rhodes* [1899] 1 QB 77; Criminal Evidence Act 1898, s. 1(a).

[130] *Davies* [1954] AC 378; *Loveridge* (1982) 76 Cr App R 125.

jury, but should warn them that each may have an interest of his or her own to serve.[131] Tapper and Cross regard the law here as inconsistent: 'On principle there does not appear to be any good reason for distinguishing the case in which an accomplice gives evidence on his own behalf from that in which he testifies on behalf of the prosecution.'[132] But this overlooks the nature of the corroboration warning, which in these cases would be superfluous. There is no need for the judge to warn of the danger of convicting on the strength of the accomplice evidence in the absence of corroboration – if the accused reach the stage of giving evidence in their own defence, there is, inevitably, evidence before the court which corroborates the accusation of one against his or her co-accused. The prosecution must have established a case to answer in order to force the defence to produce any evidence in reply. Therefore there will be evidence which implicates each accused in a material particular, and all that is required if they go on to attack one another is a reminder of what their motives are likely to be.

The assumption that alleged victims of sexual offences are more likely to be untruthful (knowingly or otherwise) than the alleged victims of other kinds of crime has been made by many eminent lawyers. Professor Williams wrote in 1963 that there was a sound reason for the requirement of a corroboration warning.[133] This view is not exclusive to men. The Heilbron Report is the work of a woman judge and is a great deal more recent: 'We are not unaware of the fact that from time to time women do make false charges from a variety of motives.'[134] But few could put the common law anxiety more colourfully than Lord Hailsham: 'The evidence of Lady Wishfort complaining of rape may be dangerous because she may be indulging in undiluted sexual fantasy. A Mrs Frail making the same allegation may need corroboration because of the danger that she does not wish to admit the consensual intercourse of which she is ashamed.'[135] Not until 1988 did the Court of Appeal finally recognize that even if that is the case, it does not explain the previous insistence on corroboration in the strict sense in cases where the fact of rape is conceded by the defence, so that the sole issue in the trial is the identity of the culprit.[136] A remaining mystery is why the

---

[131] *Knowlden* (1983) 77 Cr App R 94.

[132] Tapper and Cross, *Evidence*, p. 230; cf. Law Commission (Scotland), describing the distinction as an anomaly: *Corroboration of Evidence in Criminal Trials*, Working Paper No. 115 (1990), para. 4.18.

[133] G. Williams, *The Proof of Guilt* (Stevens, London, 1968).

[134] *Report of the Advisory Group on the Law of Rape*, Cmnd 6352 (1976).

[135] *Kilbourne* [1973] AC 729, 748.

[136] *Chance* [1988] 3 All ER 225; the correct direction is such cases is an identification evidence warning in accordance with *Turnbull* [1976] 3 ALL ER 549.

sexual offences warning has to be given where the complainant is male.[137] Are men thought falsely to cry rape as frequently as women?

There seems to be no clear evidence to support either contention.[138] Although many judges in their warning to juries stress how easy it is to invent an allegation of rape,[139] the experience awaiting complainants in court[140] gives rise to doubt.[141] It is also difficult to understand why it is frequently said that the charge is a difficult one to refute; it might be thought that, on the contrary, the burden and standard of proof on the prosecution demand an extraordinarily convincing complainant if there is to be a conviction, since there is often no other evidence. The Home Office view is that it is difficult to know to what extent, if any, false charges are made;[142] a police surgeon who acted for the Royal Ulster Constabulary claimed that of the rape allegations investigated by him sixteen out of eighteen were inventions.[143] A case study regarded by the Home Office as 'more careful'[144] found that 29 per cent of claims were definitely false, and a further 18 per cent probably were.[145] The much-publicized civil action for rape in 1988 appears to have featured an expert witness who claimed that nine out of ten allegations of rape are baseless, and that in this particular case the complaint could consist of a dream or fantasy now firmly believed.[146] The debate tends to provoke strong reactions, but is clouded by the failure to clarify one basic point. Is the argument that women (and men?) in general commonly invent sexual attacks, or is it that women who suffer from mental or emotional illness are prone to do so – in other words, that such fabrications are a symptom of disorder? The latter contention is much easier to believe, and might even be

---

137   *Gammon* (1959) 43 Cr App R 155.
138   J. Temkin, *Rape and the Legal Process* (Sweet & Maxwell, London, 1987); cf. Law Commission (Scotland) Working Paper, para. 4.31.
139   A contention which can be traced back as far as 1680: 'It must be remembered that [the] accusation [is] easily to be made and hard to be proved, and harder to be defended by the party accused, tho never so innocent': M. Hale, *Pleas of the Crown*, ed. E. Sollom (Nott & Gosling, London), Vol. 1, c. 58, p. 635.
140   See chapter 4.
141   See Law Commission (Scotland) Working Paper, para. 4.37, describing the 'stress, trauma and humiliation'. Cf. Young, *Rape Study – A Discussion of Law and Practice* (Department of Justice and Institute of Psychology, New Zealand, 1983).
142   Home Office, *Sexual Offences, Consent and Sentencing* (HORS No. 54).
143   Stewart, 'A retrospective survey of alleged sexual assault cases', *Police Surgeon*, 17 (1981), p. 28.
144   Home Office, *Sexual Offences*.
145   MacLean, 'Rape and false accusations of rape', *Police Surgeon*, 15 (1979), p. 2940.
146   *Independent*, 9 November 1988.

susceptible to verification. As it is, the position is absurd, as Cross, using the example of a summary trial involving a sexual assault has shown:[147]

> Is it not somewhat odd to require a magistrate to reason as follows on a charge of indecent assault brought by a respectable middle-aged female: 'I believe her evidence, but I must think twice before acting on it because sex is a mysterious thing'; whereas, on a charge of assault brought by a man with numerous convictions for violence, the magistrate can simply say to himself, 'I believe his evidence and I need not think twice before acting on it because there is no danger that charges of violence will be made on account of neurosis, jealousy, fantasy or spite'?

There is evidence in recent case law that the Court of Appeal is becoming more sceptical of the 'we know what women are' school of thought. In *Chauhan*[148] and *Dowley*[149] the complainant's distressed condition soon after the alleged attack was treated as evidence capable of corroborating her complaint although the earlier precedents are rigidly hostile to 'self-corroboration'.

In Scotland corroboration is required in all cases in the sense that the evidence of more than one witness is not full proof of a civil[150] or a criminal case, but it is facts, not witnesses, which must be corroborated.[151] There is no equivalent of *Baskerville*, however, and so circumstantial evidence appears to be sufficient. And a previous identification by the same witness can support identification in court.[152] Certainly, a general requirement of this nature can be defended with more ease than can the rigidity of the present corroboration rule in England, which makes it extremely difficult for the judge to adjust his or her summing up to make it genuinely helpful to the jury. Also, the warning makes little sense; on the one hand, the judge should warn the jury that it is dangerous to convict on the evidence in the absence of corroboration and, on the other, he or she must tell the jury that they may nevertheless do so.[153] Apart from the many anomalies identified by the Law

---

[147] C. Tapper and R. Cross, *Evidence*, 6th edn (Butterworths, London, 1985), p. 237; quoted Law Commission (Scotland) Working Paper, para. 4.22.
[148] (1981) 73 Cr App R 232.
[149] [1983] Crim LR 168.
[150] With the exception, under Law Reform (Miscellaneous Provisions) (Scotland) Act 1960, s. 9, regarding personal injury suits.
[151] A. B. Wilkinson, *The Scottish Law of Evidence* (Butterworths/Law Society of Scotland, London/Edinburgh, 1986).
[152] D. McBarnett, *Conviction* (Macmillan, London, 1983).
[153] Law Commission (Scotland) Working Paper, para. 4.17.

Commission,[154] there is also reason to believe that the corroboration warning as delivered at present is self-defeating in that the emphasis on the evidence which needs to be corroborated and the repetition of all the prosecution evidence capable of corroborating it accentuates the case against the defendant.[155]

The dilemma facing abolitionists is whether it is dangerous simply to scrap the common law corroboration rules with no replacement. Leaving judges unfettered discretion to warn only in respect of witnesses or evidence where they perceive a need for caution clearly would allow them more scope to influence the verdict. It could also give rise to confusion and to endless appeals. Yet, in relation to children's evidence, Parliament abolished the rules and left the courts to their own devices.[156] At one point, the Law Commission appears sanguine about relying on the judgment of the trial judge. They argue that it may be inappropriate to give the accomplice warning in some cases, for with a particular witness it might be 'obvious that he has no ill-feeling towards the accused and that he is repentant and anxious to tell the truth'.[157] But the problems which could arise from an unfettered judicial discretion are noted: 'In the absence of legislative rules defendants would have greater scope to argue that the judge had failed to give adequate warning to the jury about suspect testimony...appellate courts would then have the burden of deciding whether to formulate new rules in place of the old.'[158] The non-appearance of such problems in relation to child witnesses since the Criminal Justice Act 1988 may be because most of the cases in which they are involved concern sexual offences, currently requiring a warning, or because judges are continuing to warn juries in exactly the same way as before. It would probably be better to provide some statutory guidance; the Law Commission welcomes reactions to a framework which allows the judge some discretion, but requires a warning in the judge's own words of the risk of unreliability and the need for caution in certain cases. There could be a lively debate as to which witnesses are the appropriate candidates for this approach. A Scottish response might argue that, rather than battle over which are the prosecution witnesses least to be trusted, it might be better to acknowledge that it is always dangerous to rely to the detriment of the defendant on the unsupported evidence of one person.

---

[154] Ibid.
[155] Ibid., para. 4.24.
[156] Criminal Justice Act 1988, s. 34; see chapter 4.
[157] Law Commission (Scotland) Working Paper, para. 4.12.
[158] Ibid., para. 5.7.

Believing witnesses: reliability

The Home Office at one stage took seriously the idea of obtaining evidence under hypnosis, but more recently issued a circular to all police forces instructing them to discontinue the practice.[159] This is slightly disappointing, as, if hypnotism is an aid to memory[160] it could be helpful to the police in investigation, even though evidence so obtained would be likely to be inadmissible at trial. However, there is no apparent consensus as to whether hypnotism does facilitate recall. Wagstall suggests that the effect is not greater than that arising from any other relaxation techniques,[161] and there is research which indicates that people in a hypnotic trance are more than usually vulnerable to suggestion.[162]

The inaccuracy of eyewitness memory is now becoming known to most trial lawyers through the influence of the Devlin Report[163] and its effect on appellate decisions.[164] There is an increasing body of knowledge obtained by psychologists which has substantially undermined faith in identification evidence. For people remember action details better than descriptive details.[165] Even so, they tend to give fragmented and limited accounts of events that they have witnessed, and are prone to making errors in identifying the actors at subsequent line-ups.[166] It seems that an error-free report is the exception rather than the rule, that the more full of detail it is the more errors there will be, that time lapse increases unreliability[167] and that cross-racial identification is even more unreliable than identification within the same

---

[159] [1988] NLJ 528.

[160] Reiser, 'Hypnosis as an aid in a homicide investigation', in Wrightsman, Willis and Kassim (eds).

[161] Wagstall, 'Hypnotism and the law: a critical review of some recent proposals' [1983] Crim LR 152.

[162] Putnam, 'Hypnosis and distortion in eyewitness memory', in Wrightsman, Willis and Kassim (eds).

[163] *Report of the Departmental Committee on Evidence of Identification*, Cmnd 338 (1976).

[164] See *Turnbull* [1976] 3 ALL ER 549.

[165] Lipton, 'On the psychology of eyewitness testimony', *Journal of Applied Psychology*, 62 (1977), p. 90.

[166] B. R. Clifford and R. Bull, *Psychology of Person Identification* (Routledge & Kegan Paul, London, 1988); J. Shepherd, J. Ellis and G. Davies, *Identification Evidence: A Psychological Evaluation* (Aberdeen University Press, 1982).

[167] Clifford, 'Eyewitness testimony; the bridging of a credibility gap', in Farrington, Hawkins and Lloyd-Bostock (eds).

racial group.[168] Some psychologists have found that even a good view of a person for several minutes does not guarantee the accuracy of identification on a later occasion.[169] Confidence is no indicator of accuracy.[170] Although courts and jurors share the police assumption that their special training and experience make police officers superior eyewitnesses for detail, experimental evidence fails to confirm this.[171] Some of these findings are not unchallenged,[172] but even so, the implications are alarming, for example of the finding that accuracy of description ranges from only 25 to 35 per cent,[173] accuracy of recognition between 40 and 65 per cent, but with variations according to the conditions in which the observation was made.[174] At identification parades at which the real actor is not present, there is a one-third likelihood of a volunteer being selected. Gardner found that estimates of height varied from four feet to six feet six, with 50 per cent of subjects overestimating height by eight inches.[175] Devlin concluded that although powers of recognition are better than those of description, juries should be warned that it is not safe to convict upon eyewitness evidence unless the circumstances of the identification are exceptional or the eyewitness evidence is supported by substantial evidence of another sort.[176]

The Court of Appeal did not go so far; the guidelines in *Turnbull*[177] require the judge to withdraw the case from the jury if the prosecution consists of nothing more than poor-quality identification evidence, such as a 'fleeting glimpse'. If the identification evidence is more solid, but the case turns wholly or substantially on it, the judge should warn the jury of the need for caution and explain the reasons for it. In his or her own words the judge should ask the jury to consider carefully the circumstances in which the witness saw the offender, and remind them that even a confident witness can be mistaken. This is seen by some as a half-hearted acknowledgement of

[168] Shepherd, Deregoswski and Ellis, 'A cross-cultural study of recognition memory for faces', *International Journal of Psychology*, 9 (1974), p. 205.
[169] Shepherd, Ellis and Davies, *Identification Evidence*.
[170] Wells and Murray, 'Eyewitness confidence', in *Eyewitness Testimony: Psychological Perspectives*, eds G. Wells and E. Loftus (Cambridge University Press, 1984); Daffenbacher and Loftus, *Law and Human Behaviour* (1982).
[171] Clifford, 'Police as eyewitnesses', *New Society*, 22 (1972), 176.
[172] E.g. Lindsay and Wells, 'What do we really know about cross-race identification evidence?', in *Evaluating Witness Evidence*, eds S. Lloyd-Bostock and B. R. Clifford (Wiley, Chichester, 1983).
[173] Clifford, *New Society* (1972).
[174] Shepherd, Ellis and Davies, *Identification Evidence*.
[175] Gardner, 'The perception and memory of witnesses' (1933) 18 Cornell LQR 391.
[176] *Report...on Evidence of Identification*, para. 8.4.
[177] [1976] 3 All ER 549.

the weaknesses of identification evidence. For researchers have found that even when warned of adverse conditions, mock jurors do not make sufficient adjustment.[178] Loftus found that they were more impressed by eyewitness testimony than by any other forensic evidence.[179]

The fact is that the criminal justice system is not in a position to abandon the evidence of eyewitnesses altogether, and in some cases the defence relies on it to establish an alibi. The Devlin Committee was criticized for rejecting procedural change to reflect psychological findings[180] but there are and should be doubts about the extent to which the results of simulations for experimental purposes can be applied to concrete situations involving real crimes. Wells argues[181] that the police, unlike psychologists using human guinea-pigs, rely on those witnesses who claim that they can make an identification. The subjects who take part in experiments (often students) are selected before the event rather than after it and are not especially likely to express great confidence. Even if they did, they would do so in very different circumstances in which nothing hangs on any error they might make. Some research findings could, if adopted by the courts, give rise to distracting side-issues; for example, it is difficult to imagine the court becoming embroiled in a debate about how attractive the accused is; yet there is evidence that very attractive or very unattractive people are more identifiable than those in between.[182]

A major contributor to the apparent impasse between lawyers and those psychologists who feel that the courts could take more account of current knowledge of the reliability of evidence is the conflict between the two systems of reasoning which trials attempt to utilize jointly in uneasy harness. From an empirical point of view identification evidence is extremely suspect. But deductive logic would suggest that the testimony of a witness to a crime has very high probative value – if it is not mistaken, there is none better. A further problem which is not faced by psychologists, who stage their own

[178] Lindsay, Wells and Rumpel, 'Can people detect eyewitness and identification accuracy within and across situations?', (1981) 66 *Journal of Applied Psychology*, 66 (1981), p. 78.

[179] Loftus, 'Reconstructing memory, the incredible eyewitness' *Psychology Today*, 8 (1974), p. 116.

[180] Bull and Clifford, 'Identification evidence: the Devlin Report', *New Scientist*, 70 (1976), p. 307.

[181] Wells, 'Applied eyewitness testimony research', in Wrightsman, Willis and Kassim (eds).

[182] Cross, Cross and Daly, 'Sex, race, age and beauty as factors in recognition of faces', *Perception and Psychophysics*, 10 (1971), p. 303; Bull, 'The influence of stereotypes on person identification', in Farrington, Hawkins and Lloyd-Bostock (eds).

experiments in the best way to achieve scientifically acceptable results, is that trials involve more than one issue. *Turnbull* is an attempt by the judges to devise guidelines which bring scientific knowledge to bear on proceedings; but the note of caution to be introduced relates to identification evidence, and it is not always obvious whether a case is an identification case or not. If the judge gets it wrong, and fails to warn the jury of the dangers when the case does involve primarily identification evidence, then the conviction is likely to be quashed on appeal. Opinions tend to be divided about *Hewett*;[183] D was charged with driving with blood–alcohol concentration above the prescribed limit. He had been drinking with Mrs G and had got into a BMW with her. Police officers, following in their van, said the car did a violent U-turn. They followed the car until it halted (at a spot in Chelsea, dimly lit), and asked for a sample of breath from D, who was sitting in the driver's seat but insisted that he had not been driving. Mrs G said that she had been the driver and asked to be breathalysed. The two police officers had been sitting in the front of their van; both gave evidence that a man and a woman were in the car, and that the man was driving. They described the driver as having a leather jacket and a beard, and the woman, alleged to have been sitting in the passenger seat, as having long fair hair. Mrs G maintained that a scarf hid her hair, and that she got out of the passenger seat because she had left her shoes that side, and needed to put them on. D swapped seats with her in order to help her find her shoes, and that was why he got out the driver's side when the car stopped. The defence appealed against conviction on the ground that the jury should have had a *Turnbull* warning. The argument was dismissed by the Court of Appeal on the grounds that this was not an identification case. Even though the dispute concerned the identity of the driver of the car, the police had been observing the BMW in the dark and through two sets of glass. Although the visual limitations of the officers in the circumstances tempt many lawyers to see *Hewett* as a *Turnbull* case, the Court of Appeal was right. For the police and the court were entitled to infer that the man who was found in the driving seat immediately after being ordered to stop was responsible for the vehicle; the only reason to doubt that he was the driver came from the defence evidence – the prosecution evidence did not turn on eyewitness identification of Hewett. The police officers' descriptions were relevant only because the defence tried to rebut the commonsense inference by arguing that Mrs G had been driving all the time.

The courts have so far resolutely refused to address an apparent inconsistency in their treatment of suggestion, by the use of leading questions for example. Cross-examination makes extensive use of the leading question and is regarded as an admirable forensic skill. But the courts refuse to accept

[183] [1978] RTR 174.

evidence-in-chief so obtained,[184] and there has been considerable discussion of the issue with regard to disclosure interviews with children, designed to elicit an allegation of sexual abuse.[185] The courts are not in fact inconsistent; it is one thing to attempt to discredit witnesses' evidence by leading them to contradict themselves (even if in fact this is not as significant as lawyers think) since the effect of that is to cancel out the testimony. It is altogether different to obtain the allegation on which the court is expected to decide and possibly take coercive action by means of suggestion. There is no doubt that all potential witnesses are highly suggestible. Elizabeth Loftus has led the work in this area, and shown that not only do descriptions of events and participants alter on an alarming scale to reflect facts 'planted' by the questioner, but the questioning process can have a permanent effect on memory.[186] The style of questioning used by police officers is highly suggestive, and not without good reason. It is extremely difficult to obtain spontaneous descriptions without leading questions.[187] Memory appears to be divided into available and accessible information; a witness can provide available information without prompting, but to go further will need cues.[188] So suggestive or leading questioning reduces the number of omissions, but increases the overall number of errors.[189] To make matters worse, it appears that the more knowledgeable the interrogator appears to be about the matter in hand, the more likely is the witness to adopt any suggestion in the question asked.[190] Thus the capacity of the police, whether inadvertent or not, to influence the testimony given may depend on whether at the time of the interview they seemed to know a great deal about the offence – which may depend on the stage the investigation has reached.

[184] Although in a civil case a judge may allow it and adjust his or her perception of the evidential value of the testimony.

[185] See chapter 4.

[186] Loftus, 'Reconstruction of automobile destruction: an example of the interaction between language and memory', *Journal of Verbal Learning and Verbal Behaviour*, 13 (1974), p. 585; Loftus and Palmer, 'The malleability of eyewitness accounts', in Lloyd-Bostock and Clifford (eds).

[187] Bryden, *Identification Proceedings under Scottish Criminal Law*, Cmnd 7096 (1978), para. 1.03.

[188] Davies, 'Research on children's testimony: implications for interviewing practice', in *Clinical Approaches to Sex Offenders and their Victims*, eds C. Hollin and K. Howells (Wiley, Chichester, 1991).

[189] Marquis and Oskamp, 'Testimony validity as a function of question form, atmosphere and item difficulty', *Journal of Applied Social Psychology*, 2 (1972), p. 167.

[190] Smith and Ellsworth, 'The social psychology of eyewitness evidence accuracy: misleading questions and communicator expertise', *Journal of Applied Psychology* 72 (1987), p. 294.

It cannot be long before judges will be faced with this issue; it has already been discussed to some extent in Family Division cases which involve disclosure interviews with children. It is a growing concern in relation to confessions obtained from the accused by the police. Once advocates become aware of the effect of suggestion, they may attempt to introduce the issue into trials, with a view to discrediting evidence so obtained. If they do, all the aforementioned anxieties about extrapolating from the experimental to the real situation will surface with a vengeance.

4

Witnesses with a Legitimate Grievance; Victims of the Adversarial Trial[1]

I was terrified up there. My legs were quaking.
Witness quoted in McBarnett, *Conviction*

Giving evidence in English courts is a largely unrewarding task. Expert witnesses are paid for their services but, for others, time at work is lost and expenses are meagre.[2] Most courts do not have separate car parking space for witnesses.[3] Although it is generally accepted that giving evidence is an intimidating experience, little is done to reassure witnesses, who may find that there is no microphone to amplify their answers, in which case they are obliged to project their evidence, no matter how sensitive, into a courtroom which may be large and crowded. These problems are worst in criminal cases tried by jury, but lawyers report severe attacks of 'stage-fright' in witnesses of all kinds, even those asked to give evidence in civil cases in which they have no direct interest. Involvement in criminal trials, however, is much more traumatic. If the witness is afraid of retaliation, little can be done by the criminal justice system to reassure him or her, such dramatic measures as a change of identity and/or police protection being reserved for major matters such as the 'supergrass' informer cases in Northern Ireland. In Denmark witnesses are allowed to give evidence anonymously if it appears that they will be otherwise exposed to danger, but this operates to the

---

[1] Passages in this chapter were first published as parts of the following articles: 'Child evidence: more proposals for reform' [1988] Crim LR 813; 'In the box or on the box?' [1990] Crim LR 363, reproduced here by kind permission of Sweet and Maxwell.
[2] D. McBarnett, *Conviction* (Macmillan, London, 1983).
[3] McKittrick, 'Witnesses: the most precious resource' (1987) 51 J Cr L 192.

disadvantage of the defence.[4] In many cases where genuine fears exist, such as domestic violence, anonymity could not be achieved. Meanwhile,

> Involvement in the operation of the criminal justice system often presents witnesses with so many major inconveniences and problems such as wasted time caused by trial delays, loss of income and inappropriate physical accommodation at court that, all too frequently, even civic minded, initially co-operative witnesses wish they had never stepped forward and vow never to do so again.[5]

Witnesses of all kinds should be treated better than they are at present, but this would involve the administrators of justice in some forethought and expense. This chapter looks at those witnesses who are particularly ill-served by the English adversarial system of trial.

RAPE COMPLAINANTS

> *Once a woman sets in train a complaint that she has been raped, she has to undergo a prolonged ordeal. In the first place there will be a police interrogation, one of the purposes of which is to ensure, as far as possible, that she is not making a false charge...Next she has to answer further questioning by the police surgeon...and to undergo a thorough as well as an intimate and inevitably distasteful gynaecological examination. Furthermore, if her story of the rape is true she will, at this stage, probably be in a state of shock and possibly also have suffered painful injuries; yet she may have to spend many hours at the police station before she is able to return home...At the trial, which will take place some considerable time later, she has to relive the whole unpleasant and traumatic experience. In many cases, she will be cross-examined at length.*
>
> Report of the Advisory Group on the Law of Rape (Heilbron Report)

A combination of common humanity and the fear that a large number of rapes go unreported and therefore unpunished because of the brutal treatment to victims of which the legal system was suspected influenced the Heilbron Committee,[6] whose proposals were the spur to the introduction of the Sexual Offences Amendment Act 1976. Unfortunately, section 2,

---

[4] Anderson, 'The anonymity of witnesses: a Danish development' [1985] Crim LR 363.

[5] M. H. Graham, *Witness Intimidation* (Quest Books, Westport, Conn., 1985).

[6] *Report of the Advisory Group on the Law of Rape* (Heilbron Report), Cmnd 6352 (1975).

designed to protect complainants from degrading and irrelevant cross-examination, appears to have had astonishingly little effect. Not only is the predicament of these vulnerable witnesses largely an incident of the adversarial nature of the criminal trial, but it appears that evidential reform is ineffectual because related matters such as relevance, particularly the difference between credibility and the issue, are too complicated for many lawyers to understand them – and if the reform is not understood, it does not achieve anything.

In a rape trial the prosecution must show that intercourse took place, that it took place without the consent of the prosecutrix, and that the accused was the person responsible. Unfortunately, in some cases there is no evidence apart from that of the complainant herself. Medical evidence provides support if there was violence of a kind to cause discernible injury, but will identify the rapist only if there is material available which would enable a DNA fingerprint to be taken. In most cases it is virtually inevitable that the complainant has to give evidence. Her evidence has traditionally been regarded as highly suspect. We have already seen in chapter 3 that judges are required to give a corroboration warning. Some lawyers have advocated further safeguards. Glanville Williams has written in support of Wigmore's view that women who make allegations of sexual assault should be subject to scientific evaluation, the results of which would be revealed to the court. Rather than warn the jury of the dangers of uncorroborated evidence, it would be better, thought Wigmore, to employ 'expert scientific analysis of the particular witness's mentality as the true measure of enlightenment…No judge should ever let a sex offence charge go to the jury unless the female complainant's social history and mental make-up have been examined and testified to by a qualified physician.'[7] Such statements suggest that these gentlemen regard a complaint by a woman that she has been raped as an inconvenient and unseemly slur, and that she must anticipate a cautious and sceptical reaction from the criminal justice system before it assists her. The attitude that victims of alleged rapes are 'fair game' continues into the present day and colours the kind of cross-examination they undergo.

The nature of cross-examination of rape complainants is known to be a major source of distress. One of the most vexed questions in this context is the extent to which they can be questioned on previous sexual relationships. In a case where the issue is consent, this might be done simply to discredit the complainant, on the footing that because of her sexual habits she is not a person to be believed when she claims that she did not consent, or the object may be to show that, given the circumstances, there was in fact consent on

[7] Wigmore, *Evidence*, 3rd edn (Little, Brown & Co., Boston, 1940), pp. 924, 2061; quoted in G. Williams, *The Proof of Guilt* (Stevens, London, 1963), p. 159.

this occasion. The logic of a cross-examination on sexual history designed to discredit the prosecutrix is not obvious; the most extensive promiscuity does not suggest that a woman is not honest. Some lawyers argue that such reasoning has not been employed for many years, and that anyone who attempted to use it would only alienate the jury from his or her client's cause. Unfortunately, this view appears to be over-optimistic. The Heilbron Committee found that such cross-examinations were established practice, despite being degrading and irrelevant. In Scotland the same was more recently found to be the case, prior to the introduction of the Law Reform (Miscellaneous Provisions) (Scotland) Act 1985.[8] Most of the women interviewed by Chambers and Millar[9] found the experience of testifying confirmed their worst fears. It is not clear whether advocates employing such tactics genuinely thought that these questions were relevant to the woman's credibility; the suspicion remains that some of the motive was to cause as much distress as possible, thereby undermining her performance in the witness-box.

The solution arrived at in the Heilbron Report was to introduce a general prohibition with an inclusionary discretion. The result was section 2 of the Sexual Offences (Amendment) Act 1976:

(1) If at any trial any person is charged with a rape offence to which he pleads not guilty, then, except with the leave of the judge, no evidence and no question in cross-examination shall be adduced or asked at the trial, by or on behalf of any defendant at the trial, about any sexual experience of a complainant with a person other than that defendant.

(2) The judge shall not give leave in pursuance of the preceding subsection for any evidence or question except on an application made to him in the absence of the jury by or on behalf of a defendant; and on such an application the judge shall give leave if and only if he is satisfied that it would be unfair to that defendant to refuse to allow the evidence to be adduced or the question to be asked…

The offences to which the section applies include attempted rape and being an accessory to it, but not indecent assault.[10]

The Court of Appeal has said that leave should be refused if the object of

---

[8] S. 36 introduced a general prohibition on questions about sexual behaviour, including evidence of prostitution, but there is an inclusionary discretion where to deny the defence would be 'contrary to the interests of justice'.

[9] Chambers and Millar, 'Proving sexual assault: prosecuting the offender and persecuting the victim', in *Gender, Crime and Justice*, eds P. Carlen and A. Worrall (Open University Press, Milton Keynes/Philadelphia, 1987).

[10] S. 7(2).

the cross-examination is merely to say to the jury 'that's the kind of girl she is',[11] but has not ruled out all questioning which goes to credibility, although it is not at all clear when questions going simply to credit are permissible:[12]

> If the proposed questions merely seek to establish that the complainant has had sexual intercourse with other men to whom she was not married, so as to suggest that for that reason she ought not to be believed on oath, the judge will exclude the evidence...In other words, questions of this sort going simply to credit will seldom be allowed...On the other hand, if the questions are relevant to an issue in the trial in the light of the way the trial is being run, for instance relevant to the issue of consent, they are likely to be admitted, because to exclude a relevant question on an issue in the trial as the trial is being run will usually mean that the jury are being prevented from hearing something which, if they did hear it, might cause them to change their minds about the evidence being given by the complainant.

The impossibility of establishing a clear dividing line between matters of credit and the issue in the trial was recognized by the Court of Appeal and is manifest in this passage. The concluding words appear to bring the whole argument full circle by referring again to what the jury might think of the complainant herself, rather than the fact of consent.

An example of how utterly confused a court can become over the distinction between credibility and the issue in the case is the recent case of *Funderburk*.[13] The charge was of unlawful sexual intercourse with a girl under the age of consent.[14] D alleged that the thirteen-year-old complainant's allegations of ten or eleven acts of unlawful sexual intercourse with her were false. She described the alleged offences in detail, including a graphic account of how she lost her virginity on the first occasion. D wished to testify to conversations with himself and with others in which, he said, she had claimed to be sexually experienced, so that she could not have been a virgin as described. Whether such further evidence could be adduced depended on whether the matter of her virginity was relevant solely to her credibility as a witness, or whether it was relevant to the issue. The Court of Appeal quoted with approval the description of the former kind of evidence by Lawton LJ in *Sweet-Escott*: 'Since the purpose of cross-examination as to credit is to show that the witness ought not to be believed on oath, the

[11] *Viola* [1982] 3 All ER 73.

[12] Ibid., p. 77.

[13] [1990] 2 All ER 482.

[14] Since the offence here was not a rape offence, the complainant did not have such protection as is afforded by s. 2; the court seemed to think that nevertheless the spirit of the section should apply.

matters about which he is questioned must be related to his likely standing after the cross-examination.'[15] Applying this test, there was no doubt that the opinion of the jury of her credibility might have altered if they had heard that she had spoken of experiences which, if true, would mean that she could not have been a virgin at the material time. Her standing as a witness would have been much reduced,[16] but the court failed to recognize that this was because her alleged remarks amounted to previous inconsistent statements, which happened, in this case, to concern previous sexual relationships. The defence questions, therefore, would not have been designed to suggest that a girl with such a past ought not to be believed, but would have been directed to her consistency as a witness – a different kind of credibility issue. The Court of Appeal's confusion on this point led Henry J to conclude that the conversations in fact went to the issue in the case, and that therefore if she had denied making the statement, she could have been contradicted by other evidence. Being previous inconsistent statements, such contradictory evidence indeed could have been adduced, but not because her status as a virgin was an issue in the trial; it is not an element of the offence with which D was charged. Henry J stressed the degree of emotion shown by the complainant during her description, and seemed to think that this made whether or not she lost her virginity at that time an issue in the case:[17]

> This particular detailed account of that first incident would be the most vivid picture which the jury took back with them into their retiring room. Even disregarding the tears and the pathos it was an account of something which only happens once in a lifetime…If a detail of such significance is successfully challenged it can destroy both the account and the credit of the witness who gave it. Therefore…this is not a challenge which goes merely to credit but… to the issue.

The passage demonstrates the impossibility of establishing a clear dividing line between matters of credit and the issue in the trial. Henry J here acknowledges by implication that in some trials the credibility of the witness *is* the issue.

From the *Viola* judgment it appears that there are circumstances in which questions going to credit may properly be put.[18] The Court of Appeal does not trouble us with examples of these in that decision, but *Funderburk*

---

[15] (1971) 55 Cr App R 316, 320.
[16] [1990] 2 All ER 482, 488, *per* Henry J.
[17] Ibid., p. 491.
[18] The words 'will seldom be allowed' in the passage from the *Viola* judgment quoted above leave an unquantifiable loophole.

may be an example. Nevertheless, there appears to be an alarming void confronting the courts who have to identify appropriate cases. Adler's research at the Old Bailey in fact found judges permitting questions solidly in the 'There you are, members of the jury; that is the sort of girl she is' category.[19] But, in addition, a more sophisticated manipulation of the statute was observed. There the justification for the questions is said to be the need to establish that the woman has no aversion to intercourse, or to intercourse with an older man (such as the defendant) or to intercourse with black men (such as the defendant). It is difficult to believe that such an argument is seriously entertained, but if it is, of course, counsel could even argue that such questions go beyond the matter of credit to the issue of consent itself. A further problem arises in relation to cross-examination which seeks to establish that the complainant is a prostitute. Certain textbooks[20] assume that such questions are permissible under section 2, relying on the authority of *Krausz*,[21] a case decided before the 1976 Act. If the assumption is that such questions go to credit, it is not at all clear why this should be. Is it to be supposed that it is known that prostitutes are more prone to tell lies than most people? Or is it that prostitutes are particularly prone to make up allegations of rape? It is difficult to see why an admitted prostitute should deny consent after the event – presumably not being as subject to sexual fantasy as Lady Wishfort, or as prone to embarrassment as Mrs Frail.[22] It might equally be supposed that a prostitute would be reluctant to make an accusation of this sort in public, since it could be damaging from a professional point of view. However, in *Bashir*[23] it was held that the matter was relevant to the issue, rather than to credibility, and so not only are the questions permissible, but the complainant's denials can be contradicted by other evidence. This kind of reasoning has so little merit that it looks positively antediluvian. The consequence is that such cross-examination is allowed as a matter of course. Adler has found that some defence lawyers put it to the complainant that she is a prostitute, knowing that they will be answered (honestly) 'No'.[24] The motive is to raise a doubt in the juror's minds. It is instructive to refer at this point to the Bar's Code of Conduct:

---

[19] Adler, 'Rape: the intention of Parliament and the practice of the courts' (1982) 45 MLR 664.

[20] With the honourable exception of C. Tapper and R. Cross, *Evidence*, 7th edn (Butterworths, London, 1990), p. 235.

[21] (1973) 57 Cr App R 466.

[22] See above, p. 91.

[23] [1969] 1 WLR 1303.

[24] Adler, 'The relevance of sexual history evidence in rape: problems of subjective interpretation' [1985] Crim LR 769.

'Questions which affect the credibility of a witness by attacking his character, but are not otherwise relevant to the inquiry, may not be put in cross-examination unless there are reasonable grounds to support the imputations covered by the questions.'[25]

The alternative argument, that the complainant's occupation of prostitution is relevant to the issue of guilt, is no less difficult to fathom, yet it is propounded in the Heilbron Report itself. This particular contention will be addressed in due course, but at this stage it might be helpful to note the overriding principle in the same Report: 'In general, the previous sexual history of the complainant with other men...ought not to be introduced.'[26] Despite this, Adler reports that questions on the subject are allowed in a great many cases. In 40 per cent of the cases she observed[27] the defence made applications for leave, 75 per cent of which were wholly or partly successful. Most of the applications submitted that the previous sexual relationships were relevant to an issue in the trial; in 80 per cent of these cases, that was said to be consent. It must be the case that if the questions *are* relevant to an issue, to disallow them would inevitably be unfair to the accused, and therefore the judge ought to permit them, under the terms of section 2(2). What neither Parliament nor the Court of Appeal appears to have noticed is that it is significantly within the control of the defence what the issues in the trial actually are. In an adversarial trial, the parties decide which battlefield they wish to fight in.

The leading case of *Viola*[28] attempts to provide guidance to judges dealing with applications under section 2, but raises as many questions as it answers. In that case there were three alleged incidents on which the defence wished to cross-examine the complainant, and the trial judge refused to give leave in relation to all of them. The accused claimed that he happened to call at her flat and she made advances to him which led to consensual intercourse. His counsel wished to question her about an alleged visit by two other men, who claimed that she made advances to them when they chanced to visit her flat earlier that day. The Court of Appeal held that the incident (which appears to suffice as 'sexual experience' within the language of section 2)[29] was sufficiently similar to the circumstances of the alleged rape to merit inclusion. The reasoning there presumably was that if she made overtures to these visitors, she must have made them to Viola as well (resembling the 'not

---

[25] Code of Conduct for the Bar of England and Wales, r. 139(a).
[26] Heilbron Report, para. 134.
[27] Adler (1982) 45 MLR 664.
[28] [1982] 3 All ER 73; see above.
[29] In *Hinds and Butler* [1979] Crim LR 111, evidence of conversations about previous sexual relationships was treated as falling within the terms of s. 2.

averse to sexual intercourse' argument). The other incident, also held by the court to have been relevant to the issue of consent and which therefore should have been allowed, was that a naked man was seen in the complainant's flat about nine hours after the alleged rape. It seemed to be agreed that intercourse with her own boyfriend a day after the alleged rape was not relevant. It appears, then, that incidents of a sexual nature in the life of the complainant might be relevant to the issue on the 'similar facts' principle, that, if they are close in nature to the circumstances of the alleged rape, this suggests that there is such a pattern in her sexuality as to suggest that she consented on this occasion also. 'Evidence of sexual promiscuity may be so strong or so closely contemporaneous in time to the event in issue as to come near to, or indeed reach the border between mere credit and an issue in the case.'[30]

Also, incidents may be of more direct significance, as in the *Viola* case, where it was presumed that victims of rape do not generally choose to indulge in consensual intercourse soon after the event. Other examples of direct relevance include cases where the defence seeks to explain medical evidence of the presence of semen in the complainant at the material time by citing other acts of intercourse. In *Fenlon*[31] the trial judge was held to have been right to allow questions only in so far as they concerned the complainant's last act of sex before the alleged rape, which the Court of Appeal thought allowed D to develop his point without causing undue distress. Courts have allowed leave in cases where young girls have been found not to be virgins, which, in conjunction with their allegations against their fathers or stepfathers, is extremely prejudicial unless the defence is allowed to show that in fact relationships outside the home could explain this. It might be thought that if the defendant should deny *mens rea*, his knowledge of the complainant's habits would become relevant if he claimed that as a result he thought she consented, or, at least, that he was not reckless. For the defence can control how the trial is run, and in *Viola* the Court of Appeal stressed that issues become relevant in the light of how the trial is being run. They also held that the judge has no discretion to exclude under section 2 – he or she must use his or her judgment as to whether disallowing the questioning would be unfair to the defendant.[32]

These principles seem irreconcilable with the case of *Barton*.[33] D claimed that his belief that the complainant consented was reasonable, although it

[30] [1982] 3 All ER 73, 77, *per* Lord Lane CJ.
[31] (1980) 71 Cr App R 307.
[32] Since there is no discretion involved, the judge's decision can be overturned on appeal.
[33] (1987) 85 Cr App R 5.

was admitted that he broke down the door of her hostel bedroom, and that she screamed and kicked. He said that she had always behaved like this during acts of group sex at which he was present. The trial judge refused to allow questions on these lines, and was upheld on appeal. Whether or not a belief is reasonable must be inferred from evidence before the jury, and to allow an accused to adduce more on this issue would be to deprive complainants of the protection that section 2 was designed to give them. Although the Court of Appeal proved commendably sympathetic to the predicament of rape victims in this case, its solution does not seem to be justifiable, given the relentless logic of the adversarial trial. Although Barton's story was ludicrous, he *had* made recklessness, and therefore the reasonableness of his belief, an issue in the case. The degree to which the defence can control which issues should figure in the trial and therefore ensure exposing the alleged victim to a humiliating ordeal is one of the least appealing features of the adversarial proceeding, and the court seems to have been forced by the manifest unfairness of Barton's tactics to disregard it. It also places judges in a difficult position; they are required to adjudge whether the proposed cross-examination of the prosecution witness is relevant to the issue before they have heard the defence evidence. The Court of Appeal acknowledged the problem in *Viola*: 'at this stage it may not be easy for the judge to reach a conclusion', but Lord Lane CJ consoled himself with the thought that the trial structure frequently requires a judge to make decisions in the absence of the appropriate information, for example, on the issue of separation of trials: 'He has to reach the best conclusion that he can.'[34]

The 'similar facts' account of sexuality evinces fascinating insight into individual preconceptions; for example, Professor Elliott[35] says that any rule which could produce the result in *O'Sullivan*[36] must be a bad rule. In that case, a chapter of Hell's Angels were alleged to have raped the wife of a rival gang leader. They were refused leave to ask whether she had not voluntarily indulged in intercourse with numbers of motor cycle gang members in the past. The incidents were held not to have been sufficiently similar. But Elliott's argument appears to suggest that if the woman consented with one gang of motor cyclists, she is likely to consent to any. Temkin asks[37] whether incidents would be sufficiently similar if both involved the woman wearing a mini-skirt. The absurdity of this kind of argument is confirmed by the fact

---

[34] [1982] 3 All ER 73, 77, *per* Lord Lane CJ.
[35] Elliott, 'Rape complainants' sexual experience with third parties' [1984] Crim LR 4.
[36] (1981) CA ref. 3292/B2/80.
[37] Temkin, 'Evidence in sexual assault cases: the Scottish proposals and alternatives' (1987) 47 MLR 625.

that if the previous history is genuinely relevant to the issue, then the witness's denials of the allegations are not final and can be rebutted by evidence. Thus the court could actually be faced with evidence of what she was wearing on the previous occasion, or whether she really has a proclivity for sex in a Morris Minor as opposed to a Mirafiori. It may be that the similar facts argument is behind the assumption that evidence that the complainant is a prostitute is always admissible.[38] The Heilbron Committee seemed to think so, and concluded that to disallow questions on the subject as in *Krausz*,[39] *Clay*[40] (where the acts of prostitution were about twenty years before the alleged rape) and *Bashir*[41] must be unfair to the accused.

Adler's research shows that not only are judges consciously giving leave for cross-examination under section 2, but that questions are frequently asked without application having been made and without objection from either prosecuting counsel or the judge. The apparent indifference of the prosecutor is odd, given that it seems that juries are more reluctant to convict those accused of rape when they have heard of the complainant's sexual history.[42] This writer, having heard indefensible 'fishing' cross-examinations which caused considerable distress to complainants, found that some of the lawyers involved had not worked out what the central issue in the case was, nor, therefore, that the questions were irrelevant. The obligation to tie the cross-examination to the case actually being pleaded is not understood by every lawyer operating in the criminal courts, and this exacerbates the ordeal, not only of rape victims, but women who complain of other kinds of sexual assault – to which section 2 does not apply anyway. Another problem is that although complainants come into court as witnesses for the prosecution, they do not enjoy a lawyer–client relationship with counsel. It is inconsistent with adversarial theory to allow legal representation for prosecution witnesses, but that is not an insuperable obstacle; we have seen that there are many aspects of the criminal trial which are not strictly adversarial. In non-adversarial jurisdictions such as Germany, all victims are entitled to representation; in France, they can put in a claim for nominal damages, making themselves *parties civiles*, or co-plaintiffs, with the same effect. Certainly legal representation[43] would alleviate the position of all

[38] Heilbron Report, para. 135.

[39] (1973) 57 Cr App R 466; see above.

[40] (1851) 5 Cox CC 146.

[41] [1969] 1 WLR 1303.

[42] H. Kalven and H. Zeisel, *The American Jury* (Little, Brown & Co., Boston, 1966, p. 249.

[43] As urged by J. Temkin, *Rape and the Legal Process* (Sweet & Maxwell, London, 1987), p. 178.

victims who give evidence for the prosecution; if it were combined with a non-adversarial structure, so that the issues in the case were not dictated by the defence, their protection would be considerably improved.

CHILDREN

Vulnerability

There can be no doubt that children are particularly vulnerable witnesses. In the first place, few are likely to comprehend the exact nature and purpose of the proceedings; some children think they are there to prove their own innocence.[44] If the case involves suspected abuse of the child, he or she may have been removed from his or her home and family. The child may have been interviewed by various interested agencies,[45] and therefore required to repeat his or her story over and over again. In *Re E*[46] a child, Z, was questioned by parents, a social worker, and then seven times by a child protection officer of the NSPCC, four of which interviews were videotaped.[47] The ordeal for the child witness involves such potentially harrowing features as: facing the accused; the imposing atmosphere of a crowded courtroom; the fact that in a jury trial he or she must speak loudly enough to be heard over some distance; relating intimate and embarrassing details, if the case involves sexual abuse; in some cases, a genuine fear of the accused if there have been threats in the past; there may be a moral and emotional dilemma if the consequences of denouncing a loved relative are understood.[48] Where child victims of sexual abuse have given evidence in court, they have been found to be suffering greater psychological damage than victims who have not.[49]

[44] Cashmore and Bussey, 'Children's conceptions of the witness role', in *Children's Evidence in Legal Proceedings*, eds J. R. Spencer, G. Nicholson, R. Flin and R. Bull (Spencer, Faculty of Law, University of Cambridge, 1990).
[45] Although moves to co-ordinate inter-agency investigation are now well under way; see below.
[46] *The Times*, 2 April 1990.
[47] This despite the recommendation in the Cleveland Report that there should be no more than two interviews, and these should not be too long: *Report of the Inquiry into Child Abuse in Cleveland, 1987*, Cm. 412 (1988) para., 12.34.
[48] Libai, 'The protection of the child victim of a sexual offence in the criminal justice system' (1969) 15 Wayne LR 977, 984.
[49] T. C. Gibbens and J. Prince, *Child Victims of Sex Offences* (Institute for the Study and Treatment of Delinquency, London, 1963); cf. Dr Jane Wynne, 'The court appearance is child abuse itself', Address to the British Paediatric Association, *The Times*, 17 April 1986; Avery, 'The child victim: potential for secondary victimization' (1983) 7 Crim JJ 1.

On the other hand, the Thompson Committee[50] reported that a majority of psychiatrists and social workers who made representations to them thought that children should continue to participate in the trial, and that they were not so seriously affected by giving evidence as was generally supposed. However, there was agreement that multiplicity of interviews is damaging.

The criminal trial presents a more daunting prospect to the child witness than does the civil, partly because of its public nature and physically grand scale, the courtrooms having to be large enough to accommodate the jury, but also because of its more adversarial character. In the past, civil proceedings dealing with child abuse have been of different kinds: wardship, formerly a route by which care orders were obtained, involved the High Court invoking an ancient procedure which appeared to be entirely non-adversarial in character;[51] care proceedings, not regarded as strictly adversarial, since the participants are not necessarily those with something to deny;[52] and then there are divorce and matrimonial proceedings which, typically, take place in the county court.[53] The Children Act 1989 dramatically restricts the use of the wardship jurisdiction to prevent care or supervision orders from being given outside care proceedings, leaving the nature of welfare cases largely unresolved. But the Act has indicated a new approach – the hearsay rule is abolished as far as most child-centred hearings are concerned[54] – and will institute new procedures, much closer to an inquisitorial model, which may render care proceedings shorter and less frequent.[55] In an entirely adversarial trial the child witness must be cross-examined by the opposing side on every fact which they propose to deny, and this frequently prolongs the child's ordeal and forces the defence into a hostile posture which might in fact be counterproductive from their point of view. Advocates are not allowed to make the acquaintance of witnesses in advance of the trial,[56] so counsel find it difficult, however willing they may be, to break down the child's reluctance to discuss the abuse with strangers.

[50] Scottish Home and Health Department, *Report on Criminal Procedure in Scotland*, (1975).
[51] *Re H and Re K* [1989] FCR 356; wardship is an ancient jurisdiction which is administrative and non-adversarial in character, and so the hearsay rule does not apply.
[52] *Humberside v DPR* [1977] 3 All ER 964; although 'essentially non-adversary' in nature the hearsay rule applied. Cf. *In Re W, The Times*, 10 November 1989; see chapters 1 and 7.
[53] In *Re H and Re K* it was held that the hearsay rule applied. See chapter 7.
[54] See chapter 7.
[55] See below.
[56] 'A barrister may not discuss a case with or in the presence of potential witnesses, save for his lay client': Code of Conduct for the Bar of England and Wales, r. 142(b).

Attempts have been made to overcome some of these difficulties. The use of screens to shield the child from the defendant in criminal cases has had mixed fortunes. The Scottish Law Commission regards them as worthwhile,[57] despite the practical problems they can present. No courts have purpose-built screens; some of those produced for the purpose have gaps, filled by tacking on extra paper.[58] Prosecutors, who must make application to the court and who may benefit from their use, do not have to meet the cost.[59] More sophisticated methods are now available to assist child witnesses. Section 32 of the Criminal Justice Act 1988 allows them to give evidence through a live television link on a trial on indictment[60] if under the age of fourteen and the offence charged is one to which subsection (2) applies, but evidence may not be so given without the leave of the court. The kinds of case to which subsection (2) applies are:

(a) to an offence which involves an assault on, or injury or a threat of injury to, a person;
(b) to an offence under section 1 of the Children and Young Persons Act 1933 (cruelty to persons under 16);
(c) to an offence under the Sexual Offences Act 1956, the Indecency with Children Act 1960, the Sexual Offences Act 1967, section 54 of the Criminal Law Act 1977 or the Protection of Children Act 1978; and
(d) to an offence which consists of attempting or conspiring to commit, or of aiding, abetting, counselling, procuring or inciting the commission of, an offence falling within paragraph (a), (b) or (c) above.

Although there were gloomy predictions that giving evidence through the medium of the live video link would be almost as unnerving as remaining in the body of the court,[61] experience does not seem to bear them out. Children have not, apparently, found the exercise intimidating, and judges and counsel expressed themselves enthusiastic.[62] Whether the removal of the child

---

[57] *Report on the Evidence of Children and Other Potentially Vulnerable Witnesses* 1989, HC Paper 161, paras. 4.17–4.27.
[58] Morgan and Plotnikoff, 'Children as victims of crime: procedure at court', in Spencer, Nicholson, Flin and Bull (eds).
[59] CPS Circular 46/1987.
[60] Or an appeal to the criminal division of the Court of Appeal or the hearing of a reference under Criminal Appeal Act 1968, s. 17.
[61] Spencer, 'Child witnesses and video-technology: thoughts for the Home Office' (1987) 51 J Cr L 444. See also MacFarlane, 'Diagnostic evaluations and the use of videotapes in child sexual abuse cases' (1985) 40 Miami LR 135.
[62] Scottish Law Commission, *Report on the Evidence of Children and Other Potentially Vulnerable Witnesses* (Scot. Law. Com. No. 125, 1989), paras. 4.8–4.33.

from the immediate scrutiny of the jury makes it harder to obtain a conviction is not known. It has been suggested that a screen image of the child lacks the power of his or her actual presence,[63] the accused being a more real person to the jury, who see him or her throughout the trial. But the obvious weakness of the live video link is that it does no more than separate the child physically from the other participants in the trial. The nature of examination-in-chief and cross-examination is unaltered, and the time gap between the alleged offence and the day of the trial may mean that the court is presented with a description of events far less reliable than the child's account soon afterwards. The fact that Parliament and the courts are now alive to this problem and seem minded to deal with it may reflect increasing disillusion with the principle of orality.[64]

Reliability of child witnesses

The distinction between sworn and unsworn evidence may be somewhat mystifying in the absence of corroboration requirements for either,[65] and is soon to be abolished in criminal cases for that reason.[66] The anomaly that children in civil cases had to give evidence on oath, and therefore might have to be older than those in criminal cases, has been rectified by the Children Act 1989.[67] However, even with unsworn evidence, since *Wallwork*[68] it was long assumed that the minimum age of competency should be eight. At present the trial judge must conduct an inquiry[69] into the child's understanding in order to see whether he or she is capable of giving sworn or unsworn evidence. In order to be sworn, the child's understanding must go beyond the general social duty to tell the truth, to an awareness of the obligation to tell the truth to the court.[70] It appeared to be received wisdom that it is

---

[63] S. B. Smith, 'The child witness', in National Association of Councils for Children, *Representing Children: Current Issues in Law, Medicine and Mental Health* (1987), p. 13.

[64] See also chapter 7.

[65] Abolished: Criminal Justice Act 1988, s. 34.

[66] Criminal Justice Bill 1991.

[67] S. 96; the court must be satisfied that the child understands that it is his or her duty to tell the truth and has sufficient understanding to justify his or her evidence being heard.

[68] (1958) 42 Cr App R 153.

[69] Now see Criminal Justice Bill 1991.

[70] Children and Young Persons Act 1933, s. 38(1); *Brasier* (1779) 1 Leach 199; *Hayes* [1977] 2 All ER 288.

exceptional for children younger than eight to have sufficient awareness of the importance of telling the truth. Nevertheless, there has been considerable pressure on the courts more recently to admit the evidence of younger children in the climate of growing concern about their sexual abuse, for without the victim's evidence the offence may be difficult to prove. John Spencer[71] has argued forcefully that very young children ought to be able to give evidence in some form. If offences against them cannot be prosecuted for want of their evidence, they are not protected by the law. Some of the arguments on this issue turn on how much credence it is appropriate to give the evidence of small children; but there is also to be borne in mind that the nature of English trials, particularly criminal trials, may weigh against introducing small children as witnesses simply on humanitarian grounds. There is also the problem that civil and criminal matters are heard separately, forcing the child to give evidence twice. If, in a particular case, it is thought that the child concerned should not do this more than once, a decision would have to be made as to which is the more important – to find the most appropriate haven for the child in civil proceedings, which involve a lower standard of proof, or to bring an alleged offender to justice through a criminal trial. How trials should be altered will be discussed shortly. Recently the Court of Appeal in *B*[72] and *Wright and Ormerod*,[73] perhaps anticipating imminent reform, has declared that *Wallwork* has been overtaken by events and that the competency test is a matter of the judge's discretion. The court in *Wallwork* would have been influenced by the nature of the experience which a court appearance would represent, the five-year-old in that case not having the technological facilities now available. The judge's discretion now appears to be unfettered[74] except that the younger the child the greater the care that has to be taken before admitting the evidence.

The assumption that children's evidence is inherently suspect was behind the common law requirement that a warning of the need for corroboration be given to the jury, and the statutory requirement in relation to unsworn children that no one should be convicted solely on the strength of what such a child might say.[75] These requirements were summarily abolished in the Criminal Justice Act 1988,[76] presumably representing new faith in the credibility of child witnesses. There has been a lobby of opinion arguing that

---

[71] E.g. Spencer 'Child-Witnesses and Video Technology: Thoughts for the Home Office' (1987) 51 J Cr L 444; 'Reforming the competency requirement' [1988] NLJ 147.

[72] *The Times*, 1 March 1990.

[73] (1990) 90 Cr App R 91.

[74] And see Criminal Justice Bill 1991.

[75] Children and Young Persons Act 1933, s. 38(2).

[76] S. 34.

children are equally as reliable as adults,[77] but the question of the reliability of the evidence of children is in fact a particularly complicated one. There is no doubt that children can be helpful in identification[78] although stress reduces their performance,[79] making it advisable to screen them from the suspect during any identification parade. But tests have found that an eight-year-old is more likely than an older child to select a face from a series of photographs when that of the real subject is not there.[80] This may be because young children do not understand the object of the exercise and assume it is some sort of test of themselves,[81] increasing the likelihood that they will hazard a guess and select the person most like the subject. In a famous article,[82] Dr Jones describes the case of Susie, aged three, who was able to pick out a photograph of her attacker from six pictures. Although her ability to describe the events and to remember who was responsible is encouraging, the problem that children may be more likely to pick out the wrong person because the real one is not shown should not be forgotten.

If a child is required to describe an event rather than describe or identify a person, more is required of his or her memory, and he or she is more likely to make errors.[83] A child's capacity to remember events increases with age, apparently in direct relation to his or her understanding of what he or she observes.[84] The research on children's ability to recall and describe events suggests that they are not as good as adults at searching their memories or categorizing them to order.[85] Unprompted, children of under ten recall five

[77] Notably Spencer, 'Child witnesses and the law of evidence' [1987] Crim LR 76; [1988] NLJ 147.

[78] Parker, Hoverfield and Baker-Thomas, 'Eyewitness testimony of children' *Journal of Applied Psychology*, 16 (1986), p. 287; Davies, Stevenson-Robb and Flin, 'The reliability of children's testimony', *International Practitioner*, 11 (1986), p. 81.

[79] Davies, Stevenson-Robb and Flin, ibid.

[80] Yuille, Cutshall and King, 'Age-related changes in eyewitness accounts and photo-identification', unpublished; quoted, C. Hedderman, *Children's Evidence; The Need for Corroboration*, Home Office Research and Planning Unit Paper 41, pp. 13–14.

[81] Moston, 'The suggestibility of children in interview studies', *First Language*, 7 (1987), p. 67.

[82] Jones, 'The evidence of a three year old child' [1987] Crim LR 677.

[83] King and Yuille, 'Suggestibility and the child witness', in *Children's Eyewitness Memory*, eds S. Ceci, M. Toglia and D. Ross (Springer, New York, 1987).

[84] Davies, 'Research on children's testimony: implications for interviewing practice', in eds C. Hollins and K. Howells *Clinical Approaches to Sex Offenders and their Victims*, Wiley, Chichester, 1991.

[85] Davies and Brown, 'Recall and organization in five year old children', *British Journal of Psychology*, 69 (1978), p. 343: Perry, 'Child and adolescent development – a psychological perspective', in *Child Witnesses; Law and Practice*, ed. J. E. B. Myers (Wiley, New York, 1987).

or six times less than adults and furnish accounts which are more fragmentary and selective than do older children or adults.[86] The explanation for this appears to be that young children are only learning to think conceptually and have only a limited range of concepts.[87] The greatest development here takes place between the ages of five and ten.[88] However, if a child possesses a body of knowledge, for instance about cars, which enables him or her to organize information systematically, he or she may well be more accurate describing a car than an adult without such knowledge.[89] More significantly, his or her observation of and ability to recall details depend very much on how important the event was to the child. Being immediately involved in it has a far deeper impression on the memory than when the child is merely a bystander.[90]

Children are quicker to forget than adults, and so the younger they are the faster the memory fades;[91] this means that the principle of orality with regard to these young witnesses is entirely inappropriate. The court merely deprives itself of the most accurate account if it insists that the child relate it on the day of the trial. There is also doubt as to whether lay adults can always understand what the child means to say, which presents problems as to how the meaning can be communicated to jurors, unless some kind of interpretation is given by an expert.[92] The risk that a child will forget important details means that it is vital that evidence be obtained shortly after the event; but it may be difficult for the child to describe it unaided. It has been shown that prompting can assist children to search their memories, since the questions asked can themselves organize their thinking. Marin's study[93] found that when structured questioning guided the children's efforts to remember, they were much closer to the adults in performance.[94] How-

---

[86] Marin, Holmes, Guth and Kovac, 'The potential of children as eyewitnesses', *Law and Human Behaviour*, 3 (1979), p. 295.

[87] Davies, Stevenson-Robb and Flin, *International Practitioner* (1986).

[88] Brown, 'Learning and development: the problem of compatibility, access and induction', *Human Development*, 25 (1982), p. 89.

[89] Ibid.

[90] Goodman, Aman and Hirschman, 'Child sexual and physical abuse; children's testimony', in Ceci, Toglia and Ross (eds).

[91] Brainerd, Kingma and Lowe, 'On the development of forgetting', *Child Development*, 56 (1985), p. 1103.

[92] Murray, *Evidence from Children: Alternatives to In-Court Testimony in Criminal Proceedings in the United States of America*, Scottish Law Commission Research Paper (April 1988).

[93] Marin et al., *Law and Human Behaviour* (1979).

[94] Cf. Ceci, Ross and Toglia, 'Suggestibility of children's memory; psycho-legal implications', *Journal of Experimental Psychology*, 38 (1987), p. 116.

ever, 'structured questioning' is rather easier to achieve when the researcher knows the facts, as Marin's questioners did, and as Dr Jones did when questioning Susie about what happened.[95] This raises the question of suggestion, particularly as Tschirgi has argued that people testing a hypothesis preferentially search for evidence which will support it.[96] It is extremely difficult to put questions non-suggestively where the inquisitor does not know what, if anything, happened. Dent found that a major problem in his experiment, where the interviewers did not know the facts, was their tendency, whatever their training, to reach a premature conclusion and then attempt to elicit confirmatory information from the young witnesses. In such cases were the least accurate descriptions obtained.[97]

There are conflicting views as to whether children are more susceptible to suggestion than adults. Marin thought not,[98] but Cohen and Harnick[99] found twelve-year olds more suggestible than adults, and nine-year-olds more suggestible still. But more depends upon the strength of the impression created by the event than the child's age;[100] it is much harder to get a child to accept 'planted' information where he or she had central as opposed to peripheral involvement in it. Davies concludes that the evidence shows that suggestibility in children is more a function of setting and task than state of mind.[101] However, most of the experiments on which that conclusion is based deal with morally neutral matters. More disturbing findings were the result of an experiment[102] in which the questioner deliberately assumed guilt or innocence on the part of the actor. Children of five and six saw incidents in which a janitor was tidying up toys. In the case of half of them, the janitor became 'Chester the Molestor' in that he ceased work to play with the dolls in a suggestive way, adopting malicious and aggressive behaviour towards them. When questioned neutrally afterwards by 'Chester's boss', the

[95] Jones [1987] Crim LR 677.

[96] Tschirgi, 'Sensible reasoning: a hypothesis about hypotheses', *Child Development*, 51 (1980), p. 1. See Hedderman, *Children's Evidence*.

[97] Dent, 'The effect of interviewing strategies on the results of interviews with child witnesses', in *Restructuring the Past*, ed. A. Trankell (Kluwer, Deventer, 1982).

[98] Marin et al., *Law and Human Behaviour* (1979).

[99] Cohen and Harnick, 'The susceptibility of child witnesses to suggestion', *Law and Human Behaviour*, 4 (1980), p. 295; cf. Goodman and Reed, 'Age differences in eyewitness testimony' *Law and Human Behaviour*, 10 (1986), p. 317.

[100] Goodman, Aman and Hirschman, in Ceci, Toglia and Ross (eds).

[101] Davies, in Hollin and Howells (eds).

[102] Clarke-Stewart, Thompson and Lepore, 'Manipulating children's interpretations through interrogation', paper presented at Society for Research on Child Development, Kansas City, USA (1989). See Davies, ibid.

children were generally accurate in describing his behaviour. But in some cases, the questions were designed to incriminate the 'cleaning' Chester, or to exculpate the 'playing' character. There, fewer than half the children stuck to their story, instead adopting the questioner's interpretation or saying that Chester had both cleaned and played. This shows, says Davies, the 'devastating effect' on these children of assumptions of guilt or innocence, although the authors could not reproduce the results with older children.[103] Against this is work that shows that even three-year-old non-abused children will resist suggestions implying impropriety after an intimate medical examination.[104] Although it may be that overall there is not sufficient evidence to justify a conclusion that children are more suggestible than adults, who are extremely themselves suggestible,[105] the difficulty remains that children are peculiarly the subjects of a disclosure process which frequently uses suggestion to overcome reluctance to report abuse. No other potential witnesses are targeted by investigative agencies for intensive scrutiny in the way that children are.

Whether or not children would invent stories of abuse of their own accord is an even more vexed question. The law has been influenced by an instinctive feeling that the temptation to lie might be stronger for children than adults. Professor Williams suggests[106] they might lie for reasons such as gaining attention or because of dislike of a step-parent or new 'uncle'. It has been assumed that, if they do not understand the significance of the accusation they are making, it is less reliable – hence the nature of the questioning traditionally done by judges to assess competence, which turns on whether or not the child appreciates the importance of telling the truth *in court*.[107] Spencer and Flin, arguing that children are unlikely to lie about abuse, suggest that children lie more usually to avoid trouble than to create it.[108] But it should be remembered that children often have different concerns from adults. There is a view that children may go to extreme lengths to

---

[103] But work with adults suggests that the relationship, particularly the degree of trust, between the subject and the suggester is crucial: Gudjonsson, 'Retracted confessions: legal, psychological and psychiatric aspects' (1988) 28 Med Sci L 187.

[104] Saywitz, Goodman, Nichols and Moan, 'Children's memory for a genital examination', paper presented to the Society for Research on Child Development, Kansas City, USA (1989).

[105] See chapter 1.

[106] Williams, 'Child witnesses', in *Criminal Law: Essays in Honour of J. C. Smith*, ed. P. Smith (Butterworths, London, 1987).

[107] *Hayes* [1977] 2 All ER 288.

[108] Spencer and Flin, 'Child witnesses – are they liars?' [1989] NLJ 1601.

cover up behaviour for which they fear rebuke – for instance playing with children disapproved of by their parents, or accepting sweets from strangers, having been told not to do it – because they are unaware of the triviality of the incident about which they are concerned in comparison with the story they are telling.[109] It is not possible to devise experiments to measure a tendency to lie; psychologists typically stage events in the presence of witnesses so that they can compare the descriptions given with a known reality. There are claims that children of particular ages could not invent allegations of sexual abuse because they do not have the essential knowledge,[110] but this is doubted by the Royal College of Physicians.[111] It may be that there is a gap between what adults wish a small child to know, and what is in fact gleaned from much older friends.[112] American research suggests that interviewing techniques for children may result in a large number of unfounded allegations, particularly in cases involving warring adults, such as custody or access disputes.[113] The problem with such claims is that they can be made only where there is a reason to believe that the truth is known to the researcher. The same applies to claims the other way, as in the work of Jones and McGraw,[114] who estimate that only about 2 per cent of allegations by children of sexual abuse are false. The totality of findings is inconclusive, to say the least, but there are two legitimate conclusions which may be drawn. The first is that it is no more possible to say that children are as reliable as adults than that they are not. The second is that, although opinions may vary as to whether children would or could spontaneously invent allegations of sexual abuse, there is some cause for concern about their vulnerability to suggestion, particularly where there is an adult with considerable opportunity to influence the child who has a motive for fostering a belief that abuse has occurred.

Identifying the cases where this has happened may be especially difficult,

---

[109] Trankell, 'Was Lars sexually assaulted? A study on the reliability of witnesses and of experts', *Journal of Abnormal Psychology*, 56 (1961), p. 385.

[110] DHSS Paper, *Child Abuse – Working Together* (1986): 'A child's statement that he or she is being abused should be accepted as true until proved otherwise. Children seldom lie about sexual abuse.'

[111] Evidence to Butler-Sloss LJ, Cleveland Report.

[112] Eva Smith, 'How to deal with children's evidence', in Spencer, Nicholson, Flin and Bull (eds).

[113] Raskin and Yuille, 'Problems in evaluating interviews of children in sexual abuse cases', in Ceci, Toglia and Ross, (eds).

[114] Jones and McGraw, 'Reliable and fictitious accounts of sexual abuse in children', *Journal of Interpersonal Violence*, 2 (1987), p. 27.

as there is evidence that adults have more trouble differentiating truthful from untruthful children when they are very young.[115] It is suggested[116] that it would be safer to rely on interview evaluation techniques, such as Statement Validity Analysis, which test the contents of the child's statement against criteria based on findings that true statements share various characteristics.[117] Such assessment is employed in Canada,[118] the United States and Germany, where there are court psychologists to carry it out. Whether or not this is the way forward for England may be arguable, but judges should approve of the stance that there can be no initial assumptions about the credibility of a child who makes an allegation. One of the tests in Statement Validity Analysis is whether the statement accords with other evidence, including medical. There have been cases where conclusions about abuse were reached without any attempt being made to check the contents of the child's story against ascertainable facts. In *Re E*[119] there was ample independent evidence that the father worked in London during the week and could not have committed the acts of which he was accused. In *Re H and Re K*[120] the child referred to acts occurring while she and her father were 'in their pyjamas' and on 'Nona's bed', which could not have been true. In *Re G*[121] a boy's earlier statement was shown by a subsequent questioner to be unreliable by the simple means of asking him when and where the acts took place; his answers were fantastic. This kind of failure to attend to reality bolsters the judicial anxiety that some interviewers begin with preconceptions and are unwilling to take notice of facts which conflict with them. It is futile to make recommendations to the courts until the child's statement has been compared with all the facts. Any major inconsistency between the statements and the other evidence must be acknowledged if the interviewer's conclusions are to carry any weight.[122] Butler-Sloss LJ stresses that adults as well as children must be interviewed to obtain background information,[123]

---

[115] Westcott, Davies and Clifford, 'Lying smiles and other stories: adults' perceptions of children's truthful and deceptive statements', paper presented at the First European Congress of Psychology, Amsterdam; cited Davies, in Hollin and Howells (eds).

[116] For example by Davies, ibid.

[117] Faller, 'Criteria for judging the credibility of children's statements about their sexual abuse', *Child Welfare*, 67 (1988), p. 389.

[118] E.g. Yuille, 'The systematic assessment of children's testimony', *Canadian Psychology*, 29 (1988), p. 247.

[119] *The Times*, 2 April 1990.

[120] [1989] 2 FLR 313.

[121] [1987] 1 FLR 310.

[122] *Re H and Re K* [1989] 2 FLR 313; *Re G*, ibid.

[123] Cleveland Report, paras. 12.2–9.

but, although it is clearly vital that no conclusion is drawn before it is known, the Cleveland Report does not make it clear whether it should be known at the time of the interview itself. Specialists differ about the importance of this; the Great Ormond Street approach[124] is to consult any available information before interviewing, but the NSPCC model[125] recommends interviewers to ignore it, in order to avoid forming preconceptions. Statement Validity Analysis would, *inter alia*, systematically test the contents of the child's statement against known facts in order to evaluate its reliability.

One of the suggested ways in which the trauma for child witnesses might be reduced is to admit into evidence the hearsay record of a disclosure interview. These are often videotaped; if courts could avail themselves of such evidence, they would have the opportunity to hear the account given by the child closest in time to the alleged event, and also to see the manner in which it was given and in response to what questions. But the courts and the experts have been in fundamental disagreement over the kind of questioning appropriate to obtain disclosures of abuse from children. The earliest videotaped interviews were based on a style of questioning in fact developed at Great Ormond Street as therapy for children known to have been abused – many of whom went through a stage of denial – but which was later used to obtain disclosure where abuse was suspected.[126] Pressure and leading and hypothetical questions were used to overcome the child's resistance, which might derive from guilt, fear or love. Judges who had the opportunity to see the video records of the interviews were extremely hostile to the methods used.[127] Since the refusal of the courts to pay any heed to evidence so obtained, a great deal of work has been done to develop interview styles which would be acceptable to the judges. Unfortunately, specialists have not reached consensus on the best interviewing techniques.[128] The Home Office[129] is unable to suggest a firm format; the situation is complicated by the anticipated presence at the interview of representatives of more than one agency. The advantage of a police presence obviously is that the likelihood of a

[124] Vizard, 'Interviewing children suspected of being sexually abused; a review of theory and practice', in Hollin and Howells (eds).
[125] Bannister and Print, *A Model for Assessment of Interviews in Suspected Cases of Child Sexual Abuse*, NSPCC Occasional Paper No. 4 (1988).
[126] Vizard, 'Interviewing young, sexually abused children; assessment techniques' [1989] Fam L 28.
[127] 'Tranter cases' [1987] 1 FLR 269–310; see also Douglas and Willmore, 'Diagnostic interviews as evidence of child sexual abuse' [1987] Fam L 191.
[128] Vizard lists ten possible approaches recommended by clinicians, in Hollin and Howells (eds).
[129] Circular 67/1989.

successful prosecution can be determined without subjecting the child to further questioning once the disclosures have been made. What is not clear is the respective roles of those involved in the interviewing. Partly for this reason, the Pigot Report recently recommended that the agencies concerned select between them a single, trained interviewer, with a proper briefing on the specific needs of each agency represented.[130] A further recommendation in the Report that there should be a code of practice governing the conduct of video-recorded interviews[131] would be a vital step towards achieving some certainty in this area.

Solving the problem: criminal cases

Before the Pigot Committee was constituted, there was an influential lobby in support of the admission of videotaped interviews in criminal cases in lieu of the evidence of children, to spare them the ordeal of testifying in court.[132] But, in order to accommodate the defence, the accused and his or her lawyers would be present, although not visible to the child, behind a two-way screen. The accused's questions could then be put to the child by 'feeding' them through a trained interviewer, so that the accused could not subsequently complain that he or she had no opportunity to cross-examine the child. The videotaped record of this procedure would then be admitted at the trial as a complete substitute for the presence of the child. It was a proposal that found favour with the Scottish Law Commission in its early Discussion Paper,[133] but suffered from serious disadvantages both to the accused and to the child.[134] The fact that the exact nature of the case against the defendant must be known and that he or she must have instructed lawyers before the interview could take place, also suggested delay which could diminish the true usefulness of the account given by the child. The Scottish Law Commission[135] (SLC) and the Pigot Committee (Pigot) took account of the strength of feeling among criminal law practitioners by preferring a different solution, which is fairer to the parties but cumbersome and likely to lead to practical problems in criminal trials. Briefly, the disclosure interviews on videotape would replace the child's evidence-in-chief, but the child would be cross-examined by defence counsel at a pre-trial hearing in

---

[130] Home Office, *Report of the Advisory Group on Video Evidence* (Pigot) (1989), para. 4.14.

[131] Ibid., para. 4.8.

[132] Williams, in Smith (ed.); Spencer (1987) 51 J Cr L 444.

[133] No. 75, June 1988.

[134] McEwan, 'Child evidence: more proposals for reform' [1988] Crim LR 813.

[135] Scottish Law Commission, *Report on the Evidence of Children.*

front of the judge. The jury would not be present but would see this recorded on videotape.[136]

The intention behind the proposals is to provide the court with the most reliable evidence available,[137] bringing to justice those who commit offences against very young children, and reducing the stress suffered by children who give evidence in the present conditions. It is hoped that the proposals, which are designed to address all these matters, will lead to more pleas of guilty, making the ordeal in court unnecessary for all concerned. There is doubt whether they will have this effect; the American evidence is admitted to be ambiguous.[138] However, the desirability of constructing a system of trial where the accused cannot profit, in terms of deterrent effect, from the ordeal facing his or her victim in court, is beyond argument.[139] Both the SLC and Pigot recognize that a contemporaneous account is frequently more accurate and detailed than one given much later in court, particularly in the case of child witnesses. Given the increased co-operation between agencies working with sexually abused children, which often results in disclosure interviews being videotaped for the purposes of all concerned, Pigot feels that expansion of the process to cover other kinds of abused or neglected children could provide valuable evidence for the criminal courts. But the requirement that the taped interview should be made within a few days of the initial complaint[140] assumes an identifiable moment at which an accusation is made. The disclosure process with some sexually abused children is far less cut and dried than that,[141] and Pigot might do better to imitate the SLC, who would admit any previous consistent statement by any witness as evidence of the facts as long as it is in permanent form. As it is, the decision will have to be taken at some point that a complaint has been made, and arrangements made for a video session as soon as possible. English and

---

[136] The Pigot and SLC proposals represent a great deal of thought by the relevant bodies. Pigot in fact was a Committee especially set up by the Home Secretary to review the problem of the vulnerable witness. Yet at the time of writing, the government seems minded to dispense with key recommendations and therefore the reasoning behind the scheme as a whole.

[137] Pigot, para. 2.10.

[138] Ibid., para. 2.11: cf. Murray, *Evidence from Children*. Those few recorded changes of plea where defendants had seen videotaped interviews might have been forthcoming anyway.

[139] The unsavoury tactic of using contested committal proceedings as a baptism of fire for this purpose will be unavailable under Pigot (and see Criminal Justice Bill 1991).

[140] Pigot, para. 4.10.

[141] Vizard [1989] Fam L 28.

Scottish courts will be aware that the sooner this is done, the more accurate the statement is likely to be. Pigot makes it clear that the purpose of the videotaped interview must be recognized; it is akin to a witness statement[142] and is entirely distinct from a therapeutic interview.[143]

There is a marked contrast between the two reports in the way they deal with the conduct of interviews. The SLC is relatively cavalier; the only elaboration on the general admissibility of previous consistent statements in permanent form is that the use of leading questions should *not* be fatal to the admissibility of the statement.[144] Pigot acknowledges that many judges already allow a number of leading questions with the evidence-in-chief of child witnesses if they are having problems in court, but recommends that for the taking of videotape evidence a code of practice be drawn up. This would provide guidelines for interviewers who intend to present such evidence in criminal courts. The most appropriate model of interview is thought to be Professor Yuille's 'step-wise' approach.[145] It is vital also in these cases that the interviewer should never be the first to suggest that a particular offence was committed, or that a particular person was the perpetrator.[146] Other guidelines would include a cautious use of anatomically correct dolls,[147] and provide for the accused person to be shown the recording as soon as practically possible.[148] In its evidence to Pigot, the NSPCC asked that rigid uniformity of interviewing styles should not be advocated, since these vary a great deal depending on the age of the child, whether or not there is clear disclosure, and the personality of the questioner.[149] Given that Pigot recommends that judges dealing with child abuse cases should be 'experienced and approved',[150] there is hope of flexibility. It

---

[142] Pigot, para. 4.9.

[143] Ibid.

[144] SLC Draft Evidence (Children and other Witnesses) (Scotland) Bill, clause 8. A blanket ban would be quite inappropriate: McEwan, 'Child abuse, disclosure interviews and the courts' [1989] 2 Child L 19.

[145] Pigot, para. 4.18.

[146] Ibid., para. 4.20. In fact, in the case of a reticent child, it is doubtful whether this is a realistic requirement. It is in any case impossible to legislate against such suggestions being made before the video-recording, whether by interviewers or by anyone else.

[147] For a review of the research see Westcott, Davies and Clifford, 'The use of anatomical dolls in child witness interviews', Adoption and Fostering, 13 (1989), p. 6.

[148] Pigot, para. 4.23.

[149] NSPCC, *Submission to the Home Office Advisory Group on the Admissibility of Video Recorded Interviews* (1988).

[150] Pigot, para. 7.11.

is absolutely essential that the right judges hear these cases, if the courts are not to become bogged down in technical arguments. The code of practice is not intended to be binding[151] and therefore should not be allowed to spawn unmeritorious legal objections and appeals. However, it is difficult to see how any judge can appreciate fully the significance of this kind of evidence, without help from, and attention to the views of, those with training in child development and, particularly, the behaviour and responses of abused children. A further problem will arise in cases where a child has been receiving therapeutic counselling since the interview was recorded; although it may be acceptable as a substitute for the child's evidence-in-chief, his or her reaction in cross-examination may be regarded as tainted by the subsequent discussions, which may be redolent of 'coaching'. Counsellors even now are finding that prosecutors urge them to delay therapy until after the trial; if the needs of the child are put first, therapy may proceed at the expense of securing a conviction, since the child's evidence may be excluded. In any case, there are counsellors who regard the conviction as a necessary ingredient of the child's recovery.

Given the flexible system proposed by the SLC, Pigot seems technical and legalistic in comparison. Why restrict admissibility to statements by victims of violence under fourteen, and victims of sexual offences under seventeen? And why attempt to categorize the interviewers? If there is useful evidence in any recorded interview, why should it be excluded simply because the questioner does not have the required duties as to 'the investigation of crime or the protection of or the welfare of children'?[152] A recorded statement organized by a malevolent mother clearly should be excluded, but we do not need statutory definitions to achieve that. The problem here seems to be that although it is recommended that experienced and approved judges should deal with child abuse cases, they are even so not really trusted to understand them. The Scots seem content to let guidance develop on a case-by-case basis without constraints on the judicial discretion. If Pigot fears a lack of judicial consistency, we really will have to look carefully at the whole issue of the training of judges in this field, and the selection of judges for that training. Experience at the Family or Criminal Bar is not on its own a guarantee of suitability for this kind of work.

The admissibility of the videotaped interview would be decided by the trial judge at the preliminary hearing. Its admission would not deprive the defendant of the right to cross-examine, since the child has to attend to give evidence, albeit by virtue of a new procedure (see below). This enables the defence to investigate the possibility of suggestion, and the presence in court

---

[151] Ibid., para. 4.8.
[152] Pigot, *Recommendations*, 1.

of the interviewer allows questioning about the circumstances of the interview, and, if relevant, multiplicity of interviews.[153] Pigot argues that the child is not worse off if he or she is cross-examined on discrepancies between the earlier statement and what he or she says in court, since the child could in any case have been cross-examined on any previous inconsistent statement.[154] But Pigot cites only one known instance of a videotape being used for this purpose in a criminal case; some lawyers feel that it is ill-advised to alert the jury to the existence of a videotape which they have not seen. And the time lapse does make it more than likely that inconsistencies will emerge, thus giving new opportunities to the defence.

Regarded as a deposition procedure by the SLC, the proposal is that whether or not a videotaped interview is available for evidential purposes, a child witness should be examined by counsel before the trial judge (any videotape largely having replaced his or her evidence in chief) in informal conditions. The proceedings would themselves be videotaped and shown to the jury. Thus the jury would see two videotapes in succession, the earlier statement and then the examination and cross-examination which would have taken place shortly before the opening of the trial. The trial judge, therefore, would deal in the preliminary hearing with the admissibility of any videotaped interview and then go on to supervise the taking of the child's evidence. The Home Secretary's letter of invitation to Pigot made it clear that the accused's right to cross-examine must be preserved; the Committee concluded that the judge should control the nature of the cross-examination with 'special care',[155] another recommendation which could usefully apply elsewhere.[156] Pigot does not explain what the manner of this special care might be. It is doubtful whether in the present climate judges would step in to stop some of the varieties of cross-examination of children currently employed; children can be led to contradict themselves without bullying, and the danger is that juries may make too much of discrepancies which have been induced by the forensic skills of the lawyer. It would assist them if some means were found to explain the effect of seductive leading questions in the context of cross-examination as well as how significant they are in the course of a diagnostic interview.[157] Pigot proposes that in order to avoid alarming the child, the accused would not be present at the hearing although

---

[153] 'The inherent defects of hearsay may be argued to be cured by the presence in court of the maker of the statement and the person to whom it was made': Pigot, para. 2.8.

[154] Ibid., para. 2.21.

[155] Ibid., para. 2.29.

[156] E.g. with rape complainants. See above.

[157] Suggestion that an expert witness act as *amicus curiae*; see below.

he or she could watch through a two-way mirror or television link. This means that an accused person representing him- or herself would not be able to cross-examine a child witness, and effectively is forced to secure legal representation. There is no constitutional right to confrontation[158] in English law, and no problem is contemplated with the European Convention on Human Rights, which requires that an accused person must have the opportunity to 'examine or have examined' witnesses against him or her.[159]

There may, however, be problems with that Convention, and there will certainly be controversy, over the recommendation made in the face of resistance from the Bar representative on Pigot, Miss Rafferty. This would allow the judge who felt that the witness could not cope even in the informal context proposed to protect him or her from direct questioning by lawyers. Questions could be relayed through a person who has the confidence of the child, for example a social worker. It is not clear whether this person might have conducted the original diagnostic interviews.[160] It is difficult to agree with the majority view that it is not a conclusive objection that counsel is hindered in developing his or her line of questioning without interruption and without his or her own intonation, timing and delivery.[161] It would appear, also, to flout the principles of natural justice if that individual was identified in any way with the prosecution of the case, directly or indirectly, and a defendant was nevertheless forced to conduct his or her defence though him or her. Any proposal, through a change in the Bar Code of Conduct, giving counsel pre-trial access to the child in order to familiarize the child with his or her intended interrogator, would need careful consideration to avoid abuse.[162]

Use of these two reforms together would allow the courts to drop the minimum competency requirement for children, which is causing so much trouble. Pigot suggests that the fiction of the oath be abandoned altogether for any child under the age of fourteen; age, intellectual development and maturity would go to weight. In general, if a child's evidence is available, it should be heard.[163] Pigot makes some justifiably sharp criticisms of the corroboration requirements for sexual complainants, with a proposal that they should go, as did those for child witnesses. An admonition to 'tell the truth' from the judge should be sufficient,[164] with no requirement for a warn-

---

[158] *Smellie* (1919) 14 Cr App R 128; *X, Y, and Z, The Times*, 3 November 1989.
[159] Art. 6(d).
[160] Pigot, para. 2.32.
[161] Ibid., para. 2.33.
[162] Miss Rafferty's suggestion: ibid., para. 2.34.
[163] Ibid., para. 5.12.
[164] Ibid., para. 5.15.

ing as such. It might be thought that a judge would inevitably give some direction relating to young children, particularly as under this proposal the jury will not see the child in the flesh at all; at present, judges appear to be giving a warning which merges the sex offence warning with emphasis on the fact that the complainant is a child. This formula is probably inevitable, given that child witnesses are called upon almost exclusively in sex offence cases. And it is difficult to see how judges could properly fulfil their function in the case of an unsworn child who in their own judgment does not suffiently understand the gravity of the proceedings to be put on oath, if they did not stress to the jury that the evidence may be suspect.[165] This is not to argue for the strictness of the *Baskerville* corroboration test; merely for recognition of the fact that children *are* in a significantly different position from that of other witnesses. Not only have they comparatively undeveloped cognitive abilities, but they are, in sexual abuse cases, subject to a process of suggestion and repeated interrogation in a way no other potential victims are likely to be.

The SLC assumes that the 'deposition' or pre-trial hearings will be the exception, rather than the rule: 'In many cases children will be able to give evidence by conventional means.'[166] The reason for this belief is not clear; but in the SLC Report the availability of the deposition procedure depends upon the discretion of the judge after application (from whom is not specified). The judge should take account of the circumstances of the particular child in making his or her decision. In Pigot the judge has no discretion to refuse if application is made by the prosecutor, subject to the wishes of the child. The difference of emphasis is puzzling, and Pigot appears to have got it right. Judges are not experts on the issue of how stressful a court appearance would be for particular children, and there should be a presumption that it is so in every case.

These proposals have endless potential for legalistic debate, which may result in the videotaped interview being excluded, and run the risk that the jury will feel alienated from a child who appears to them only as a face on a screen.[167] Retention wherever possible of procedures based on adversarial principles will result in an unwieldy and cumbersome scheme which relies heavily on technological personnel and equipment with a potentially pro-

---

[165] Although Murphy doubts with regret whether in the absence of statutory requirement judges will continue to give corroboration warnings over children's evidence: P. Murphy, *A Practical Approach to Evidence*, 3rd edn (Blackstones, London, 1988), p. 485.

[166] SLC, *Report on the Evidence of Children*, para. 4.7; this may be from behind a screen or through closed circuit television if appropriate.

[167] Smith, in National Association of Councils for Children.

hibitive cost. This probably explains why the present Criminal Justice Bill contains only a heavily watered-down version of the Pigot proposals, whereby cross-examination will be carried out in the ordinary way rather than in an informal setting in the absence of the jury. It is not surprising that bitter disappointment is being expressed; however, some observers would have been amazed if the money for the full Pigot scheme had been found. It seems beyond our capability to devise a simple solution; the basic adversarial trial is adhered to irrespective of how inappropriate it manifestly may be to the kind of case which is primarily concerned with the protection of vulnerable members of society. The committees responsible for these reports felt it beyond their scope to consider an entirely different procedure which would be primarily inquisitorial, allowing informal questioning by the judge, who could also examine any available hearsay evidence. Rather than put children through a formal cross-examination, which would prove little in many cases beyond how easy it is to confuse a child, the judge would ask the pertinent questions to establish what opportunities for suggestion there might have been, and the accused would be able to raise further points, about which he or she would request the judge to ask.[168] Utter devotion to the adversarial trial might appear somewhat irrational in ordinary circumstances; to insist on retaining it while going to such lengths to escape its traditional features as do these committees, bound as they are by terms of reference designed to confine discussion to narrow limits, might seem thoroughly eccentric.

Solving the problem: civil cases

One of the advantages of developing an inquisitorial method of trial in criminal cases if there were no jury[169] is that the same judge could hear the criminal charge concurrently with any civil case founded on allegations of abuse. This would mean that the child would be required to give evidence only once. The Children Act 1989 has stopped short of establishing children's courts with jurisdiction to hear all such civil matters, but this is plainly on the way. Judges are already developing specialized expertise in abuse cases both on the criminal and the civil side. The procedures currently being devised for the operation of the Children Act 1989 are more inquisitorial than the old-style care proceedings; they require pre-trial disclosure of evidence and preliminary hearings. The object is to reduce the duration of the final hearing, and ensure that the court is as fully informed as possible. Adopting a generic procedure would be simpler and more humane, and, it is submitted, the absence of a jury would not make the verdict less reliable. But

[168] See McEwan [1988] Crim LR 813.
[169] Ibid.

such a revolution is a long way off; there appears to be widespread political and emotional support for trial by jury, even for the kind of fraud trial which jurors cannot possibly understand.[170] Meanwhile, the operation of the hearsay rule in relation to child witnesses in civil cases, despite reforms, is more complicated than is necessary. This matter will be dealt with in detail in chapter 7; at this stage suffice it to say that whether or not the court is entitled to rely on a child's out-of-court statement in any form depends entirely upon the nature of the proceedings, and therefore which court hears the case.

OTHER VULNERABLE WITNESSES

Here Pigot is a grave disappointment. Without apparent reason and unlike the SLC, the English report tends to concentrate upon the problems of child witnesses in particular, unnecessarily[171] leaving other vulnerable witnesses to one side. The hot-house atmosphere surrounding the issue of child abuse should not blind lawyers to the fact that there are other witnesses who may be at least as vulnerable as children. The predicament of rape complainants, addressed above, would clearly be eased by applying the proposals to them. The SLC is aware of this and seems to have had little trouble incorporating relevant provisions in its draft bill. In Scottish courts, given the wide range of measures which would be available, the judge could select whichever is most appropriate to the witness required to give evidence in any given case. The SLC considers that a flexible discretion for the judge is the best way to achieve this, and that courts would be cautious in authorizing the use of special procedures for adult witnesses:[172]

> [They] will do so only where the circumstances clearly require them both in the interests of justice and in the interests of the witnesses themselves. Such caution will, we think, impose its own restrictions, but will do so more flexibly and more appropriately than would be the case if somewhat arbitrary restrictions were to be imposed by statute.

Pigot is apparently irretrievably committed to exhaustive statutory definitions, and is content to leave the extension of the new measures to include

---

[170] See *Fraud Trial Committee's Report*, HMSO (1986); the recommendation that a judge should hear fraud trials with two lay assessors rather than with a jury has fallen on stony ground.

[171] The Home Secretary's letter of invitation does not so limit their scope.

[172] SLC, *Report on the Evidence of Children*, para. 5.19.

adult vulnerable witnesses until a future development to occur 'eventually'. The Home Secretary's letter expressly addresses the Committee to 'other victims of crime',[173] so the political climate is not entirely hostile.

A neglected group of victim–witnesses easily as vulnerable as children are the mentally handicapped. Vizard has shown that there is a reluctance to accept that symptoms of abuse indicate adult interference, placing the mentally handicapped in a position previously occupied by battered wives and children, who were similarly the subjects of denial by society.[174] The problems of the mentally handicapped in communicating their distress and describing their experiences can be just as acute; if in institutions, it seems that they may be just as vulnerable to physical and sexual abuse as children.[175] There may be communication difficulties more difficult to overcome than is the case with children, particularly as the reaction to abuse may involve withdrawal, creating the impression of a more severe handicap than is in fact the case.[176] The disclosure techniques used with young children – play and the use of anatomical dolls – may be necessary to uncover abuse. The additional problem of competence,[177] which could be alleviated, although not solved, by the Pigot proposals, exacerbates the problem of proof, as does the obligation to warn the jury about the reliability of those of defective intellect.[178] Although it was thought that the mentally handicapped were poor at retaining information over time,[179] it subsequently appeared that, as with children, difficulties related to the level of initial understanding of the event itself, rather than to deficiencies in memory capacity.[180] The court would inevitably benefit in these cases from the assistance of an expert to interpret the

---

[173] The explanation may be the very English assumption by the Committee that these witnesses must be fitted into legally defined categories, a problem avoided by the SLC. The judge would decide whether particular witnesses required the protection of the new procedures, taking account of their age, physical condition and mental capacity.

[174] Vizard, 'Child sexual abuse and mental handicap: a child psychiatrist's perspective', in *Thinking the Unthinkable; Papers on Sexual Abuse and People with Learning Difficulties*, eds M. Brown and A. Craft (FPA Education Unit, London, 1989).

[175] Sinason, 'Uncovering and responding to sexual abuse in psychotherapeutic settings', in ibid.

[176] Ibid.

[177] Gunn, 'Sexual abuse and adults with mental handicap; can the law help?', in Brown and Craft, (eds).

[178] Ibid.

[179] Ellis, 'The stimulus trace and behavioural inadequacy', in *Handbook of Mental Deficiency*, ed. N. R. Ellis (McGraw-Hill, New York, 1963).

[180] Belmont and Butterfield, 'Learning strategies as determinants of memory deficiencies' *Cognitive Psychology*, 2 (1971), p. 411.

witness's behaviour; there is no legal authority against it, as long as the expert does not usurp the function of the court by expressing an opinion as to whether or not abuse took place.

EXPERT WITNESSES

There can be no doubt that courts could improve their assessment of child and mentally handicapped complainants by allowing experts to explain how their memories work; this is permissible under current case law, but the fact that witnesses are called by the parties, and that therefore the expert has been selected because of the compatibility of his or her views with the arguments to be put forward by that party, undermines the authority with which experts speak. Anecdotal tales of American trials being dominated by queues of 'hired gun' expert witnesses lined up for either side have led not to judges questioning the wisdom of a trial structure under which there is no other means to hear expert evidence, but to a reluctance to allow experts to express opinions except within narrowly and obscurely drawn limits. Judicial restrictiveness is particularly noticeable in the cases concerning expert evidence on the credibility of witnesses. This field which, naturally, is the domain of the 'trick cyclists'[181] is wide open to the scepticism and disdain of lawyers.

> The fact that an expert witness has impressive scientific qualifications does not by that fact alone make his opinion on matters of human nature and behaviour within the limits of normality any more helpful than that of the jurors them-selves; but there is a danger that they may think that it does...Jurors do not need psychiatrists to tell them how ordinary folk who are not suffering from any mental illness are likely to react to the stresses and strains of life.[182]

Thus psychiatrists may not explain what the effect of provocative acts would be on a 'normal' person,[183] nor may they give an opinion on whether there was intention behind such a person's act.[184] Where he or she has an expertise outside the experience of the tribunal of fact, as a psychiatrist has with the

---

[181] Psychiatrists and psychologists are still so regarded in certain quarters of the legal profession: Clapham, 'Introducing psychological evidence in the courts: impediments and opportunities', in *Psychology in Legal Contexts*, ed. S. Lloyd-Bostock (Macmillan, London, 1981).

[182] Lawton LJ in *Turner* [1975] 1 All ER 70, 74.

[183] *Turner*, ibid.

[184] *Chard* (1971) 56 Cr App R 268.

defences of diminished responsibility[185] or insanity,[186] the expert may express an opinion on the ultimate issue, but only on the presence or absence and nature of the condition in question. Thus in *Re S and B*[187] a psychiatric social worker could legitimately describe the witness's illness, which involved a tendency to fantasize, and express the belief that the witness's claim to have been abused as a child herself was true. But, even as an expert witness, she could not go on to say that she believed the witness's evidence in the case, namely an allegation that her brother had abused his children. In *Toohey v MPC*[188] medical evidence was held by the House of Lords to be admissible to show that a witness's own hysterical personality was as likely to have caused his hysteria as the defendant's alleged attack, but not whether the witness could be believed on oath or not. On the other hand, if there were a disease present that actually prevented a witness from telling the truth, then the condition should be brought to the notice of the court.[189] In *DPP v A and BC Chewing Gum*[190] the evidence of a child psychiatrist was held to be admissible on the question whether allegedly obscene material was likely to deprave and corrupt children who saw it. Thus child development is regarded as specialist although many people have children. So in a case of alleged abuse, an expert may describe the symptoms of abuse, and add that this particular child displayed such symptoms; but must not go on to say that in his or her opinion the child has been abused – that is a matter for the court to decide. Even so, some Family Court judges allow expert witnesses to offer such opinion evidence, on the basis that they are assisted and not bound by it.

An interesting facet of the case law in this area is that an expert may give evidence on personality only if the personality in question is unusual or abnormal, and that is for the judge to decide. This means that there is a legal definition of mental abnormality which may have little to do with psychiatric assessment. For example, in *Reynolds*[191] the court rejected expert evidence on a subject who allegedly could not separate fantasy from reality. Yet in the

---

[185] *Matheson* (1958) 42 Cr App R 145; an opinion on the ultimate issue is in strict theory inadmissible, but allowed in such cases 'time and again without any objection': Lord Parker CJ in *DPP v A and BC Chewing Gum* [1968] 1 QB 159.

[186] *Holmes* [1953] 1 WLR 686.

[187] *Independent*, 1 June 1990.

[188] [1965] AC 595.

[189] Compare *MacKenney* (1981) 72 Cr App R 78; May J refused to allow a psychologist to say that the principal prosecution witness was a psycopath and therefore highly likely to lie.

[190] [1968] 1 QB 159.

[191] [1989] Crim LR 220.

well-known case of *Lowery*[192] the Privy Council approved the admission of evidence of the sadistic tendency of one co-defendant and the passive dependent personality of the other, the object of which was to suggest that the first led the other into murder.[193] In *Masih*[194] the Court of Appeal upheld the trial judge's refusal to admit expert evidence on the mental capacity of a man with an IQ of 72 (the boundary between dull-normal and subnormal intelligence) on the issue of his alleged recklessness; if the defendant had had an IQ of 69 or less (mental defective) the evidence might have been admissible. Psychologists object to this assumption that low intelligence is relevant only when the level is of this extreme kind. Higher, but significantly low IQs are often ignored by judges who do not appreciate their effect, and refuse to be persuaded to the contrary by the expert in the field. It is astonishing to find that lawyers are able and willing to prefer their own views of human nature and mental disorder – psychiatrists constantly complain that judges think they know more about psychiatry than they do. The reality appears to be that judges have invented techniques for excluding experts whom they do not trust. There is a select band of expert witnesses, including psychiatrists, who are known to the judges and are treated with enormous respect. The whole problem is a result of judicial fear of the 'hired gun' syndrome, and could be avoided completely by detaching expert witnesses from the interests of the parties to the cause.

The adversarial trial appears to be designed to hinder judges who wish to hear expert evidence. In *Bayer v Clarkson Puckle Overseas Ltd*[195] the issue was whether the defendants acted with proper professional skill and care in underwriting on the plaintiff's behalf environmental impairment liability insurance in relation to a lead-smelting plant. Saville J proposed to hear expert opinion on that issue, but observed that there was a dispute about the facts on which the plaintiff's experts based their opinion. He suggested that therefore both sides should first present their evidence on the facts, and then call their experts in turn. He met with considerable resistance from the plaintiff, who argued that in an adversarial system counsel can call witnesses in the order he or she chooses – an objection which the judge decided to ignore. He also decided that all the expert witnesses should hear one another give evidence, so that the basis of the dispute could be clarified. It is becoming increasingly common for judges to let the experts hear the whole of the

---

[192] [1974] AC 85.

[193] Decided on its own special facts, according to Lawton LJ in *Turner*; a cynic might regard it as significant that, unusually, deciding that the evidence was admissible enabled the conviction to be upheld.

[194] [1986] Crim LR 395.

[195] [1989] NLJ 256.

case. The difficulty of giving evidence when the expert witness has not heard the rest of the case is a frequent criticism; for example, Professor Gee doubts the value of testimony of an expert who is unaware of the context into which it fits, and of many significant facts.[196] The Police and Criminal Evidence Act 1984[197] to some extent alleviates this problem in criminal trials by providing for disclosure of expert evidence from each side; this allows the experts the opportunity to consider each other's findings, and prevents the theatrical trick of suddenly producing conflicting results like a rabbit out of a hat. The most common complaint of experienced forensic scientists and psychiatrists, however, is the way that counsel can use his or her ability to control what they say in court. The witness depends on counsel to ask the right question; this presupposes that counsel has a grasp of the scientific issues involved – increasingly difficult in view of the pace of technological development. The accuracy of the evidence may be undermined if the witness is not allowed to qualify or explain his or her answer; expert witnesses are frequently cut off precisely because the qualification is unhelpful to counsel's case, and some advocates insist on 'Yes' and 'No' answers which are entirely misleading in areas of complexity. It has been said that lawyers love to emphasize the witness's expertise in glowing terms, thus making it psychologically difficult to admit that he or she does not know the answer.[198] There are other well-known tricks; one is to ask the witness whether he or she knows a particular book (usually old and obscure), pour scorn on the expert if he or she has not heard of it, read aloud apparently contradictory passages out of context and then ask the expert to explain them. Others include humiliation, even going so far as demanding to inspect a doctor's extremely grubby handkerchief, bullying, complaining if the witness cannot be more precise when it would be wrong to do so, calling an expert who uses entirely inappropriate techniques which yield no result and suggesting that therefore there is something suspect about a technique which does, and translating testimony into simpler language which makes it sound absurd.[199] Although lawyers may reply that expert witnesses are often well paid for their pains, the hostile reception from lawyers to their evidence and the resultant publicity have made some experts reluctant to have anything at all to do with cases such as child abuse.[200]

The amount of weight attached by courts to expert evidence probably

---

[196] Gee, 'The expert in the criminal trial' [1987] Crim LR 307.

[197] S. 81.

[198] Gudjonsson, 'The psychology of false confessions', *Medico-Legal Journal*, 57 (1989), p. 93.

[199] See e.g. L. R. Haward, *Forensic Psychology* (Batsford, London, 1981).

[200] Vizard [1989] Fam L 28.

depends on the tribunal and the issue. Courts with no claim to superior expertise are entitled to reject even unanimous expert opinion;[201] jurors may choose to rely on their own view of the defendant's mental state in a diminished responsibility case notwithstanding the view of all the psychiatrists called,[202] depending on their own assessment from his or her performance in court (even unsworn), the circumstances of the killing and his or her conduct at the time. This has led to the curious fact that 'sympathy' cases such as mercy killing are more likely to result in a diminished responsibility verdict than horrific crimes such as those of Peter Sutcliffe (the Yorkshire Ripper), who was found to be insane by every psychiatrist who saw him. In a study where half the subjects, who all acted as jurors in mock trials, heard psychological evidence on the weakness of identifications and the other half did not, the first half were more reluctant to believe the identification witness. But they were no better at discriminating between accurate and inaccurate testimony.[203] It seems that the expert evidence there was too non-specific; what was needed was more individualized opinion as to who was most likely to be reliable – the very ground into which experts are not allowed to tread. Although lawyers have a traditional distrust of the 'head-shrinking' branch of the medical profession, one reason for the reluctance to admit more direct evidence on witness credibility than is at present permitted is almost certainly the identification of the expert with the interests of one party or the other.

To alleviate the impasse, it has been suggested that experts should be summoned by the court rather than the parties. In France, Germany and many other countries the expert witness is selected by the court, although in France the parties may jointly nominate someone. These witnesses may give an opinion on the credibility of a witness. Even in the English system it is sometimes possible for experts to be independent, as in wardship (non-adversarial) proceedings, and Chancery judges have called of their own volition[204] every kind of scientist, also accountants and engineers.[205] However, there is much cause for concern in those cases where expert evidence is squeezed into the adversarial model. Many experts quite properly

---

[201] *Lanfear* [1968] 1 All ER 683.

[202] *Walton v R* [1978] 1 All ER 542.

[203] Wells, Lindsay and Tousignant, 'Effects of expert psychological advice on testimony', *Law and Human Behaviour*, 4 (1980), p. 275.

[204] Under the authority of Supreme Court Act 1981, s. 67 and RSC Ord. 40, r. 12.

[205] Phipson, *Evidence*, 14th edn (Sweet & Maxwell, London, 1990), para. 32.32; but in *A-G v Slingsby* (1916) 33 TLR 120 the House of Lords regarded it as irregular that the judge had called a sculptor to give his opinion as to the resemblance of the child in a legitimacy case to its alleged parents.

take serious exception to the way their opinions are distorted or suppressed, and question whether criminal trials in particular have any interest in the scientific truth. An independent expert, who is allowed to explain him- or herself without dependence on the questioning techniques of counsel, would serve the interests of justice a great deal better. The spectre of 'rent-an-expert', apparently the American nightmare, would be avoided. For criminal cases perhaps the Home Office could keep a list of approved persons, one of whom should be present throughout the trial in an *amicus curiae* role. In cases of sexual abuse he or she could explain to the court how accurate and/or suggestible a child of that age (or handicapped person) might be, and what behaviour patterns have been found to be symptoms of abuse. Allowing parties unlimited scope to go 'expert-shopping' (bearing in mind that they have no obligation to disclose how many experts were consulted and gave unwelcome advice) does little to enhance the prestige of the courts; meanwhile, a distinguished forensic scientist has said: 'A court is not an instrument for ascertaining the truth; it's a game – a deadly game – which is played between adults.'

5

The Accused in the Criminal Trial

NOT AN ORDINARY WITNESS

The principles which normally apply to adversarial trials are modified in the case of someone facing trial for a criminal offence. The accused's position is also to some extent protected by the operation of the presumption of innocence; other qualifications of adversarial theory may flow from recognition that he or she is not a voluntary participant in the proceedings, and therefore to treat him or her as a free agent would be unfair. The accused's duty to disclose evidence is, as we have seen in chapter 1, much less onerous than that of the prosecution. But there are other limits to the duty to disclose, which he or she shares with other kinds of witness: there is a privilege against self-incrimination, a principle of confidentiality where it is in the public interest, and legal professional privilege.

There can be no doubt that in some cases legally privileged material could be of probative value, but is excluded from the trial. Although privilege operates only to resist discovery of documents and privileged material is in fact admissible if it comes into the hands of the other party by any means, the holder of the privilege can recover his or her material or restrain its use in breach of confidence at any point during the case.[1] No privilege attaches to information in the hands of a lawyer which is actually held to further some criminal purpose.[2] But if a lawyer hears his or her client confess to the crime charged, that revelation is entirely confidential even though it might be

---

[1] *Nationwide v Goddard* [1986] 3 WLR 734; although the exercise of the court's power to order an injunction may not in fact be automatic, *per* Scott J in *Webster v James Chapman & Co (a firm) et al* [1989] 3 All ER 939.

[2] Police and Criminal Evidence Act 1984, s. 10(2).

thought significant at the trial.[3] If the client changes his or her story a dozen times, a fact which would be suggestive of unreliability were the court to hear of it, his or her lawyer may not disclose it. On the other hand, there is a principle that legal professional privilege cannot be invoked where it would prejudice the case of the accused – an indication of the imbalance of procedural rights at criminal trials which follows from the presumption of innocence. But the principle was watered down recently by the Court of Appeal in a case where the competing interests were those of two co-defendants. In *Ataou*[4] H, originally a co-defendant, gave evidence against D on a charge of conspiracy to supply heroin. At first, the alleged conspirators had shared the same solicitor, who still represented D. A member of the firm passed a note to counsel during D's trial, to the effect that H had told his original solicitor that D was not involved. The trial judge refused counsel leave to cross-examine H on his previous inconsistent statement, since he declined to waive his privilege. The Court of Appeal quashed D's conviction, not because the questions should necessarily have been allowed, but because the judge had failed to recognize that each case requires a balancing of competing public interests: the due and orderly administration of justice against the production of all evidence supporting the defence. The Court of Appeal did take note of the fact that H had already pleaded guilty and therefore was unlikely to be prejudiced by such a breach of confidence. There has been criticism of this case on the grounds that it is entirely inappropriate to balance against the risk of convicting the innocent the somewhat nebulous public interest in a general freedom to communicate in confidence with one's lawyers.[5] The existence of a privilege in relation to lawyer–client communications could be seen as a reinforcement of the adversarial pattern of trial. Free from any obligation to disclose what their clients tell them, lawyers can prepare a case for trial with as much of a 'surprise' element as they can muster. It is entirely up to the other side to gather their own evidence in support of their case; therefore they cannot expect to rely on their opponents' lawyers to provide it for them. (The usual justification for the privilege, that clients would not be frank with their lawyers without it, is not supported by any known evidence.) However, Continental jurisdictions such as Germany adopt a similar approach in relation to communications between lawyer and client in order to encourage frankness and thereby to enhance the effectiveness of legal advice.

The privilege against self-incrimination may have its roots in the right

---

[3] Counsel should not represent his or her client on a plea of not guilty in such a case.
[4] [1988] 2 All ER 321.
[5] Allen, 'Legal privilege and the accused: an unfair balancing act' [1988] NLJ 668.

of accused persons to remain silent.[6] It may be the rationale of the rather mysterious terms of section 1(e) of the Criminal Evidence Act 1898: 'A person charged and being a witness...may be asked any question in cross-examination notwithstanding that it might tend to criminate him as to the offence charged.' The simplest interpretation of this provision is that once an accused person elects to exercise the right, bestowed by section 1(1), to give evidence in his or her own defence, he or she may not pick and choose which questions to answer on the basis of what will serve the interests of his or her case. The provision may have been thought necessary because otherwise the privilege against self-incrimination might have been invoked (although probably unsuccessfully), or because in Continental trials, which have no general right to silence, a defendant *can* decline to answer any question he or she chooses. Section 1(e) thus ensures that, in this respect at least, once in the witness box an accused is in the same position as other witnesses.

THE RIGHT TO SILENCE

Silence during investigation

The right to silence during interrogation, and the right to choose whether or not to give evidence, are applications of adversarial principles. There can be no duty on an adversary to supply an explanation unless he or she chooses to do so. Yet the last few years have seen considerable erosion of the right to silence. Reforms to date have tended to be justified on pragmatic grounds, the foremost of which is that convictions of the guilty are too difficult to achieve if suspects are entitled not to co-operate with investigations. Given the utilitarian approach, it is perhaps not surprising that the right to refuse to answer questions has been effectively removed in the case of serious and company frauds – cases which may not be the most heinous of crimes, but may be particularly difficult to unravel. The Department of Trade and Industry can now ask persons to attend, to answer questions, furnish information and produce documents;[7] the sanction is punishment for contempt of court.[8] The Serious Fraud Office has rather less sweeping powers, but can

---

[6] L. W. Levy, *Origins of the 5th Amendment* (OUP, Oxford/New York, 1968); doubted by MacNair, 'The early development of the privilege against self-incrimination' (1990) 10 Oxford JLS 66.

[7] Companies Act 1985, ss. 431, 432 and 434, as amended by Companies Act 1989, s. 56.

[8] Companies Act 1985, s. 436.

demand attendance before the Director and a description of the location of documents. Failure to comply is an offence.[9] The most notorious of the recent changes to the law is the abolition in Northern Ireland of the right to silence when questioned by the police. This was especially controversial since it was achieved by statutory instrument and therefore without full Parliamentary debate.[10]

The controversy surrounding the right to silence is curiously overheated; extreme statements which bear little proportion to the issue have been made by both sides. The right to remain silent represents to some a bastion of liberty, so that its removal would 'dismantle the venerable fortress built by many generations of British lawyers to protect the innocent'.[11] For the other side, representatives of the abolitionist school of thought have certainly exaggerated the extent to which the right to silence hampers criminal investigation. Sir Peter Imbert, the Commissioner for the Metropolitan Police, said that abolition would be the most important single step legislators could take to control and reduce crime.[12] It appears to be virtually impossible to prove the contention frequently made by police officers that the right is used exclusively by guilty men, and is effective in helping them avoid conviction.[13] In fact, there are grounds for believing that the 'right to silence' is of little practical importance.

Research shows few criminals avail themselves of the right to silence even though the caution reminds them of it. American research suggests that suspects either take no notice of the caution or, hearing it, assume that the police know everything and confess at once.[14] Research carried out for the Policy Studies Institute found that not one subject remained silent under questioning, and remarked that the caution had so little effect that there was no incentive for the police not to caution.[15] Paul Softley's research for the Phillips Report, also prior to the Police and Criminal Evidence Act, confirmed that rarely did the caution encourage silence. About 12 per cent of

[9] Criminal Justice Act 1987, ss. 2–3.
[10] Criminal Evidence (Northern Ireland) Order 1988.
[11] M. Manfred Simon, letter to *The Times*, 5 October 1972.
[12] *Daily Telegraph*, 16 September 1987.
[13] See the debate on conviction rates of 'professional criminals', Zander, 'Are too many professional criminals avoiding conviction? A study in Britain's two busiest courts' (1974) 34 MLR 26; Mack, 'Full-time major criminals and the courts' (1976) 39 MLR 241.
[14] Wald et al., 'Interrogations in New Haven: the impact of *Miranda*' (1967) 76 Yale LJ 76.
[15] D. J. Smith and J. Gray, *Police and People in London*, Vol. 4: *The Police in Action* (Policy Studies Institute, London, 1983).

those he saw interviewed exercised the right to some degree, but only 5 per cent of those aged under seventeen did so.[16] Irving commented:[17]

> To remain silent in a police interview room in the face of determined questioning by an officer with legitimate authority to carry on his activity requires an abnormal exercise of will...When it does occur, the observer would be forgiven for making the fallacious assumption that the abnormal behaviour is associated with some significant cause (in this context guilt as opposed to innocence).

The psychological pressure was acknowledged in the Phillips Report, which concluded that, rather than remind a suspect of a right which it is almost impossible to exercise, it would be better to have safeguards designed to increase the reliability of what he or she says.[18] To this end, the Police and Criminal Evidence Act reinforced the right to legal advice and began the move towards tape-recording of all police station interviews.

Since the Act, research has shown discrepancies between the exercise of the right to silence and the right to legal advice in different areas and between different police stations.[19] But both are more likely to be exercised in relation to a serious offence,[20] and the discrepancies may therefore be attributable partly to the nature of crime prevalent in particular localities.[21] The figures from the West Yorkshire and Metropolitan Police[22] show between 12 and 23 per cent, respectively, of suspects exercising the right to silence to some degree; this figure suggest a slight increase since the Act. There is an increase in the number of suspects receiving legal advice in some form – from about 7 to 24 per cent.[23] It would be reasonable to assume that increased access to legal advice must increase the number of suspects refus-

---

[16] Softley, *Police Interrogation: An Observational Study in Four Police Stations*, Royal Commission on Criminal Procedure Research Study No. 4 (1980).

[17] Irving, *Police Interrogation: A Case Study of Current Practice*, Royal Commission on Criminal Procedure Research Study No. 2 (1980).

[18] *Report of the Royal Commission on Criminal Procedure* (Phillips Report), Cmnd 8092 (1981), para. 4.51.

[19] Home Office, *Report of the Working Group on the Right of Silence* (1989).

[20] Ibid.

[21] Maguire, 'Effects of the PACE: provisions on detention and questioning' (1988) 28 Br J Crim 19.

[22] Home Office, *Report of the Working Group*, App. C, pp. 60–2.

[23] Brown, *Detention at the Police Station under the Police and Criminal Evidence Act 1984*, Home Office Research Study No. 104 (1990); similar figures, Sanders, Bridges, Mulvaney and Crozier, *Advice and Assistance at Police Stations and the 24 Hour Duty Solicitor Scheme* (Lord Chancellor's Department, 1989).

ing to answer at least some police questions, although it appears that the nature of legal advice given depends partly on the solicitor's assessment of the strength of the police case.[24] Only a small minority of suspects refuse to answer any police questions at all (from 2 to 6 per cent), but police concern centres on their conviction that it is experienced criminals suspected of serious crime who are the greatest problem, and who tend to rely on the right to silence. Indeed, the take-up rate is greater for those with criminal records, but the difference is slight.[25] Irving and McKenzie record a lower rate of admissions of guilt after the Act in serious cases, but concede that their sample is a small one.[26]

The legal effect of exercise of this right suggests that suspects who choose that course do not necessarily protect their interests. In some circumstances, remaining silent in the face of an accusation is tantamount to an admission of guilt, and can corroborate evidence against them.[27] The Eleventh Report of the Criminal Law Revision Committee assumed that silence in the face of an accusation by a police officer could never amount to an acknowledgement of guilt,[28] but Wolchover has shown that this is an over-simplification.[29] He suggests that the Committee view is correct in cases where a suspect has been cautioned,[30] for to explain to a suspect that he or she is entitled to say nothing and then draw an adverse inference if he or she does so is clearly unacceptable. Apart from that, whether or not remaining silent is tantamount to an admission of guilt depends on whether or not the accuser and the accused are 'on even terms', which depends entirely on the context. If Wolchover is right, the terms of the caution are an exaggeration of the legal position, but by uttering them the police render any subsequent silence justifiable, making the caution a self-fulfilling prophecy. Even in these cases, however, the judge may comment on the refusal of the accused to answer police questions, as long as he or she does not invite the jury to infer guilt. The judge may say that the failure to raise a defence now relied on at trial, or the failure to give a fuller account to police at the time, deprived them of the opportunity to investigate the accused's version.[31] In *Gerard*[32] D was stopped

---

[24] B. Irving and I. K. McKenzie, *Police Interrogation: The Effects of the Police and Criminal Evidence Act 1984* (Police Foundation, London, 1989).

[25] Home Office, *Report of the Working Group*, App. C, pp. 60–2.

[26] Irving and McKenzie, *Police Interrogation*, p. 180.

[27] *Hall v R* [1971] 1 All ER 322.

[28] *Evidence (General)*, Eleventh Report of the Criminal Law Revision Committee, Cmnd 4991 (1972), pp. 28–30.

[29] Wolchover, 'Guilt and the silent suspect' [1988] NLJ 396.

[30] As in *Chandler* [1976] 3 All ER 105, *Lewis* (1973) 57 Cr App R 860.

[31] *Moran* (1909) 3 Cr App R 25; *Parker* (1934) 24 Cr App R 2.

[32] (1948) 32 Cr App R 132.

in possession of a lorryload of spirits, and ran away. At the police station, he was asked to explain the origin of the spirits, and replied, 'What I have to say I will say to the court.' The trial judge remarked that if he were innocent it was curious that he had made that statement when not yet charged, if he had merely run away because he lost his head. The conviction was upheld. Wolchover concludes that to achieve the ends of the police lobby, the only reform necessary is to abolish the obligation to administer the caution. This would not reverse the burden of proof since a 'requirement to proclaim is hardly equivalent to a requirement to prove'.[33] He admits, however, that juries might find it easier to convict where the silence is seen to be significant, but this will not always be the case.

In Scotland any 'special defences' such as alibi, insanity, self-defence or incrimination of another must be lodged at least ten days before the trial date. Such a provision would assist those police officers and prosecutors who complain of the 'ambush defence' which is concealed from them until the last minute, effectively preventing them from gathering the appropriate evidence and arguments to deal with it on the day of the trial. The issue of the ambush defence is closely linked with that of the right to remain silent during interrogation. For although it is one thing to refuse to answer police questions when held at a police station and another to introduce a procedure whereby the defence must disclose its case or the identity of its witnesses in advance, the fact remains that at present a suspect is entitled to raise a matter such as self-defence at trial having said nothing about it at the police station, even though it is reasonable to assume he or she knew the relevant facts at the time. If the suspect had been cautioned, the trial judge seems to be confined to pointing out to the jury that the police have had no opportunity of investigating this defence. Last-minute alibis presented such a problem that they were specifically dealt with in the Criminal Justice Act 1967;[34] the justification for withholding other kinds of defence is not immediately apparent. Nevertheless, the Criminal Bar Association takes considerable exception to any move to extend the obligation on the defence to disclose information. The Association's argument is that the Crown might shift its ground once the information is received, being in a better position to define or redefine the charges. As far as the prospect of actual disclosure of the defence case is concerned, the Association's objection is that if the prosecution case is defective in law, the defence is reluctant to show its hand because that enables the prosecution to put its house in order before the trial starts.[35] The fact that English lawyers feel able to present publicly an argu-

---

[33] Wolchover [1988] NLJ 396, 434.

[34] S. 11. For other duties of the defence to disclose, see chapter 1.

[35] David Cocks QC, *Counsel* Nov./Dec. 1988.

ment which presupposes that defeat of the prosecution on surprise or technical points which have nothing to do with the facts is an end in itself
demonstrates how deeply the adversarial tradition is entrenched in their
psyche. Outsiders may be astonished that it is considered not only perfectly
respectable but positively desirable to retain a system that places surprise
and tactics above moral guilt and the truth.

The Phillips Report was against any change in the law unless interrogation
procedures were dramatically reformed, so that suspects were given at all
stages of the investigation full information about both their rights and the
nature of the evidence against them.[36] Inevitably, the Committee concluded,
this would involve a move towards an inquisitorial system of trial, for the
interrogations would have to be supervised by a judicial official to ensure
that the suspect was indeed so informed. The obligation to answer could be
justified 'only if the critical phase of the investigation, that is the phase at
which silence could be used adversely to the accused, was to become more
structured and formal than it is now; in effect responsibility for and conduct
of this phase of the investigation, close to charge, would have to become
a quasi-judicial rather than a police function'.[37] The Committee drew a
distinction between questioning before arrest, where there should be no obligation to answer, and afterwards, where the suspect would be fully informed
as to his or her position. Although the suggestion envisages a considerable
step towards an inquisitorial process, there is support for this approach even
now.[38] According to Zuckerman, requiring answers from a suspect who does
not know the nature of the case being assembled against him or her is tantamount to ambush by the police, since the suspect must reveal the nature of
his or her case when the case against him or her may not have been clearly
explained.[39] This approach seems over-protective of suspects; there are some
basic questions which innocent persons ought to be able to answer in a
straightforward way without prejudicing their interests. Failure to answer in
more sinister circumstances would be understood by the jury and not detract
from the defence case. The ethics of police interrogation is now a vexed
issue; the question whether they are entitled to lie about the strength of the
evidence in their hands is not settled,[40] and the courts are currently having to
address the question of the way in which admissions are to be obtained if the
police have to operate according to a set of moral standards going beyond the

[36] Phillips Report, para. 4.53.
[37] Ibid., para. 4.52.
[38] Editorial [1988] NLJ 737.
[39] Zuckerman, 'Trial by unfair means: the Report of the Working Group on the
Right of Silence' [1989] Crim LR 855.
[40] See chapter 6.

basic provisions of the Police and Criminal Evidence Act and the codes of practice.

The Home Office Working Group

In 1989 the Report was published of a group set up by the Home Secretary to advise him on how to change the law on the right to silence – the Group was not empowered to discuss the desirability of such a change.[41] Perhaps because of this the proposal is modest in scope; the Group will not countenance effective reversal of the burden of proof, so failure to answer will neither amount to evidence of guilt nor corroborate any prosecution witness. The fact that the Northern Ireland provisions[42] go further necessitated the drafting of elaborate cautions which the province's officers carry around on printed cards.[43] Instead, the proposal for England and Wales is that the adverse inference which the jury is entitled to draw is confined to the credibility of the accused, or, if he or she relies on a specific defence which could easily have been mentioned during interview but was not, the jury may infer that the defence is not true.[44] In relation to the ambush defence, the Report is of particular interest. The inescapable need for disclosure of defences (which assumes disclosure by the prosecution) to ensure a balanced, rather than a gimmicky, trial is accepted, so that the remaining debate concerns feasibility. If a workable procedure could be introduced, the judge could comment adversely on failure to disclose, although it would not be evidence against, and therefore could not amount to corroboration. But many witnesses thought that the fraud trial procedure would be too cumbersome for ordinary cases. There was consensus also that the Scottish system whereby the procurator fiscal may cause the accused to be brought before the sheriff for judicial examination before or after bail is allowed, was complicated and, in any case, rarely used.[45] The Working Group therefore suggests that pilot studies be set up, where a judge could order disclosure on his or her own initiative, or on application from either side, and should do so only where an ambush defence seems likely.

These proposals reflect disillusion with the adversarial trial, with its

---

[41] Nevertheless many protests were received; Home Office, *Report of the Working Group*, p. 26.

[42] Criminal Evidence (Northern Ireland) Order 1988.

[43] Ibid., arts 3–6.

[44] A distinction doubted by Zuckerman, [1989] Crim LR 855.

[45] There the suspect is not obliged to answer questions but if he or she offers replies at the trial which he or she could have given at the examination, his or her failure to do so may be commented on by the judge and the prosecutor.

emphasis on tactics. The more disclosure takes place, the less will depend on the performance of advocates and witnesses on the day. The Working Group notes that early attention by counsel to the issues may concentrate the minds on both sides on the question of the adequacy of the whole case[46] – and that may lead to fewer cases coming to court. Zuckerman argues that disclosure would be a purely procedural reform, and the sanction for non-disclosure should therefore be a procedural one, that the accused should not be allowed to run the defence in question at all. Such a rule would be catastrophic for a defendant with inept lawyers. It would represent a move even further away from the adversarial tradition; a case could be won or lost according to the way the paperwork is done. And in civil cases courts do not generally ignore reality and refuse to hear a defence which was not pleaded; an amendment and adjournment are the proper course. Clearly the impact in terms of costs and the difficulty in retaining the same jury presents practical problems on a scale making such a procedure inappropriate for most criminal offences. Apart from the disclosure issue, there can be no doubt that to require a suspect to answer police questions is a move towards an inquisitorial process which begins long before the trial. The police, for many years treated as private individuals who happen to have an organized machinery for law enforcement,[47] are seen to be acting as quasi-judicial officials, heavily regulated and circumscribed by the Police and Criminal Evidence Act, who launch an investigation ultimately concluded by the criminal court. Refusal to co-operate with them could in future lead to hostile reaction in the court itself.[48]

Silence in court

Since 1851[49] a party to civil litigation has been in a position to insist that the other gives evidence; the extension of the principle to proceedings instituted in consequence of adultery[50] suggests that the availability of relevant evidence was regarded as more important than allowing litigants to decide entirely for themselves how and to what extent they will participate in the trial. Such an erosion of adversarial principles has not yet affected the right of a defendant in a criminal trial not to give evidence. In Continental trials

---

[46] Home Office, *Report of the Working Group*, p. 108.
[47] St J. Robilliard and J. McEwan, *Police Powers and the Individual* (Blackwell, Oxford, 1986), pp. 1–9.
[48] Likewise, prosecutors are increasingly being regarded as distinct from private parties, and to have special responsibilities, see chapter 6.
[49] Evidence Act 1851, s. 2.
[50] Evidence Further Amendment Act 1869; *Tilley v Tilley* [1949] P 240.

the accused cannot decline to be questioned, but can decline to answer. If he or she does elect to explain him- or herself, he or she does this unsworn. In most systems the courts may not draw adverse inferences from a refusal to answer all or any of the questions put, but there is considerable psychological pressure to answer because unfavourable commonsense inferences are almost inevitable, given that the refusal always relates to a particular question.[51] The position of a Continental defendant may at first sight appear to be similar to that of the Anglo-American, but the decision whether or not to answer is in fact more difficult; since he or she is questioned before any of the prosecution witnesses, he or she is to some extent in the dark. The defendant is in fact being treated as a primary evidentiary source,[52] which many adversarially trained lawyers would regard as entirely incompatible with the presumption of innocence. But although it is true that at the trial itself the prosecution has no need to show a case to answer, the preparatory stages of Continental proceedings will have established that already, and acquainted the accused with the nature of the case against him or her.

In theory, if the accused is a poor witness, his or her performance in the witness box should go only to credibility, and not indicate guilt. This is small consolation in the light of the obvious risk that, once the jury regard the accused as a person not worthy of belief, he or she will be convicted. But prosecution witnesses have to perform as well as they can, and must satisfy a higher standard of proof before they may be believed. The accused needs only to raise a doubt.

It is interesting to note that many advocates insist that a particular client is innocent and is telling the truth but that they know that he or she would be 'a disaster' in the witness-box, and must at all costs be excluded from it. The limited ability of individuals, including lawyers, to distinguish lies from the truth has been the object of recent scrutiny;[53] the jury, too, may attach too much importance to factors such as fluency and confidence, but that is something which could be addressed by allowing expert assistance on the subject of credibility. In Singapore the law was changed in 1976 so that failure to give evidence could give rise to unfavourable inferences.[54] The unsworn statement from the dock was abolished at the same time. Since there is no jury, it is not clear how judges are reacting to defendants who keep out of the witness-box.

---

[51] Damaska, 'Evidentiary barriers to conviction and two models of criminal procedure: a comparative study' (1973) 121 U Penn LR 506.
[52] Ibid.
[53] See chapter 3.
[54] Criminal Procedure (Amendment) Act.

The leading case on the judge's summing-up in such cases is *Bathurst*,[55] where it was established that a judge may comment on A's failure to give evidence[56] as long as he or she points out that it is A's right. Lord Parker CJ said that the accepted form of comment was:[57]

> To inform the jury that, of course, he – the defendant – is not bound to give evidence, that he can sit back and see if the prosecution have proved their case, and that while the jury have been deprived of the opportunity of hearing his story tested in cross-examination, the one thing they must not do is to assume that he is guilty because he has not gone into the witness box.

These remarks were observed to have been *obiter* in a later case, *Sparrow*,[58] in which Lawton LJ concluded that the Lord Chief Justice could not have intended the judges to parrot a rigid formula in every case; what is said must depend on the nature of the case before him. In *Sparrow* a police officer was shot dead by a gun which the defence claimed was not intended to do more than frighten anyone who tried to apprehend the two accused. Sparrow declined to enter the witness-box. Lawton LJ said that if the trial judge had not commented on this in strong terms he would have been failing in his duty, given that he must not expressly or impliedly suggest that a defence cannot succeed unless the defendant gives evidence. Despite the fact that keeping the accused out of the witness-box runs the risk of alienating the jury, the 1972 recommendation of the Criminal Law Revision Committee that adverse inferences should be legitimized by reform was received with shock in some quarters. The Committee thought that the case for allowing inferences to be drawn was 'even stronger in the case of failure to give evidence' than for failure to respond to police interrogation.[59] The judge should warn the accused about the consequences of a failure to give evidence, and these would include corroboration of any prosecution witness requiring to be corroborated.[60]

The Home Office Working Group concludes that the judge's existing power to comment on the defendant's failure to enter the witness-box is sufficient, but recommends that the prosecution should also be able to comment in similar terms, giving the defence the opportunity to explain the

---

[55] [1968] 2 QB 99.
[56] Prosecutor may not do so; Criminal Evidence Act 1898, s. 1(b).
[57] [1968] 2 QB 99, 107.
[58] [1973] 1 WLR 488.
[59] Eleventh Report, Para. 110.
[60] Although it would not assist the prosecution in establishing a case to answer.

defendant's absence.[61] The Report anticipates difficulty with unrepresented defendants, but disposes of this by requiring that unspecified but 'adequate safeguards' be devised. The cure seems rather worse than the disease, particularly since the disease which necessitates such changes is never identified. The essential dilemma facing the defence has never been properly addressed. The Eleventh Report ignored the impact of its own suggested reforms on the cross-examination of the accused on his or her criminal record. As will be seen below, the accused may be cross-examined on previous convictions if he or she attacks the character of any witness for the prosecution.[62] The abolition of the right of the accused to make an unsworn statement from the dock (on which he or she could not be cross-examined)[63] leaves any defence counsel faced with a prosecution witness whose bad character he or she wishes to expose with a tactical problem more appropriate to a game of Risk than a criminal trial. The options are these:

1. Client has no criminal record – savage the prosecution witness with impunity.
2. Client has criminal record:
   (a) keep him or her out of the witness-box to avoid cross-examination on record, therefore forfeiting the opportunity for the client to present his or her version of the facts, and running the risk that the jury will (illegitimately) draw an inference of guilt;
   (b) put client in the box and ride the storm of the criminal record; if this option is selected, it is often wise to mention the previous convictions early on, for example while cross-examining the police witness;
   (c) leave the prosecution witness alone.

THE ACCUSED'S GOOD CHARACTER

It has been argued[64] that adducing evidence of the accused's previous good character whether or not relevant to the charge allows the jury to reach a verdict which may reflect his or her moral standing rather than the evidence adduced. There have been recently some notable acquittals which appeared to be based on a moral judgment by the jury on the character or behaviour of the accused, or indeed the accusers, rather than the evidence. It is sometimes said that one of the principal arguments in favour of trial by one's peers is

[61] Home Office, *Report of the Working Group*, p. 116.
[62] Criminal Evidence Act 1898, s. 1(f)(ii); see below, p. 156.
[63] Criminal Justice Act 1982, s. 72.
[64] Zuckerman, 'Similar facts: the unobservable rule' (1987) 104 LQR 187.

that it makes possible 'perverse' verdicts which nevertheless implement the reaction of the community. Hence the jury must know the nature of the individual whose fate they are to determine. The fact that they may be kept ignorant of the dark side of a defendant who chooses to keep his or her character out of the debate is more difficult to defend. In Continental trials the antecedents of the defendant are the first items of information presented; it is thought imperative that the tribunal of fact should know with what sort of person it is dealing.

The legal effect of evidence of merit in the accused is far from clear. It was recognized by Viscount Sankey in *Maxwell*[65] that inevitably it would in some cases establish more than credibility, and would be taken to suggest that the accused is a person unlikely to have committed the offence charged. His remarks indicate a realistic acceptance of the likely reaction of jurors to disposition evidence.[66] But the courts have become increasingly persuaded that only out of tolerance do judges allow evidence of good character to be called in the first place, and then to go to the issue of guilt;[67] this has led them into disarray. Although there are cases to the effect that such evidence goes only to credibility,[68] the earlier common law was that such evidence went to the issue of guilt, a natural consequence of the fact that before 1898 defendants were not allowed to give evidence and so the issue of their credibility as witnesses did not arise. However, judges are increasingly giving directions that it is relevant to credibility, as in *Mendez*,[69] where the Court of Appeal upheld the practice as correct. The conviction was quashed because the trial judge had in fact told the jury to give the evidence of good character such weight as they saw fit. They should have been told it went to credibility, although if the accused does not give evidence they may then be asked whether he or she is the sort of person likely to have committed the offence charged. To enhance the incoherence of this reasoning, the court added: 'That may also be done when he does give evidence but should be done in cases where he does not give evidence.'

In *Redgrave*[70] the Court of Appeal was completely confounded by the conflicting case law on this point. D was accused of importuning for an immoral purpose in a public convenience. He sought to adduce evidence of

---

[65] [1935] AC 309, 315.

[66] A reasoning process rarely permitted if the disposition evidence is negative in effect.

[67] *Rowton* (1865) Le & Ca 520; *Hurst v Evans* [1917] 1 KB 352; *Miller* [1952] 2 All ER 667; *Redgrave* (1981) 74 Cr App R 10.

[68] E.g. *Falconer-Atlee* (1973) 58 Cr App R 348.

[69] [1990] Crim LR 397; contradicts *Bryant* [1979] QB 108.

[70] (1981) 74 Cr App R 10.

heterosexual relationships to rebut the inferences of homosexuality derived from his conduct as observed by the police. It was held that he could not adduce evidence that he was of a particular disposition, only that by way of general reputation he was not the kind of young man who would behave in the way charged. This was said to be an application of the decision in *Rowton*,[71] a case which was too frequently being ignored. From *Rowton*, character witnesses should confine themselves to evidence of the reputation of the accused, and not of specific meritorious acts. Although character witnesses can be cross-examined about particular matters within their know-ledge which reflect badly on the accused, they may not, in evidence-in-chief, speak from their own experience or opinion, but may only testify as to that of the neighbourhood or community in which the accused has a good repu-tation. Also, the character proved must be of the specific kind impeached and should relate to a period proximate to the date of the alleged offence. Finally, the evidence relates to credibility, not guilt. Phipson[72] objects that it is impossible for anyone to give evidence of his or her own reputation, and therefore *Rowton* does not apply to the accused giving evidence him- or herself.[73] The preference for reputation evidence, which by definition relies on hearsay composed of gossip and speculation rather than direct knowledge, is itself baffling. A further objection to *Redgrave* is that it is nonsense to argue that evidence of heterosexuality, however established, has something to do with credibility on oath. Redgrave was not asking the court to believe what he said in the witness-box because he was really a heterosexual. He was suggesting that his sexual proclivities made it unlikely that he would approach men in a public lavatory. The fact is that 'character' evidence is a broad category, at times relating to honesty and at others to very different attributes. A defendant might suggest that he has a gentle disposition incom-patible with the violent offences alleged. He might wish to establish lifelong patriotism in order to suggest that he would not betray his country. He might even argue that as a committed homosexual he is an unlikely rapist. None of these arguments has anything to do with credibility as a witness; whether or not he gives evidence has absolutely no effect on its relevance. The proper direction to the jury must therefore depend on the purpose for which the evidence is admitted, rather than some *ex post facto* categorization by the judge. It would be absurd, as Phipson argues, to demand that if the accused gives evidence of these matters he or she should do so by way of establishing his or her own reputation, and he or she should not be depend-ent on the generosity of judges to get it in. The Court of Appeal thought that

---

71   (1865) Le & Ca 520.
72   Phipson, *Evidence*, 14th edn (Sweet & Maxwell, London, 1990), para. 18.15.
73   Citing *Samuel* (1956) 40 Cr App R 8.

Redgrave's trial judge 'might, as an indulgence', have allowed evidence of marriage or a relationship with one girl. It would be better simply to acknowledge, as Continental courts do, that it is irrational to try an individual without knowing what sort of person her or she is. The chop-logic characteristic of the cases on the significance of cross-examination on the accused's criminal record or general bad character proves this.

PREVIOUS CONVICTIONS

The accused who gives evidence at his or her own trial may find him- or herself being asked about his or her criminal record even though the previous offences bear insufficient logical relation to the current charge to justify their admission as similar fact evidence in the prosecution case in chief. We have seen in chapter 2 that the similar facts principle excludes evidence of previous misconduct by an accused person where that evidence is more prejudicial than probative. The logic is that whether or not the previous misconduct resulted in a criminal conviction, it may form part of the prosecution's case if its effect is to supply evidence that the accused is guilty of the offence currently charged.[74] It has been argued above that the similar fact decisions are inevitably incoherent and inconsistent; this is a result of the fallacious assumption that the amount of probative value can be weighed in an imaginary scale against the amount of prejudicial effect. That exercise is all the more difficult given that it relies heavily on the imaginary divide between evidence which goes merely to disposition and evidence indicative of guilt. These confusions are apparently given statutory approval in the more well-trodden field of cross-examination of an accused person on his or her record. This is a less rarefied area than similar facts. It is a matter for the everyday criminal court. It is a creature of statute, and therefore the courts cannot be blamed if the philosophical framework in which it operates is obscure. The legislature has, in fact, added confusion to confusion; not only is the similar fact doctrine apparently imported wholesale, but the creation of categories of case in which the accused can be cross-examined on previous convictions which would not have been admissible as similar fact evidence created a new minefield in which even the Lord Chief Justice had to declare defeat.

The statute in question was a landmark which allowed for the first time

---

[74] The previous offences may in some cases not be at all similar and nevertheless provide a link between the accused and the offence for which he or she is being tried. Yet the courts insist that they eschew reasoning from proof of a generally bad disposition to a conclusion that therefore he or she must be guilty. See chapter 2.

every accused person to give evidence in his or her own defence.[75] Previously, it was thought that no one should be placed in a position where he or she might be tempted to commit perjury in order to escape a human punishment. This was the Criminal Evidence Act 1898; section 1 reads as follows:

(1) Every person charged with an offence, shall be a competent witness for the defence at every stage of the proceedings, whether the person so charged is charged solely or jointly with any other person provided as follows −...

   (e) A person charged and being a witness...may be asked any question in cross-examination notwithstanding that it might tend to criminate him as to the offence charged.

   (f) A person charged and called as a witness in pursuance of this Act shall not be asked, and if asked shall not be required to answer, any question tending to show that he has committed or been convicted or been charged with any offence other than that wherewith he is charged, or is of bad character unless −

      (i) the proof that he has committed or been convicted of such other offence is admissible evidence to show that he is guilty of the offence wherewith he is charged; or

      (ii) he has personally or by his advocate asked questions of the witnesses for the prosecution with a view to establish his own good character, or the nature or conduct of the defence is such as to involve imputations on the character of the prosecutor or the witnesses for the prosecution; or

      (iii) he has given evidence against any other person charged in the same proceedings.

The obscure relationship between subsections (e) and (f)(i) is discussed in detail in all leading textbooks. The courts are seen gamely to continue to maintain that bad character, if it does not fall into the similar facts class of disposition evidence, is not indicative of guilt. In *Cokar*[76] the prosecution was not allowed to ask D about his previous acts of trespass, which led to acquittals, to show that D knew trespass without intention to steal was not a crime. In *Jones v DPP*[77] the House of Lords found it difficult to justify the cross-examination of the accused in his trial for murder of a girl guide about his previous conviction for the rape of another girl guide. He had given a

---

[75] Other statutes, such as the Metalliferous Mines Regulation Act 1872 and the Criminal Law Amendment Act 1885, had allowed accused persons in specific kinds of trial to do so. These statutes appeared to permit unfettered cross-examination.
[76] [1960] 2 QB 207.
[77] [1962] AC 635.

provenly false alibi for the murder. When that was exposed, he gave an alibi improbably identical to the one he gave at the rape trial. Lord Denning took the commonsense view that the history of Jones and his alibis incriminated him as to the offence charged, and therefore fell within section 1(e). But the majority stuck to the received view that disposition is not indicative of guilt, and confined section 1(e) to questions tending directly towards guilt, not questions about previous misconduct. The admissibility of this vital evidence, therefore, had to turn on the way in which Jones conducted his defence; he had to throw away his shield under section 1(f)(ii). The only alternative depended on the willingness of the prosecution to ask the rape victim to describe the offence anew as part of the evidence-in-chief under the similar facts rule.[78]

Section 1(f)(i) assumes that evidence of the commission of previous offences may be indicative of guilt. Bad character *simpliciter* and charges which did not lead to conviction are not included here. The courts have dealt with this omission somewhat haphazardly,[79] but generally the wording mirrors their conviction that such evidence does not indicate guilt. This effectively limits the operation of section 1(f)(i) to matters of similar fact. The House of Lords in *Jones* held that if the subsection is used to justify questions about similar fact evidence, then the prosecution should have laid a proper foundation by adducing that evidence as part of its case.[80] The reason for this is explained in the judgment of the Court of Criminal Appeal:[81]

> It might in general be undesirable that such matters should first be addressed in cross-examination; in such a case…in which the accused desired to dispute or explain the alleged similarity of circumstances or pattern of the two offences he would thereby be deprived of any opportunity to cross-examine prosecution witnesses and be exposed to the gravely prejudicial effect of suggestive questions to which his negative answers might be of no avail.

Tapper suggests that questioning might be permitted under the subsection even in the absence of evidence-in-chief from the prosecution, for example if

---

[78] The House concluded that these problems did not arise since the cross-examination did not 'tend to show' the jury about the conviction, Jones having already mentioned that he had been in trouble with the police before in order to explain why he gave a false alibi.

[79] See Tapper, 'The meaning of section 1(f)(i) of the Criminal Evidence Act 1898', in *Crime, Proof and Punishment: Essays in Memory of Sir Rupert Cross*, ed. C. Tapper (Butterworths, London, 1981).

[80] [1962] AC 635, 685, *per* Lord Morris, 697, *per* Lord Devlin.

[81] [1962] AC 635, 646.

the defence is sprung on it at a late stage.[82] However, the argument that the defence is prejudiced if unable to cross-examine on the extent of the alleged similarity is no less persuasive in such a case. It would be better to allow the prosecution prior notice of all special defences. Going further, the Continental practice of acquainting the court with the defendant's history before proceeding any further could be followed. The facts could be established without the artificial division into evidence-in-chief and cross-examination which causes so many problems. One of them is that the logic of the *Jones* decision seems less apparent when the general terms of section 1(f) are examined. The words 'tending to show', if they mean 'make known to the jury', as the House of Lords decided,[83] render the whole of section 1(f)(i) otiose; for if the evidence has been presented as part of the prosecution case, the jury know about the previous misconduct already, the exclusionary preamble in section 1(f) does not apply and therefore the exception in section 1(f)(i) is unnecessary.[84]

Losing the shield

Defendants can escape from the terms of section 1(f)(ii) in three ways: they can avoid throwing away their shield by not bringing their character into issue or attacking that of the prosecution witnesses; they can decline to give evidence in their own defence so that they cannot be cross-examined at all; or, if they appear prima facie to have brought themselves within the subsection, they can appeal to the discretion of the trial judge,[85] who may decide that justice would be best served by refusing leave to cross-examine on record. The theory behind the first limb of section 1(f)(ii) is reasonably clear. After all, at common law the prosecution is entitled to rebut evidence of the defendant's good character whether or not he or she gives evidence.[86] The purpose of the questioning is to rebut the favourable impression caused by the defence evidence, even if the aspect of character presented for the defence bears no logical relation to the defendant's previous convictions. At least, so runs the decision in *Winfield*,[87] where Humphreys J announced that

---

[82] Tapper, in Tapper (ed.).

[83] Cf. *Anderson* [1988] 2 All ER 549.

[84] It might in any case be thought that if similar fact evidence is introduced by the prosecution in its case in chief, then it would be absurd if the prosecution could not follow it up by referring to it when the accused, should he or she elect to give evidence, is cross-examined.

[85] *Selvey v DPP* [1970] AC 304.

[86] *Butterwasser* [1948] 1 KB 4.

[87] [1939] 4 All ER 164.

'there is no such thing known to our procedure as putting half a prisoner's character in issue and leaving out the other half'. The Court of Appeal thus upheld the trial judge in allowing cross-examination on previous offences of dishonesty when, on an indecent assault charge, D had called a witness to establish his proper conduct towards women. Although criticized,[88] the decision was upheld by the House of Lords in *Stirland v DPP*.[89]

The notion of indivisibility of character appears to have popular support. For example, in the early days of the community service order claims for its success were based not on improved reconviction rates, but on reports that some of the offenders wished to continue with work such as taking handicapped children swimming after the order terminated. There appeared to be a popular assumption that such generous instincts must indicate 'cure' – an inveterate burglar would not be interested. Although it is argued elsewhere in this book[90] that the similar fact cases are too narrow, and that some kinds of propensity are significant in themselves, *Winfield* is indefensible in the context within which it was decided. To exclude offences close in nature to the current offence because D chose not to throw away his shield under section 1(f)(ii), but to admit totally irrelevant ones because he has, does the criminal justice system no credit.

The rationale of the second limb of the subsection is rather more elusive. The fact that the defence has tried to discredit prosecution witnesses is taken to justify a reciprocal discrediting of the defendant on a 'tit for tat'[91] basis; if the defence has asked the court to disbelieve the witness for the prosecution because of his or her bad character or criminal record, the court would be misled when it came to assess the evidence as a whole. The accused, in contradicting the witness, would appear to have a greater claim to belief if his or her credit were artificially high in that his or her own criminal record had not been brought to light. Although at first sight it would appear that the subsection restores proper balance, there is a problem in that the accused is in greater jeopardy from prejudice than are the prosecution witnesses. Also, the balance will not be restored properly if the defendant escapes cross-examination by choosing not to give evidence at all; although he or she runs the risk of jury disapproval, the effect of the two prejudices is not necessarily even.

Since the courts are adamant that disposition is generally not evidence of

---

[88] E.g. Nokes: 'If a man is charged with forgery, cross-examination as to his conviction for cruelty to animals can have no purpose but prejudice': G. D. Nokes, *Introduction to Evidence*, 4th edn (Sweet & Maxwell, London, 1967), p. 140.

[89] [1944] AC 315.

[90] Chapter 2.

[91] *Powell* [1986] 1 All ER 193.

guilt, but here may go to the credibility of the accused as a witness,[92] the cases have come to a logical impasse. We have seen that any kind of previous conviction may be brought into the cross-examination under section 1(f)(ii); attempting to impose rationality upon this contradictory state of affairs led the Lord Chief Justice into error in *Watts*.[93] D was being tried for indecent assault. He made imputations on the police evidence which lost him his shield, so the prosecution sought and obtained leave to cross-examine on his previous convictions, which were for sexual offences against children. Lord Lane CJ conceded that the judge has a discretion once the shield has been lost, and therefore was reluctant to interfere, but could not swallow the notion that these convictions could or would be treated by the jury, even with the most correct of directions from the judge, as evidence going to credibility rather than to the issue. They should, therefore, have been excluded as more prejudicial than probative. However, in the subsequent case of *Powell*[94] Lord Lane announced that he had been wrong. He had not appreciated the 'tit for tat' principle, and therefore that in fact previous convictions should not be analysed for their logical relationship with credibility as such, but admitted whatever their nature. In *Powell* D was accused of living off immoral earnings. He claimed ignorance, that having worked hard to build up his business he had no need of money gained in such a way, and that police descriptions of his conduct were fabrications. He had previous convictions for allowing his premises to be used for the purpose of prostitution. The trial judge was held to have been right to allow cross-examination on these offences, despite their resemblance to the charge. This case shows the paucity of the similar fact principle, which forces courts, who can see that sometimes the record of the accused does have probative value but does not satisfy the perceived requirement of striking similarity, to manipulate the 1898 Act to allow the jury to hear it. It is absurd to argue that Powell's record had anything to do with his credibility on oath. It was probative, not in itself, but in the light of the defence he ran, which the trial judge said was crucial to his decision to give the prosecution leave under section 1(f)(ii). If there was insufficient 'pattern', as in *Powell*, to allow the evidence to be given in chief as similar fact, the prosecution must wait to see how the defence is run, and then obtain leave to cross-examine D *if he decides to give evidence*. Not only does this leave the admissibility of valuable evidence to chance, but it prevents the defence from showing any significant difference between the offence charged and the previous ones – the unfairness indicated by the Court of Criminal Appeal in *Jones v DPP*. Lord Lane CJ was unable to indi-

---

[92] *Selvey* [1970] AC 304.
[93] [1983] 3 All ER 101.
[94] [1986] 1 All ER 193.

cate in *Powell* just what the record had to do with D's credibility; this is understandable. But it had everything to do with whether D was likely to be guilty – an inference described as 'sheer prejudice' in *Watts*.

The same problem arises on a different question in *Duncalf*.[95] The issue was whether the prosecution, cross-examining under section 1(f)(ii), is entitled to go into the details of the offence rather than the mere fact of the conviction. A previous case, *France and France*,[96] had apparently established that the prosecution may not.[97] In *Duncalf* D was charged with conspiracy to steal. The defendants admitted being at the scene, but denied intent to steal, claiming that they were window-shopping. D lost his shield by attacking the character of police witnesses, and the prosecution cross-examined on his record, which consisted of offences of theft committed with his co-accused, in which their *modus operandi* was that they waited outside shops until the opportunity arose to run in and snatch goods off the counter. The House of Lords concluded that it was legitimate to introduce details of the *modus operandi*, distinguishing *France and France* on the grounds that there the issue was identity, here intention.[98] There can be no doubt that here their Lordships were allowing quasi-similar fact evidence by the back door; it is submitted that section 1(f)(ii) is an inappropriate vehicle for this, for the reasons given above.

Recently the Court of Appeal overturned a conviction for affray and for assault on a police officer because of the nature of the cross-examination under section 1(f)(ii). The defendant lost his shield by alleging that police witnesses had lied. The Court of Appeal rightly held that the prosecution should not have been allowed to ask questions on the details of his previous conviction for assaulting a police officer, reasoning that such facts could have no bearing on the issue of his credibility. No mention was made of *France* or *Duncalf*.[99]

The elaborate minuet between prosecution and defence provoked by this legislation, the progeny of the adversarial trial, is indefensible. It is even less so in the light of the inexcusable manner in which courts have interpreted the words 'involve imputations on the character' in section 1(f)(ii). We are told that the accused is entitled to defend him- or herself, which necessarily involves denying the truth of the prosecution case, without losing the shield.

---

[95] [1979] 2 All ER 1116.

[96] [1979] Crim LR 48.

[97] In *Watts* Lord Lane CJ dismissed *France* on the grounds that the transcript was so inaccurate that he couldn't be sure what the decision was.

[98] But *France* is consistent with *Bradley* [1980] Crim LR 173, interpreting Theft Act 1968, s. 27(3).

[99] *Khan* [1991] Crim LR 51.

Thus, calling a prosecution witness a liar is not an imputation.[100] Yet explaining to the court the reason the witness would want to lie in this context apparently is.[101] We are told that the accused is entitled to describe events in order to develop his or her defence, even though he or she emerges creditably from the account, since the accused is not making his or her character an issue.[102] The same should apply if a prosecution witness emerges *discreditably* from the account,[103] since the defence is not making that witness's character a separate issue in the trial. Yet a defendant who denies ever making the admissions he or she was described as making by police witnesses will lose the shield unless it is obvious that his or her story is consistent with them having made a mistake. If the denial amounts to an implied suggestion that they are in fact conspiring to fabricate evidence against him or her, the defendant will lose the shield.[104] It appears to be legitimate for the trial judge to lure the accused into this trap.[105] These decisions are justified by the Court of Appeal on the grounds that they can afford to be strict in the interpretation of section 1(f)(ii), since the trial judge has a discretion to exclude the convictions even after the shield is lost. But the manner in which the discretion was exercised in *Selvey*, the House of Lords case generally cited as authority for this proposition, does not encourage expectations of generosity from trial judges. The complainant in a buggery case, according to D, told him that he would go to bed with him for a pound, and that he had already gone on the bed for that sum with another man earlier that day. When D refused, he dumped indecent photographs in D's room out of pique. The trial judge asked D whether he was asking the jury to disbelieve the witness because he was 'that sort of young man'. D agreed that he was. The House of Lords upheld the judge in concluding that the shield was lost, and the fact that in his discretion he allowed cross-examination as to D's political views, which included approval of illegal activities. Yet no evidence had been introduced of the complainant's character extraneous to the events D had to describe in order to present his case (apart from that provoked by the judge). Despite this, Lord Pearce thought the 'attack on the chief witness was very thorough and very serious. There was even added to the attack contained in the alleged admissions of the prosecution witness a suggestion that he was inventing the whole charge

---

[100]   *Rouse* [1904] 1 KB 184.

[101]   *Rappolt* (1911) 6 Cr App R 156.

[102]   *Malindi v R* [1967] 1 AC 439.

[103]   *Selvey v DPP* [1970] AC 304.

[104]   *Tanner* (1977) 66 Cr App R 56; *Britzman and Hall* [1983] Crim LR 106.

[105]   *Tanner*, ibid.; observers have seen judges deliberately do this – see D. McBarnett, *Conviction* (Macmillan, London, 1983).

because the accused would not give him a pound.' It is difficult to see how the accused in the absence of legal training could describe the events which gave rise to suspicion without describing the admissions made by the complainant.[106] And yet the House of Lords thought the trial judge was right to allow the cross-examination.

The answer to all these difficulties cannot be to define further the already complicated rules on the defendant's criminal record. The eagerness with which the courts misinterpret them to reach the result they want shows that in some cases previous criminality is relevant, though not, strictly, admissible. It would be much simpler and more intellectually honest to place the record before the jury, as Continental courts do. There is clearly a risk that improper inferences will be drawn,[107] but it is difficult to see that the situation would be worse than in cases such as *Powell*, where the jury are presented with evidence of guilt and instructed to apply it to the credibility of the accused. The admissibility of the evidence would not depend on defence tactics, schooling defendants not to criticize the police or any other imponderable. And the criminal record would be seen in relation to all the defendant's history, his or her education and employment (if any) and might be more comprehensible as a result. Also, since it would come out in every case, rather than sprung on the defendant while giving evidence, the defence would be able to dispose of inconsequential information and make any material point about the nature of the criminal record.

THE CONVICTIONS OF ACCOMPLICES: SECTION 74 OF THE POLICE AND CRIMINAL EVIDENCE ACT

Prior to the enactment of sections 73 and 74 of the Police and Criminal Evidence Act 1984, the effect of the rule in *Hollington v Hewthorn*[108] was – in criminal cases – to prevent a criminal conviction from being admissible evidence that an offence had been committed. Thus, in a prosecution of D for handling stolen goods, the prosecution had to prove afresh that the goods were stolen. Now the conviction, proved by producing a certificate of convic-

---

[106] Cf. *Bishop* [1974] 2 All ER 1206; accounting for his fingerprints in the room of the prosecution witness, D claimed to have had a homosexual relationship with him. This was held to have been an imputation on his character because, 'unless [the Court is] behind the times...most men would be anxious to keep from a jury...the knowledge that they practised such acts'.

[107] Damaska (1973) 121 U Penn LR 506, 518 argues that drawing of inferences contrary to common sense is not likely.

[108] [1943] KB 587.

tion,[109] of a person (other than the accused) may be admitted as evidence that the offence described in the certificate was committed by that person,[110] although the accused may disprove it by adducing evidence of his or her own.[111] These provisions appear at first sight innocuous and sensible, but have had implications not generally anticipated; at their worst they reverse the burden of proof in criminal trials, effectively convicting an accused person by means of evidence adduced and challenged, if at all, at proceedings to which he or she was not a party.

There is a principle that one person's confession is not evidence against another; therefore, if the police statement made by B, D's co-defendant, is read out in the usual way but appears to implicate D, the judge should warn the jury that it is not evidence against D.[112] In practice prosecutors usually omit the passage placing blame on D. Otherwise, the nature of the statement may be a ground for separating the trials. The problem caused by section 74 is that if the trials of co-defendants are separated, and one is convicted before the other on a guilty plea or otherwise, it could be argued that the conviction of the first to be dealt with is admissible at the trial of the other, to show that the offence was committed or that there was a conspiracy. The acts and declarations of a conspirator are admissible against a fellow conspirator to prove the nature and scope of the conspiracy, but there must be independent evidence to implicate the latter in the conspiracy.[113] However, if one conspirator has already pleaded guilty to conspiring with D, evidence of this fact, if admitted under section 74, is very damaging. If such a conviction is admitted, the burden is on the accused if he or she wishes to challenge the presumption that the co-defendant is guilty of the offence. The courts have in some cases of this kind felt that the only way to avoid the danger of prejudice is to exclude the evidence concerning the co-defendant altogether, under section 78.[114] Inconsistent use of the discretion has precipitated a haphazard collection of cases.

The traditional view was that a plea of guilty by one co-accused is not in any sense evidence of another's guilt although at the trial of the latter the jury could be told of the other's plea to explain his or her absence from the dock.[115] The courts have been forced to look at the principle again in the

---

[109] Police and Criminal Evidence Act 1984, s. 73.

[110] Ibid., s. 74(1).

[111] Ibid., s. 74(2).

[112] *Gunewardene* [1951] 2 KB 600.

[113] *R v Governor of Pentonville Prison, ex p Osman* [1989] 3 All ER 701.

[114] For the court's power to exclude evidence which would adversely affect the fairness of the proceedings, see chapter 6.

[115] *Moore* (1956) 40 Cr App R 50.

light of section 74. In *O'Connor*[116] D was charged with conspiracy to obtain property by deception. He was alleged to have taken part with another man in a scheme to defraud an insurance company by falsely reporting a vehicle as stolen. He initially admitted the offence but then retracted. The co-defendant pleaded guilty to the offence of conspiracy to defraud before D's trial, and that conviction was admitted under section 74. The defence argued on appeal that this enabled the prosecution to put before the jury a statement made by one co-accused in the absence of the other, and that the evidential effect of the guilty plea was only that the co-defendant had conspired with D, so that it was not open to the jury to infer that D had conspired with him. The Court of Appeal held that section 74 was clearly designed to deal with the situation where it was necessary as a preliminary matter for it to be proved that a person other than the accused had been convicted of an offence as a condition precedent to the conviction of D, for example proof of theft by another in a trial for handling. Section 75 provides that where the conviction is admitted in evidence it is admitted with all the detail contained in the relevant count in the indictment. Once that went before the jury in this case, it was not realistic to stress that they would not be entitled therefore to infer that D conspired with the co-defendant. Without deciding the full scope of section 74, it was sufficient for the purposes of the present case to say that the evidence should not have been admitted under the discretion given in section 78. (The proviso was applied.)

In *Robertson*,[117] however, section 78 was not invoked. D was charged with conspiracy to burgle. There were convictions of P and L for burglary, allegedly in relation to acts in pursuance of the conspiracy. Their guilt was therefore neutral as far as D was concerned, but there was other evidence implicating him in the agreement, including an eyewitness who saw him with them at about the material time. Taken together, the evidence showed what the object of their joint plan was. The Court of Appeal held that the evidence was rightly admitted, and section 78 was inapplicable. The court distinguished *O'Connor*, where the conviction tended to lead the jury to the conclusion that D had conspired with the other accused. The appeal was dismissed also in *Bennett*,[118] where D was jointly charged with theft. The co-accused pleaded guilty, and the resulting conviction was used in evidence against D. The Court of Appeal held that this was acceptable; to omit the guilty plea would 'mystify the jury'. But since the allegation was that the co-accused, who worked in a supermarket, had passed goods worth £85 to D for a price of £4.99, the damage to D's case was substantial. As Birch has

---

[116] [1987] Crim LR 260.
[117] [1987] 3 All ER 231.
[118] [1988] Crim LR 686.

noted, juries managed not to be mystified before 1984, when they were told nothing about the fate of the co-accused.[119]

Kempster[120] represents a wish to keep the new law more in line with that of before 1984; there were eight charges, and the Crown led evidence that D had been seen in the company of his co-accused close to the time of the offences. There was also other evidence, none of which was sufficient *per se* to identify any of the offenders. The trial judge admitted the guilty pleas of the co-accused without imposing a limit on the purpose for which the prosecution could use those pleas. D's appeal was allowed; the Court of Appeal followed *Moore*[121] in holding that a plea of guilty by a co-defendant is not evidence against the other accused. Section 74 allows the admission of the plea where relevant. Here it was relevant to the issue whether D had taken part in the robberies/burglary to which the co-defendant had pleaded guilty, the offences occurring when the co-defendant was said to have been in D's company. The application of section 78 was an entirely different question. The cases show that whilst evidence which of itself established complicity should be excluded under section 78, evidence which did not of itself have that effect but which was used as a basis for other evidence to that end need not necessarily be excluded. If it is intended to use the plea as evidence against D, the intention must be clear, and may attract section 78. Here it was not clear what use the prosecution wanted to make of it, therefore section 78 was not argued on that point. Here in the light of less than over-whelming evidence against D, there was a suspicion that the prosecution did intend to use the other's conviction against him and therefore the conviction was unsafe. Another strong case is *Mattison*,[122] involving a charge against D and one Davis of gross indecency in a public lavatory. Davis pleaded guilty but D pleaded not guilty. D's case was that he had been falsely accused by the police who burst into his cubicle, which he had been using for orthodox purposes. He denied any contact with Davis. The trial judge allowed evidence of Davis's guilty plea, and the jury seemed unsure how to deal with it. They returned a note to the judge inquiring whether D had been charged with indecency with anyone other than Davis. Saville J concluded that in such a case the admission of the evidence was inevitably unfair. 'If A commits an act of gross indecency with B, it is a strong inference that the converse is also true, in the absence of special circumstances to indicate otherwise.'

Why did Parliament place the burden of proving someone else's innocence

[119]   Birch [1988] Crim LR 687.
[120]   [1989] Crim LR 747.
[121]   (1956) 40 Cr App R 50.
[122]   [1989] NLJ 1417 (CA).

on the defendant? Not being a party to the other's trial, the defendant could not influence the way it was conducted. In *O'Connor* Lord Lane CJ thought that the intention of the legislature had been merely to reverse *Hollington v Hewthorn*, to deal with offences such as handling stolen goods or impeding arrest of an offender. But in *Robertson* it was observed that the court was not entitled to ignore the plain meaning of Parliament's words.[123] Although it seems likely that cases such as *Robertson* were unforeseen, the effect is of significance for two reasons. First, it is a further instance of the erosion of the *Woolmington* principle that the defence should not bear the burden of proof.[124] Second, judicial reaction to the perceived unfairness of the provision has involved use of section 78 in a way which was entirely unforeseen,[125] with the result that the judge's discretion is becoming more important and more visible in criminal trials. We may see development in the direction that any evidence ultimately will depend for its admissibility on the court's opinion of its probative value against a general principle of fairness. If this were so, Parliament could feel free to introduce more rules which appear to strike at the presumption of innocence, in the knowledge that they would be invoked only in those cases where the judges regard their use as appropriate.

---

[123] See Munday, 'Proof of guilt by association under s. 74 of the Police and Criminal Evidence Act' [1990] Crim LR 236.
[124] [1935] AC 462; chapter 2.
[125] See chapter 6.

6

The Prosecutor in the Criminal Trial

A FORMIDABLE OPPONENT

Adversarial theory presupposes two contestants equally matched in a struggle in which the state, which provides them with a forum for the contest and a machinery to enforce victory, takes no direct interest. A curious irony is the fact that the proceedings which most closely resemble this model are civil trials, in which the state has no interest unless it is a party; but these are far less committed to the principle of orality than are English criminal trials, the closest thing to an adversarial proceeding that exists within any jurisdiction but in which the state does have a direct interest. The trend in civil cases towards greater pre-trial exchange of information and advance notification to the judge of intended arguments and evidence suggests a move in the direction of the Continental or European Court mode of trial. Consequently, the rules of evidence diminish in importance as the emphasis on orality declines. Meanwhile, advocates in criminal trials hang on doggedly to the adversarial tradition, despite increasing pressure to change[1] and a gradual movement away from many of its fundamental features through piecemeal statutory reform.[2] Yet the parties in a criminal case are not independent, and they do not have equal potency as litigants.

It is certainly possible to devise criminal proceedings which encompass the concepts of equality of risk and independence. Taking a lesson from the Anglo-Saxons, in cases where a suspect is remanded to gaol, the accuser

---

[1] E.g. Ludovic Kennedy's address to the Conference of the Liberal Democratic Party, 17 September 1990.
[2] E.g. of the hearsay rule; see Chapter 7.

could also be so remanded, in order to be fair, and – if the prosecution fails – could be made to suffer the penalty he or she sought for the defendant.[3] But although equality of risk may appear fairer than a system where the prosecutor hazards nothing, it does little to further the interest of society as a whole in the prevention of crime. In England, however, the state was slow to take on responsibility for the prosecution of crime. There were private associations for the prosecution of offences until the nineteenth century, although there were efforts to involve representatives of the community such as justices of the peace as early as 1349.[4] Public resistance to the introduction of a police force delayed an organized system of prosecution for many years, but once such forces were set up it was obvious that they would make more effective prosecutors than private individuals or associations, and would establish a consistency of approach whereby an offender's prospects of being prosecuted did not depend on the identity of the victim.

It is still assumed, however, that any private citizen is wronged by the commission of crimes, whether or not directly injured by them, and therefore may prosecute in the criminal courts. In complex cases costs are now prohibitive, and even straightforward cases are beyond the means of most people. In 1981 the Phillips Commission noted that the majority of private prosecutions were launched, not by individuals, but by shops which employed their own store detectives, or charities such as the RSPCA and the NSPCC.[5] The commissioners regarded private agencies as inappropriate prosecutors for shoplifting cases, since many offenders are elderly or have medical or personal histories which justify non-prosecution, and recommended that the practice of private prosecution by retailers should cease.[6] Prosecution is regarded as an area where discretion should be exercised in a responsible way, and in which agencies should be accountable.[7] Thus, the citizen who wishes to initiate a private prosecution finds that he or she does not have an entirely free hand. In well over a hundred Acts of Parlia-

[3] *Lex talionis*; F. Pollock and F. W. Maitland, *History of English Law* (Cambridge University Press, 1895).
[4] Ordinance of Labourers. See De Gama, *A Social History of Prosecutions in England* (doctoral thesis, in preparation).
[5] Royal Commission on Criminal Procedure, *The Investigation and Prosecution of Criminal Offences in England and Wales: The Law and Procedure*, Cmnd 8092-1 (1981), para. 171.
[6] *Report of the Royal Commission on Criminal Procedure* (Phillips Report), Cmnd 8092 (1981), para. 7.46.
[7] Ibid., para. 7.3.

ment the right to prosecute is subject to the consent of a minister, official or a judge.[8] Government agencies may ensure that the case is discontinued, either by the Attorney-General entering a *nolle prosequi*,[9] or by the Director of Public Prosecutions taking over the prosecution, which he may continue or drop by offering no evidence.[10] Also, if the individual is regarded as a vexatious litigant with a penchant for launching unmeritorious criminal proceedings, the Attorney-General may apply to the High Court for an order to prevent him or her from laying an information in future without the leave of the court.[11]

There is a recognition, then, that criminal proceedings are not a matter from which the state can stand back with magnificent disinterest. And once the police began to take on the work of prosecution, having the funds and the organization (although no increased powers) to do it, the question naturally arose whether they had special responsibilities in that regard. The public interest in the bringing of criminal prosecutions was acknowledged by the courts. In *R v Metropolitan Police Commissioner, ex parte Blackburn (No. 1)*[12] Lord Denning in the Court of Appeal conceded that a chief constable was entitled to make his own decision as to whether or not to prosecute in a particular case. But his discretion was not absolute. There might be decisions of policy with which a court could interfere, if they amounted to a failure to enforce the law. However, although Lord Denning thought that the writ of *mandamus* provided the individual with the legal equipment with which police prosecution policy could be challenged, the problem of *locus standi*[13] has never been satisfactorily addressed. The police are certainly subject to the law in the way cases are investigated; their powers, which were defined in the main in a series of cases on civil liberties, are now primarily set out in the controversial Police and Criminal Evidence Act 1984. This Act was the product of recommendations of the Royal Commission on Criminal Procedure in 1981; the Commission's review of prosecution concluded that the lack of accountability and, in some cases, inefficiency of then current arrangements demanded the creation of a specialist prosecution service.

---

[8] Ibid., para. 7.48.

[9] A power not subject to any scrutiny by the courts; *R v Comptroller of Patents* [1899] 1 QB 909.

[10] Prosecution of Offences Act 1985, s. 6(2).

[11] Supreme Court Act 1981, s. 42, as amended by Prosecution of Offences Act 1985, s. 24; there is a similar power to ban a litigant with a history of vexatious civil proceedings.

[12] [1968] 2 QB 118.

[13] An interest which the party seeks to defend, and entitles him or her to seek an administrative remedy.

The creation of the Crown Prosecution Service in 1985[14] may have succeeded in providing a more professional prosecution system, although there is heated debate on the subject. But the Service is subject to a scrutiny which shows that prosecutors are no longer to any extent regarded as equivalent to private litigants.[15] However, since the police retain the responsibility to investigate offences and gather evidence, they have a substantial influence on the cases which appear in court. The Crown Prosecutor decides whether or not to proceed with cases *as presented to him* by a police officer. The police, then, still act as a filter which may lead to many cases never being produced to the Crown Prosecution Service at all. Prosecution is in fact an enterprise conducted jointly by the police and the Service. Since the Service is not involved with a case at the investigation stage unless advice is specifically sought, there is no opportunity to control how the evidence is obtained, although police conduct is subject to the restraints of the Police and Criminal Evidence Act, the common law, and the police disciplinary code. The relative liberty of the police appears to be inevitable in an adversarial system. Although the Procurator Fiscal in Scotland and the District Attorney in the United States of America are involved at an earlier stage of an inquiry, 'in practice the police retain a very large measure of control over the the decision to prosecute and, especially where the volume of cases puts pressure on the system...the lawyer's decision tends to be little more than an endorsement of that of the police'.[16] For the purposes of gathering evidence, police officers might be thought to be in a position of privilege, with powers of search and seizure not possessed by the ordinary citizen. But many police officers complain that the safeguards in the Police and Criminal Evidence Act too often tie their hands. A journalist told John Stalker that an investigation by the press was far 'deeper and more searching than anything MI5 or Special Branch could undertake..."You have", he said, "survived the Fleet Street vetting machine."'[17]

In a strictly adversarial system, a decision to prosecute would be based entirely on the merits and potential consequences of an individual case. In fact, however, some decisions are to some extent influenced by considerations of the public interest. There have been protests that some notorious fraud trials in recent months have been influenced by utilitarian

[14] Prosecution of Offences Act 1985.

[15] The regional structure with local supervisory authorities recommended by the Royal Commission (Phillips Report, paras. 7.21–37) was not adopted. But the head of the CPS, the DPP, is answerable to Parliament through the Attorney-General.

[16] Ibid., para. 7.11.

[17] J. Stalker, *Stalker* (Penguin, Harmondsworth, 1988), p. 163.

concerns, such as the need to prove to investors that the City of London is not immune from investigation, and therefore their money is safe. It is alleged that, to this end, practices which have long been tolerated and are in fact widespread have suddenly become the object of attention; individual businessmen, investment consultants and company directors have been sacrificed to the greater good of community confidence. Similarly, the 1990 investigation into the dealings of Liverpool councillors has been described as a witch-hunt designed to encourage industrialists to base operations in Liverpool, secure in the knowledge that the widely rumoured corruption in the area has been stamped out. There is a danger that political expediency may direct prosecution policy, for example where there has been a vocal campaign in the press about a particular sort of crime, or where for some other reason there is considerable public concern, as with the Zeebrugge ferry disaster. In that case, the prosecution case against company officials was thrown out by the trial judge, causing observers to wonder why the case against them had been brought in the first place. In the defence of Kevin Taylor and his co-defendants, who included his bank manager and his accountant,[18] it was argued forcefully that the case had been brought to justify the earlier pursuit of his friend John Stalker, the former Deputy Chief Constable of Greater Manchester.[19] Whether or not the allegations contain any truth, the risk remains that close association between the government and a highly organized, centralized prosecution service could allow influence to be exercised.

There are other bodies which investigate offences and carry out prosecutions, such as the Serious Fraud Office,[20] the Department of Social Security, the Commissioners of Customs and Excise and the Inland Revenue. Some of these agencies have sweeping powers the police would envy, and which add further weight to the argument that the prosecution in a criminal case has a might on its side which unbalances the criminal trial and demands that strict adversarial theory be modified to protect the accused. The imbalance of power as between the state apparatus and the single suspect has led to significant departures from adversarial principles; the greater duty on the part of the prosecution to disclose evidence has been discussed in chapter 1. The most obvious difference, however, is the duty to obtain evidence by legitimate means, although the law on this is unclear from the point of view of both principle and content.

The fact that prosecutors are now supported by a funded and specialist service with exclusive access to investigative agencies may account for the

---

[18] *Bowley et al* Case No. 88.6607, 10 October 1989.
[19] See Stalker, *Stalker*.
[20] Criminal Justice Act 1987, s. 1(5).

scrupulousness with which courts examine some of their activities. If a defendant were to obtain valuable evidence by burgling the police station, there is no reason to think that he or she could not use it. In general, relevant evidence is admissible whatever its provenance.[21] If, however, it is so unreliable that it ceases to be relevant, it will be excluded. If the rules of evidence in criminal cases had developed exclusively along those lines, a reasonably coherent system would have emerged. Continental rules did this; oral evidence obtained by oppression is inadmissible, but physical evidence, such as documents unlawfully obtained but reliable in themselves, is not. But the common law and now the Police and Criminal Evidence Act and the cases which interpret it are less straightforward. Unreliability is not the only factor at work, a state of affairs conceded by the Criminal Law Revision Committee, who nevertheless concluded that it was the most important one.[22] Other concerns are not easily identified; it may be that judges are using the rules of evidence to deter unlawful police practices; it may be that they are mindful of the institutional might of the prosecutor, and wish to even things up; it may be that they would feel themselves or the integrity of the trial contaminated if they admitted evidence discovered by means they regard as repugnant. This is a factor in the extreme position of the American courts: 'Out of regard for its own dignity as an agency of justice and custodian of liberty the court should not have a hand in such a "dirty business"...It is morally incongruous for the state to flout constitutional rights and at the same time demand that its citizens observe the law.'[23] But once evidence which is itself reliable is excluded for any or all of these reasons, the issue of guilt or innocence has been made a secondary matter in the proceedings: 'What bothers me is that almost never do we have a genuine issue of guilt or innocence today. The system is so changed that what we are doing in the courtroom is trying the conduct of the police and that of the prosecutor all along the line.'[24]

These remarks of Judge Walter V. Shaefer indicate the anxiety of many American judges during the heyday of the doctrine of the 'fruit of the

---

[21] *Lord Ashburton v Pape* [1913] 2 Ch 469; *Nationwide v Goddard* [1986] 3 WLR 734.

[22] *Evidence (General)*, Eleventh Report of the Criminal Law Revision Committee, Cmnd 4991 (1972), para. 56. Mirfield suggests that the more extreme examples of exclusion of perfectly reliable confessions at common law were the result of a preference for generalized principles rather than scrutiny of the facts of each case: P. Mirfield *Confessions* (Sweet & Maxwell, London, 1985), p. 62.

[23] *People v Cahan* 282 P 2d 905, 912 (1955), *per* Justice Traynor.

[24] Judge Walter V. Shaefer, quoted in McDonald, 'A Center report: Criminal Justice', *The Center Magazine*, November 1968, p. 69 at p. 76.

poisoned tree', by which the courts would have nothing to do with any evidence obtained improperly. Even minor breaches which led to the discovery of reliable evidence might fall foul of this doctrine, as in *Orozco v Texas*.[25] Four police officers burst into the defendant's bedroom immediately after a shooting. They regarded him as under arrest, and asked where the gun was. He told them, and they found the murder weapon in his washing machine. Since in the heat of the moment they had not reminded him of his rights to silence and to legal advice, all this evidence was inadmissible. Widespread belief that this approach was leading to undeserved acquittals has led the American courts to adopt unconvincing reasoning to escape the rigours of *Miranda v Arizona*,[26] the case which demanded elaborate warnings to be given to suspects as soon as there were grounds for suspicion.[27]

The Phillips Report rejected the argument that it was necessary to exclude unlawfully obtained evidence as a sanction against improper police conduct. The intended result would, apparently, be best achieved by 'contemporaneous controls and good supervision'[28] and 'effective arrangement for the investigation of complaints against the police' plus the usual civil remedy.[29] The complaints procedure has (fairly or unfairly) had a poor press, and therefore victims of police malpractice may be unenthusiastic about participating in it, especially as they gain nothing more than vindication and revenge even if the complaint is upheld. To bring civil proceedings for trespass would require extraordinary determination, given the effort and expense likely to be involved. Litigation, therefore, tends to be reserved for the most extreme cases. On the other hand, the Report rightly anticipated that the system established by the Police and Criminal Evidence Act would provide better controls over what happens to suspects in the police station. The increasing use of tape-recording is designed to reduce the number of allegations that oppression was used to extract a confession; this works to the benefit of suspect and interrogator.[30] But it is more difficult to control what happens outside the police station.

The Royal Commission decided against a general discretion to exclude

---

[25] 394 US 324 (1968).

[26] 384 US 436 (1966).

[27] *Harris v New York* 401 US 222 (1971); it was held that although a confession was inadmissible as evidence of the facts stated, the accused could be cross-examined on it. Further dilution of the spirit of *Miranda* is found in the Omnibus Crime Control and Safe Streets Act 1968, amending United States Code (Title 18, Ch 3501 (a)).

[28] Phillips Report, para. 4.118.

[29] Ibid., para. 4.119.

[30] Increased police enthusiasm for tape-recording noted, Baldwin, 'Police interviews on tape' [1990] NLJ 662.

improperly obtained evidence, chiefly because it would be exercised in very few cases: only a minority of those stopped and searched are arrested; a sizeable minority of those whose premises are searched are never charged; most defendants plead guilty; and of the rest, who deny guilt, only a small proportion challenge the legality of the manner in which the investigation was conducted. This argument is startling; first, it ignores the fact that, since at the time of the Commission's inquiry such evidence was admissible, this would have encouraged guilty pleas and discouraged any challenge to admissibility. Also, the fact that so few of those searched were subsequently charged or prosecuted is more alarming than reassuring. And to allow the police to make use of evidence obtained where there were no grounds for the search is to encourage 'fishing' expeditions, and to maintain a high number of fruitless searches. Lord Hailsham, having stated that one ground for objecting to a discretion to exclude would be prolonged and expensive *voirs dires*, added that the penalty for police misconduct would be levied on the public rather than the police if it led to the acquittal of guilty men.[31] It is understandable that some are persuaded by the argument that the rules of evidence should not be used as a means to discipline the police force, since the purpose of the trial is to establish guilt or innocence, but it would be a great deal stronger if the relationship between the rules of evidence and the truth were more clearly established than it seems to be in the adversarial trial.

RELIABILITY OF EVIDENCE OR FAIRNESS?

The lack of a consistent approach to the admissibility of evidence unlawfully obtained by the prosecution predates the Police and Criminal Evidence Act 1984 and has to some extent been embodied in its provisions on confession evidence. The Criminal Law Review Committee argued that reliability was the dominant common law principle; this explained why evidence discovered as a result of a confession obtained by threats or promises was admissible even though the confession was not.[32] That position was restated in section 76(4) of the 1984 Act. But if the confession is proved to be true by subsequent discovery of physical evidence such as a corpse or stolen goods, the confession was not thereby rendered admissible at common law, and the position under the Act is the same. The Committee supported this, on the grounds that to admit confessions in these circumstances would involve the judge in a ruling on the truth or falsity of the confession, which might

---

[31] 1983/4 HL Deb., Vol. 455, col. 668 (26 July).
[32] *Warickshall* (1783) 1 Leach 263.

affect the jury, although it would not be binding on them.[33] The Committee was less happy that 'there is a good deal of obscurity as to how far the discovery of facts may be linked with the fact that the confession was made'[34]; there was confusion in the case law as to whether the court could be told that the evidence was discovered on the strength of what the accused had said. Yet the 1984 Act makes it clear that the discovery of facts, even though it may have been possible only because the accused described the location, may not be linked with his or her confession, if that is inadmissible. Section 76(5) states that evidence that a fact was discovered as a result of the statement made by an accused person shall not be admissible against him or her if the confession itself must be excluded under section 76. This provision looks suspiciously like a prohibition on accepting the 'fruit of the poisoned tree'. So does a further, curious, feature of section 76, contained in subsection (2), the provision which excludes improperly obtained confessions:

> If, in any proceedings where the prosecution proposes to give in evidence a confession made by an accused person, it is represented to the court that the confession was or may have been obtained –
> (a) by oppression of the person who made it; or
> (b) in consequence of anything said or done which was likely, in the circumstances existing at the time, to render unreliable any confession which might be made by him in consequence thereof,
> the court shall not allow the confession to be given in evidence against him except in so far as the prosecution proves to the court beyond reasonable doubt that the confession (notwithstanding that it may be true) was not obtained as aforesaid.

The proviso in parentheses appears to explode the reliability principle in favour of a disciplinary one. It might be assumed that judges are not in a position to know whether the confession was true or not, particularly at the *voir dire* stage at which they have to adjudicate on admissibility; but in that case the proviso is unnecessary. Also, there have been cases where the accused has admitted at the *voir dire* that his confession, despite the claims of police misconduct, was true.[35]

The theoretical position is further confused by the enactment of section 78 of the 1984 Act, inserted into the Bill at a late stage by an unwilling government who appeared to think that it had nothing to do with disciplining the police.[36] The section reads:

[33] Eleventh Report, para. 69.
[34] Ibid., para. 56.
[35] *Wong Kam-Ming v The Queen* [1980] AC 247; *Brophy* [1981] 3 WLR 103.
[36] St J. Robilliard and J. McEwan, *Police Powers and the Individual* (Blackwell, Oxford, 1986), pp. 224–6.

(1) In any proceedings the court may refuse to allow evidence on which the prosecution proposes to rely to be given if it appears to the court that, having regard to all the circumstances, including the circumstances in which the evidence was obtained, the admission of the evidence would have such an adverse effect on the fairness of the proceedings that the court ought not to admit it.

(2) Nothing in this section shall prejudice any rule of law requiring a court to exclude evidence.

Although, in debate on the Bill, the Home Secretary emphasized that section 78 was not addressed to the history or origin of evidence, but was concerned only with the fairness of the trial itself, it appears to be used rather more flexibly than that. It is arguable that the provision would otherwise be meaningless, since an accused is entitled to a fair trial in any event.[37] The retention of any common law discretion to exclude under section 82(3) adds a further complication in theory, but in practice judges have used section 78 to give themselves such a wide discretion that it is rarely mentioned. A flexible discretion such as this seems ideal to protect rights which, Ashworth argues, exist independently of either reliability or disciplinary concerns.[38] For it is one thing to argue that devising exclusionary rules of evidence is not an appropriate means of disciplining the police – there are other ways of doing this – but another to identify an alternative method of protecting and enforcing the right of the private citizen to be fairly treated by law enforcement officers. Evidence which is obtained by unlawful procedures, he argues, places the suspect at a disadvantage which can effectively be mitigated only by disallowing its use in court. The 'protective principle', unlike the disciplinary one, does not depend on whether or not the misconduct was deliberate; the relevant factors are matters such as the seriousness of the breach and its consequences for the accused. However, to allow such a judgment to dictate whether evidence is admitted or excluded introduces into a trial concerns other than the reliability of evidence and the pursuit of the truth. The protective principle is not therefore an application of adversarial reasoning.

The reliability principle at work

The research commissioned by the Phillips Royal Commission clearly established that being held under arrest at a police station is intimidating, to an extent where many suspects would rather confess and end the uncertainty than suffer prolonged questioning. Although the definition of oppression in

---

[37] Ibid.

[38] Ashworth, 'Excluding evidence as protecting rights' [1977] Crim LR 723.

section 76(8) of the 1984 Act requires deliberate impropriety[39] of quite an extreme kind,[40] judges, in their interpretation of sections 76 and 78 appear mindful of the helplessness of suspects, and therefore quite willing to exclude confessions because of breaches of the Police and Criminal Evidence Act Codes of Conduct; they may be rather less willing to do so where the factor which indicates unreliability arises in the absence of any misconduct by police, a matter discussed below. There are two aspects of unreliability. A confession may be given which is not true; this is the concern of section 76(2). But many court cases involve discussion about whether a confession was made at all; anything which, whether by tape-recording or other means, may spare the court the time and energy spent investigating allegations of 'verballing' by police would be welcome on a pragmatic level.

Cases in which the courts have been rigorous in excluding evidence obtained in breach of the Codes of Conduct are varied, but breaches which appear to be taken especially seriously are failure to allow access to legal advice, whether the breach consists of failure to remind the suspect of the right or of excluding a solicitor, and failure to show the suspect a con-temporaneous record of the interview. There is an obvious connection between the latter category with the authenticity–reliability problem. The courts are anxious to encourage accurate records to be kept, and if possible, agreed, so that there will not be disputes about whether admissions were in fact made. The police obligation to make an interview record and, unless it is impracticable to do so, require the suspect to sign it as correct, has recently[41] been revised to cover interviews outside as well as inside the police station.[42]

> The importance of the rules relating to contemporaneous noting of interviews can scarcely be overemphasized…Not merely is it to ensure, so far as possible, that the suspect's remarks are accurately recorded and that he has an opportunity when he goes through the contemporaneous record afterwards of checking each answer and initialling each answer, but likewise it is a protection to the police, to ensure, so far as possible, that it cannot be suggested that they induced the suspect to confess by improper approaches or by improper promises.[43]

But surely the presence of a legal adviser also ensures or increases

---

[39] *Fulling* [1987] 2 All ER 65.

[40] 'Torture, inhuman or degrading treatment' or violence or threats of violence.

[41] Revised Codes issued in 1990 took effect from 1 January 1991.

[42] Although interviews should not take place outside the police station except in circumstances requiring urgency of action; Code C, para. 11.1.

[43] *Canale* [1990] 2 All ER 181, 184, *per* Lord Lane CJ.

reliability in terms of the accuracy of the record? Yet in *Alladice*[44] wrongful denial of access to a solicitor's advice was not regarded as sufficient reason to exclude the confession, because D said he already knew what his rights were, and so wanted a solicitor present only in order to see 'fair play' at the interview. The leading cases where confessions were held by the Court of Appeal to be inadmissible if the right to legal advice had in any way been thwarted by the police[45] appear to turn on the importance of the right to silence, which is diminished if one's lawyer is not there to advise on when it is advantageous to answer, and when it is not. In *Dunn*[46] D denied the offence throughout the interview, but police witnesses claimed that he admitted it while checking through the record afterwards, and while his legal adviser, who denied hearing this, was present. It was held that the evidence was admissible, although there was no contemporaneous note of the admission. The absence of the note in this case did not handicap the defence (although in most it would) since the lawyer could give evidence that she was there and did not hear it. Here the issue should be tested in the normal way, by introducing evidence and cross-examining witnesses. It was not considered necessary to exclude the evidence altogether. In other words, the requirement for contemporaneous note-taking was seen to be only one way of guarding against the manufacture of admissions by the police; here the presence of the legal adviser filled the gap, although she could not confirm that any admission had been made! But the approach taken here does not depend at all upon the witness's status as *legal adviser*, for any disinterested third party present could in theory have testified as to whether or not the accused made the alleged admissions. If the function of the solicitor in the police station is ultimately and exclusively to remind the suspect of his or her right to silence, then the purpose of section 58 of the 1984 Act and its relationship with section 78 will be thrown into doubt if the right to silence is effectively abolished.

The right to silence is itself connected with the reliability–truth principle in that without it a suspect who is under even legitimate pressure from the police may be more tempted falsely to confess. However, it appears that the right is seldom exercised by those who might be thought to need it most.[47] The attempts in the 1984 Act to ensure that a suspect is fully aware of his or her rights, which in turn enhances the accuracy of the record and the reliability of admissions of guilt, may be doomed to failure unless greater

[44] [1988] Crim LR 608.
[45] *Samuel* [1988] 2 All ER 135; *Absolam* [1988] Crim LR 748; *Mason* [1987] 3 All ER 481.
[46] [1990] Crim LR 572.
[47] Chapter 5.

effort is made to understand the comprehension problems of the majority of suspects. The Code of Practice requires that the mentally disordered or mentally handicapped should not be interviewed in the absence of the appropriate adult, and that special care should be exercised in questioning them. There is no doubt that persons of below average intelligence have difficulty in understanding the words of the caution and frequently construe it as an injunction to speak,[48] but it appears that a detained person of even average intelligence is likely to find it difficult to grasp the nature of his or her rights when held on arrest. Gudjonsson[49] applied the Flesch Statistical Formula to analyse the reading ease of the 'Notice to Detained Persons' issued by the Metropolitan Police, which is partly read out to suspects, and then handed to them. The Notice contains the caution, the right to have someone informed, the right to legal advice, mention of the Codes of Practice, and the right to a copy of the custody record. Although understanding of these matters would increase the probable reliability of statements made in detention, only a minority of suspects are likely to fathom them. Gudjonnson found that the Notice required an IQ of at least 111 to understand it – and that would cover about 24 per cent of the population.[50] The position with the Codes of Practice is even worse. Code C, which directly deals with the detention, treatment and questioning of detained persons and which demands that detained persons and members of the public should be able to consult it,[51] is unlikely to be understood without an IQ of 126; so fewer than 5 per cent of the general population would be able to follow it. To make the Codes more comprehensible, shorter and less involved sentences would be needed.

In *DPP v Sang*[52] the House of Lords preferred the reliability principle to any notion of deterring police misconduct; Lord Diplock said that to allow a discretion to exclude the evidence of an *agent provocateur* would be absurd, since the mere fact that the witness is alleged to have provoked the crime indicates that a crime was indeed committed. More recent cases, decided since the introduction of the 1984 Act, follow the same line.[53] It is possible, despite this emphasis on reliability, that in an extreme case the court might use section 78 to exclude evidence by an *agent provocateur* who went too

---

[48] Gudjonnson, 'The notice to detained persons, PACE Codes and Reading Ease', *Applied Cognitive Psychology* (in press); Beaumont, 'Confessions, cautions and experts after *R v Silcott and Others*' [1987] NLJ 807.

[49] Gudjonnson, ibid.

[50] This was confirmed by an exploratory study, ibid.

[51] Code C, para. 1.2.

[52] [1980] AC 402.

[53] E.g. *Harwood* [1989] Crim LR 285; cf. *DPP v Marshall* [1988] Crim LR 750.

far. In a case decided before *Sang, Ameer and Lucas*,[54] a police informer approached D and asked him to sell him some cocaine. D refused, but the informer, who on his own admission used 'every trick in the book' to persuade him, eventually got D to agree to supply him with cannabis for a fictitious client who was described as extremely keen. The trial judge excluded the evidence of the *agent provocateur*.

The disciplinary principle at work

The case of *Kuruma v R*[55] is generally taken as authority for the common law position, before the 1984 Act, that if evidence is relevant and reliable, it matters not how the prosecution came by it. But even that decision accepted that there are varieties of conduct so unacceptable that the prosecution can never profit from them.[56] The conviction that the court has more to do than merely to ensure that evidence is relevant has influenced the Court of Appeal in its interpretation of section 78 of the Act. For example, in *Quinn*, Lord Lane CJ said:[57]

> The function of the judge is…to protect the fairness of the proceedings, and normally proceedings are fair if a jury hears all relevant evidence which either side wishes to place before it, but proceedings may become unfair if, for example, one side is allowed to adduce relevant evidence which, for one reason or another, the other side cannot properly meet, or where there has been an abuse of process, for example where evidence has been obtained in deliberate breach of procedures laid down in an official code of procedure.

In *Matto v Wolverhampton Crown Court*[58] real evidence contained in a sample of breath, which appeared perfectly reliable, was excluded because D was unlawfully breathalysed on private property. The Divisional Court distinguished *Fox v Chief Constable of Gwent*,[59] where the House of Lords held that an unlawful arrest was not a ground to exclude evidence obtained from a breath test subsequently administered. And in *Fennelley*[60] the unlawfulness of an arrest, in that the suspect was not told the reason for it,

---

[54] [1977] Crim LR 104.
[55] [1955] AC 197.
[56] Cf. *Callis v Gunn* [1964] 1 QB 495; *King v R* [1969] 1 AC 304.
[57] [1990] Crim LR 581, 583.
[58] [1987] RTR 337.
[59] [1985] 3 All ER 392.
[60] [1989] Crim LR 142.

led to the exclusion of the subsequent discovery, when he was searched at the police station, of heroin in his underpants. No other breach of the Act had occurred, but the Court of Appeal held that the illegality arising from the unlawfulness of the arrest ran through everything that followed. When Kevin Taylor, the businessman whose relationship with John Stalker led to the police inquiry into the conduct of the Deputy Chief Constable,[61] was tried with others over a loan he negotiated with his bank,[62] the trial collapsed when His Honour Judge Sachs excluded bank documents under section 78. The reason for this was that the court which ordered disclosure of the bank accounts had been deliberately misled by the police. The refusal of the courts in these cases to countenance use of contaminated although reliable evidence suggests an attempt to force prosecutors and their agents to adopt a higher standard of behaviour than any other party going before a court.

In *Kuruma* itself, a case decided before *Sang* laid down that there was no general discretion to exclude beyond the *nemo debet* principle, Goddard LJ said that evidence obtained by a trick might be excluded, whether it be an admission or any other kind of evidence. In *Mason*[63] police officers falsely told D while he was being questioned that his fingerprints had been found on a piece of glass from the bottle used to start the fire under investigation. They told his solicitor the same lie. D's confession was held by the Court of Appeal to be inadmissible under section 78, partly because as a result of the deception of the solicitor M was advised to explain himself to the police, and therefore his right to silence was undermined. The court denied that it was disciplining the police, arguing that the decision merely ensured fairness in the proceedings:[64]

> It is obvious from the undisputed evidence that the police practised a deceit not only on the appellant, which is bad enough, but also on the solicitor, whose duty it was to advise him. In effect they hoodwinked both solicitor and client. That was a most reprehensible thing to do. It is not however because we regard as misbehaviour of a serious kind conduct of that nature that we have come to the decision [to quash the conviction]...A trial judge has a discretion to be exercised, of course on right principles, to reject admissible evidence in the interests of a defendant having a fair trial.

Here the trial judge had paid insufficient attention to the deception of the solicitor, and therefore had omitted to consider a vital factor affecting the

---

[61] Stalker, *Stalker.*

[62] *Bowley*, Case No. 88.6607; the trial ended on 18 January 1990.

[63] [1987] 3 All ER 481.

[64] Ibid., p. 484, *per* Lord Lane CJ.

fairness of the trial; if he had considered it, Lord Lane CJ had 'not the slightest doubt' that the confession would have been excluded. Since there was no other prosecution evidence, this would have inevitably resulted in an acquittal. As for the lie to Mason himself, the Lord Chief Justice concluded: 'Despite what I have said about the role of the court in relation to disciplining the police, we think we ought to say that we hope never again to hear of a deceit such as this being practised on an accused person, and more particularly possibly on a solicitor.'[65] This reaction to the interrogation method used throws into doubt the whole issue of what are and what are not legitimate police tactics. For although the deception of the solicitor was taken more seriously because of its effect on the quality of his legal advice, misleading a suspect into thinking that the police have more evidence against him or her than they in fact have appears also to be proscribed. It is not clear whether this is because of judicial distaste for the dishonesty involved, or whether it stems from an assumption that suspects may react by making admissions which are not true.

A lay opinion might be that an innocent suspect would not fall into such a police trap, because he or she would know that they could not possibly have the evidence they claim to have. However, there are considerable risks of false confessions being made by persons who either temporarily or permanently become persuaded of their own guilt or, who react to the deception with a gloomy conviction that they will not be believed, and admit everything to avoid further interrogation. Irving and McKenzie[66] report an increased tendency since the 1984 Act in police interrogation to use tactics they describe as 'witness manipulation' – convincing the suspect that the case is a foregone conclusion so that he or she has no option but to confess. But 'lying was always seen by expert interviewers as a crude tactic, which, if discovered, handed the advantage immediately to the interviewee. In outlawing it in *Mason* the judiciary happened to be following good police practice.'[67] Thus police exaggeration of the strength of their case, which could provide a source of unreliable confessions, appears to be a problem only where less skilled interrogators have been at work; but unfortunately, emphasizing to the suspect the telling case against him or her is capable of inducing a false confession even where the police are being perfectly truthful.

[65] Ibid., p. 485.
[66] B. Irving and I. K. McKenzie, *Police Interrogation: The Effects of the Police and Criminal Evidence Act 1984* (Police Foundation, London, 1989), p. 175.
[67] Ibid., p. 177.

FALSE CONFESSIONS

The law is not designed to cope with those who confess, not as a result of police misconduct, but by reason of their innate personality making them acutely vulnerable to suggestions made during questioning. Particularly vulnerable suspects are protected in the Codes of Practice issued under the Police and Criminal Evidence Act in so far as they require that an appropriate adult attend the interviewing by police of the mentally disordered or handicapped[68] or if there is any doubt about a suspect's mental capacity. But it may be that the very intricacy of the Act's arrangements to protect suspects backfire in the sense that previous informal procedures which might have been less distressing,[69] have been abandoned. The finding that police are conducting fewer interviews with people in an intoxicated state,[70] which suggests that admissions should be more reliable, may appear to be a cause for celebration. But factors such as low intelligence and more hidden psychological characteristics are potential sources of unreliability, apart from the difficulty, discussed above, that many suspects are unlikely to be able intellectually to grasp the nature of their legal rights.

Work on false confessions is inevitably hampered by the difficulty of knowing whether a confession which is subsequently withdrawn, and which may or may not be excluded by the judge, is genuine or not. Under section 76 of the Act, as we have seen, impropriety by the police would require the exclusion of even genuine confessions. But work done on confessions which were the basis of convictions subsequently quashed or set aside with a pardon shows that the confessions tend to fall into three main groups:[71]

1 Voluntary confessions, offered to the police by someone not under investigation, and usually to publicized crimes. The reason for this may be a desire for notoriety, or to relieve a general feeling of guilt, or an inability to distinguish fact and fantasy.
2 Coerced-compliant confessions, which account for most false confessions. The best explanation is the desire to escape from a highly stressful situation. The immediate gain, which may include the need to establish some short-term certainty of future events,[72] becomes a more powerful influence

---

[68] Code C, para. 11.14.
[69] Irving and McKenzie, *Police Interrogation*.
[70] Ibid.
[71] Gudjonsson and MacKeith, 'Retracted confessions: legal, psychological and psychiatric aspects' (1988) 28 Med Sci L 187.
[72] Gudjonsson, 'The psychology of false confessions', *Medico-Legal Journal*, 57 (1989), p. 93.

on the subject's behaviour than the uncertain long-term effects of the confession, even when the alleged offence is serious.

3 Coerced-internalized confessions: the person is temporarily persuaded that he or she might have or did commit the crime because he or she does not trust his or her own memory and begins to accept the suggestions of the police. Such a confession is more likely to be elicited by gentle rather than aggressive interviewing. It may be retracted later on, although the subject is more likely to stick to it than is the coerced-compliant, but even if it is withdrawn later the subject's memory may be permanently distorted.

Gudjonsson and MacKeith argue that interrogative suggestibility and compliance are enduring psychological characteristics relevant to erroneous testimony. The effect of such a trait during police questioning may be to elicit a false admission which could form the basis of a conviction. Gudjonsson's study of 100 cases of people who retracted their confessions and were referred to him suffers from the risk of selection of particularly vulnerable subjects by the solicitors who sought psychological testing. But he compared these defendants with another 100 cases referred to him, and involving persons referred in relation to similar offences. The group which had retracted its confessions had a lower mean IQ, and far higher levels of suggestibility and compliance. These characteristics are to some extent inherent in the personality and can be measured by a reliable test[73] but they can be aggravated by conditions. Gudjonsson defines the dangerous characteristics as follows: acquiescence, which is the tendency of the person to answer questions affirmatively irrespective of content. This characteristic is most common with people of low intelligence.[74] Suggestibility is a tendency to accept uncritically information communicated during questions.[75] It is greatest in people of low intelligence. Compliance is a tendency to go along with requests of the person perceived to be in authority, even though the subject does not necessarily agree with them.[76] However, analysis of an individual's general personality does not give the whole picture: 'People are generally not

[73] Gudjonsson, 'A new scale of interrogative suggestibility', *Personality and Individual Differences*, 5 (1984), p. 303.

[74] Sigelman, Budd, Spankel and Schoenrock, 'When in doubt say yes: acquiescence in interviews with mentally retarded persons', *Mental Retardation*, 19 (1981), p. 53; Gudjonsson, 'The relationship between interrogative suggestibility and acquiescence: empirical findings and theoretical implications', *Personality and Individual Differences*, 7 (1986), p. 195.

[75] Gudjonsson, ibid.

[76] Gudjonsson, 'Compliance in an interrogative situation: a new scale', *Personality and Individual Differences*, 10 (1989), p. 535.

passive recipients of suggestive influences from others – they are constantly in a *dynamic* relationship with their social and physical environments.'[77]

Suggestibility is increased in certain situations. The stressfulness of the police interrogation at the police station may increase it, depending on the coping strategy of the detainee. He or she may become resistant, but if not, then many other factors apart from a generally suggestible personality may operate. The effect of a leading question depends on whether the subject is uncertain what the true answer is. Suspicion of the interviewer makes the subject less suggestible, and so does anger. But if the interviewer is trusted, suggestibility increases.[78] Where there is a high level of suggestibility, even questions requiring only a Yes/No answer are dangerous since, when in doubt, some people have a tendency to give affirmative answers.[79]

To some extent the police use fear as an interrogation device, although Irving and McKenzie found since the 1984 Act a reduced tendency to display authority and use the custodial conditions themselves as a means to intimidate.[80] But CID officers privately admitted using fear as a tactic, and experienced officers 'are well aware of the power of suggestion'.[81] In 1979 Irving reported that about 12 per cent of detained suspects showed visible symptoms of fear such as trembling, sweating, hyperventilation or incoherence. However, in 1986 the number had increased to about 22 per cent; this proportion dropped in the 1987 study to 10 per cent.[82] The authors explain this by suggesting that the safeguards under the Act were becoming better understood and therefore suspects were more confident that they would not be abused after arrest. But they found in the 1986 study that a great deal of tension was caused by the requirement that a contemporaneous note be made of the interview (the police stations where the studies were carried out did not have tape-recording), in the interviewer as well as the interviewee, and this was partly cured by 1987, when interviewers had found ways to compile a note not involving conducting the whole interrogation at laborious dictation speed. There is no suggestion that the police observed by Irving and McKenzie were deliberately generating tension, particularly since it was their own frustration at the note-taking procedure which caused the atmosphere picked up by the suspect. And some degree of apprehension is inevit-

---

[77] Gudjonsson and Clark, 'Suggestibility in police interrogation: a social psychological model', *Social Behaviour*, 1 (1986), pp. 83, 86.

[78] Ibid.

[79] Gudjonsson, *Personality and Individual Differences* (1984).

[80] Irving and McKenzie, *Police Interrogation*, p. 176.

[81] Ibid., p. 169.

[82] Ibid., p. 167.

able in someone placed under arrest and held at the police station powerless to alter his or her situation. The symptoms of fear described indicate only the extreme cases where physical manifestations of near-panic were shown. The most frequently occurring false confessions are the coerced-compliant, where the admission is known to be untrue by the person making it, but who makes it for his or her own neo-pragmatic reasons. Without being made aware of the research in this area, courts are unlikely to be persuaded that a confession not induced by threats or promises, but uttered during the course of a properly conducted interview is not true.

The work of Gudjonsson and other psychologists shows that the most innocuous interrogation techniques could adversely affect the reliability of admissions so obtained. Yet it is conceded that the police must be able to utilize at least some pressure:[83]

> I think it is important to realize that unless there is some kind of perceived pressure or that people believe that the police have something on them in the majority of cases people would not confess; but clearly the greater the pressure that you place people under the greater the risk that some people falsely confess, particularly if you are dealing with vulnerable individuals. Some people cope very badly with pressure, so that if you put them under even more pressure they may agree with anything that you say. Other people you can place under a great deal of pressure and they would not confess to anything…
> I do believe that a certain amount of pressure is essential in police work.

It is clearly pointless, then, to argue for a change in police methods of interrogation. The danger already exists that police officers are abandoning vigorous or 'persuasive' interviewing, preferring to go through the motions rather than face criticism.[84] The answer to this dilemma depends on an increased willingness in the courts to hear expert evidence in relation to personalities not clearly identified as 'abnormal'. For example, Gudjonsson and Haward have shown how 'forensic stylistic techniques can be used to identify the true authorship of written confession statements when their authenticity is challenged'.[85] But the judicial reluctance to accept expert opinion without clear indication of mental illness[86] effectively turns judges themselves into experts on the subject since they ultimately decide whether or not the defendant has such an illness, and therefore whether expert

---

[83] Gudjonnson, *Medico-Legal Journal* (1989).
[84] Irving and McKenzie, *Police Interrogation*. But for resistant personalities such a style is necessary.
[85] Gudjonnson and Haward, 'Psychological analysis of confession statements', *Journal of the Forensic Science Society*, 23 (1983), p. 113.
[86] See chapter 4.

evidence is admissible. In the matter of mental handicap, Gudjonsson accuses lawyers of a tendency to depend heavily on certainties, such as the fact that an IQ of under 70 suggests a serious reliability problem. However, some judges will accept evidence of the relationship between low IQ and suggestibility. But lawyers tend to give up if told that the accused is average in any way.[87]

Another safeguard would be to introduce a requirement that confession evidence on its own may not provide sufficient evidence for a conviction, so that further evidence indicating guilt would be needed. For the 1984 Act is simply not designed to deal with the problem of self-induced unreliability. In *Fulling*[88] D was arrested on suspicion that she and her lover had invented a burglary in order to defraud her insurance company. She initially declined to answer police questions, but alleged that during breaks she fell into conversation with a woman named Christine, who had the cell next to hers. She claimed that a police officer then informed her that her lover for the previous three years had been having an affair with a woman who was being held in the cell next to D. She had in fact known that some time before there had been a relationship with a woman named Christine, but had been assured by her lover that it was over. Discovering that she had been deceived and that she had been placed next to her rival, she claimed, distressed her greatly and made her desperate to leave the police station. The defence argued that a confession obtained in that state of mind should be excluded from her trial. However, it was held in the Court of Appeal that the ground for exclusion put forward under section 76(2)(a) did not apply; the confession was not obtained by oppression, since that involves misconduct by police. Further, although section 76(2)(b) was not argued at trial, it would probably not have succeeded as the confession was most unlikely to have been rendered unreliable by D's discovery. Yet her evidence was that she was desperate not to go back to the cell, and the court seemed to overlook the fact that the police presumably told her about the affair in order to get an admission, and to get D to incriminate her lover. Section 78 was not referred to in the judgment.

In *Goldenberg*[89] a heroin addict alleged that his confession was given because he was suffering withdrawal symptoms. Here the Court of Appeal held that section 76(2)(b) requires the unreliability to be a result of something *said or done*, and by someone other than the suspect. Thus the confession cannot be excluded under section 76 even if the suspect has

---

[87] Gudjonsson, *Medico-Legal Journal* (1989); cf. *Masih* [1986] Crim LR 395 where an IQ of 72 was treated as 'normal' by the Court of Appeal.

[88] [1987] 2 All ER 65.

[89] [1988] Crim LR 678.

inadvertently hurt him- or herself at the police station, or is feeling ill, or has an embarrassing digestive problem. If such a confession is to be excluded, that must be done under section 78, which was not referred to in this case, and which has two disadvantages for the defence. First, the advantage of the burden of proof being placed on the prosecution, as in section 76, is lost. Second, the matter turns on the exercise of discretion by a particular trial judge, which takes us back to the difficulty of convincing judges that stress combined with a compliant or suggestible personality could result in a confession so unreliable that fairness demands it be not admitted.

There is little guidance as to how the courts will exercise their discretion in cases of self-induced unreliability. In the common law cases before the 1984 Act courts have considered the question of the accused's own mental state. In *Isequilla*[90] the Court of Appeal held that although the accused at the time he made admissions was so hysterical that he was frothing at the mouth, there was no reason to exclude them. The court went on to say, however, that there could be cases where the accused's mental state at the time he confessed was such that the confession should be excluded, but described them as 'extreme', for example 'where the man is a mental defective'. In *DPP v Ping Lin*[91] the Privy Council commented on the decision in *Isequilla* in these terms: 'A confession which is simply blurted out by a criminal caught in *flagrante delicto* is not the sort of thing to which [the exclusionary principle at common law] applies; if it were, anyone caught red-handed who admits "it's a fair cop" could probably plead self-induced fear and have his remark excluded.'

There are, however, cases where unreliable confessions have been excluded, following *Isequilla*, such as *Davis*[92], where expert evidence at the *voir dire* suggested that D at the time of his questioning was still under the influence of the drug Pethidin. In *Kilner*[93] D had a low IQ, epilepsy and became hysterical when he found himself in difficulties. Although there had been no misconduct by the police, the confession was not admitted at trial. There may be instances of similarly unreliable confessions being excluded expressly on the grounds that to admit them would render the trial unfair under section 78 of the 1984 Act. However, the language in *Isequilla* and the willingness of the Court of Appeal to uphold the convictions in *Fulling* and *Goldenberg* suggest that the judicial perception of unreliability is a very limited one. Using section 78 rather than section 76 leaves everything to the inevitably uncertain exercise of judicial discretion, which would be satisfac-

---

[90] [1975] 1 WLR 716.
[91] [1976] AC 574, p. 602, *per* Lord Hailsham.
[92] [1979] Crim LR 167.
[93] [1976] Crim LR 740.

tory if all judges gave the available scientific research the respect it deserves.

The thrust of the Working Paper of the Law Commission[94] is to abolish the existing rules on corroboration rather than to add to them. The Commissioners' attention appears to be directed mainly to the question whether there should be a broad requirement to warn the jury in some cases, not the question whether in some cases convictions should be ruled out where the prosecution evidence is from only one source. Discussion of confession evidence is specifically ruled out,[95] apparently because the question of the reliability of such evidence may be discussed elsewhere.[96] However, the Commission acknowledges that in Scotland there is a general requirement for evidence in support in criminal cases, and that in all but a few United States jurisdictions an extra-judicial confession by the defendant without corroboration is not considered sufficient to sustain a conviction. It is submitted that the doubtful reliability of all confession evidence demands a requirement of evidence in support, or a mandatory warning at least.

---

[94] Law Commission, *Corroboration of Evidence in Criminal Trials*, Working Paper No. 115 (1990).

[95] Ibid., para. 1.3.

[96] The reliability of convictions based entirely on confession evidence is, at the time of writing, being considered by the Royal Commission on Criminal Justice (chairman Lord Runciman). They will consider the findings of May J's *Inquiry into the Circumstances Surrounding the Convictions Arising out of a Bomb Attack in Guildford and Woolwich in 1974.*

7

Hearsay[1]

There is no advocate who has not experienced countless cases where a story that seemed consistent and watertight down on paper was destroyed by a proper and skilful cross-examination. Trials conducted on paper, on the whole, represent second-rate justice.

Lord Irvine of Lairg, *Hansard* (House of Lords Debates)

HEARSAY AND THE ADVERSARIAL TRIAL

Judicial loyalty to the principle of orality has undermined successive legislative attempts to extend the range and application of exceptions to the hearsay rule. Statutes which were intended to facilitate the reception of hearsay in civil cases have not had the desired effect:

> The liberalizing aim of the Evidence Act 1938 was frustrated by restrictive interpretation, and led to dissatisfaction eventually culminating in the passage of the 1968 [Civil Evidence] Act. The approach now adopted by judges at first instance seems to be in danger of duplicating that entire saga, though fortunately it is not yet too late for the Court of Appeal to reaffirm the intention of the legislature by adopting a broader approach to the meaning of 'record' in s. 4.[2]

In the House of Lords debates on the Criminal Justice Bill, the government found that opposition lawyers would not easily countenance major

---

[1] Some passages in this chapter were first published as part of an article, 'Documentary hearsay: refuge for the vulnerable witness?' [1989] Crim LR 629, reproduced here with kind permission of Sweet and Maxwell.

[2] C. Tapper and R. Cross, *Evidence*, 7th edn (Butterworths, London, 1990), p. 555.

departures[3] from traditional grounds for exclusion: 'To mitigate the rule against hearsay and permit documentary hearsay is sensible. To destroy the rule altogether is to damage irretrievably the fairness of the criminal trial.'[4] The Law Reform Advisory Committee for Northern Ireland, on the other hand, considered all possible improvements to the present unsatisfactory legislation governing the admissibility of hearsay evidence in civil trials in the province, and provisionally concluded that the most sensible course would be to abandon the rule except for the safeguard that hearsay evidence should not normally be admissible in civil proceedings where it is reasonable and practical for the maker of the relevant statement to be called as a witness.[5] The qualification is thought necessary to reflect the right of a party to insist on the production of the best reasonably available evidence against him or her.[6]

At first sight, it seems curious that lawyers are so much more ready to dispense with orality requirements in civil than in criminal trials. The issues are not inevitably so very different from those dealt with in criminal cases. However, we have already seen throughout this book that, although criminal trials venture some way from adversarial theory in the matters of independence of parties and equality of risk, they remained, until recently, far more committed to adversarial procedures than civil trials. Civil trials adhere more closely to the adversarial model in terms of the equal position of the litigants, but have developed a more informal and flexible approach to the procedures, presumbly because the judge sits alone. However, although there are signs of new attitudes in the civil sphere, they are not universally held. Some statutory reforms have been narrowly interpreted in reported decisions, despite the absence of a jury.[7] On the other hand, recent reforms concerning documentary hearsay allow criminal courts to admit varieties of evidence not covered in civil cases.

The evolution of the hearsay rule appears to be historically tied to that of jury trial; although Morgan argues[8] that it is a consequence of the trial structure in an adversarial system, so that it is the adversary, rather than the jury,

---

[3] Although less exception was taken to the provisions concerning business documents than to those regarding first-hand hearsay documents.

[4] Lord Hutchinson of Lullington, HL Deb., Vol. 489, col. 74 (20 October 1987).

[5] Law Reform Advisory Committee for Northern Ireland, *Hearsay Evidence in Civil Proceedings*, Discussion Paper No. 1 (1990), para. 5.38.

[6] If enacted, Northern Ireland civil courts would in this respect resemble many Continental jurisdictions, which have an equivalent of the 'best evidence' rule.

[7] Many judges sitting alone in civil cases tend to disregard the hearsay rule, preferring to see or hear all the evidence and then to rely on their own judgment.

[8] E. M. Morgan, *Some Problems of Proof Under the Anglo-American System of Litigation* (University of North Carolina, New York, 1956).

who is protected from hearsay evidence because of the importance of cross-examination. His conclusion is doubted by Baker,[9] who amasses an impressive body of evidence to show that, historically at any rate, the origin of the rule is clearly linked to the development of trial by jury. In the leading cases, judges tend to explain the reasons for the rule in terms of the potential effect that hearsay evidence could have on the jury. A modern judicial statement to the same effect can be found in the judgment of Lord Bridge in *Blastland*:[10]

> The rationale of excluding [hearsay] as inadmissible, rooted as it is in the system of trial by jury, is a recognition of the great difficulty, even more acute for a jury than for a trained judicial mind, of assessing what, if any, weight can properly be given to a statement by a person whom the jury may not have seen or heard and which has not been subject to any test of reliability by cross-examination...As Lord Normand put it,[11]...'The rule against admission of hearsay evidence is fundamental. It is not the best evidence and it is not delivered on oath. The truthfulness and accuracy of the person whose words are spoken to by another witness cannot be tested by cross-examination and the light which his demeanour would throw on his testimony is lost.'

The alleged superiority of oral testimony is not universally accepted. Like historians, Continental jurisdictions prefer documentary sources. A French treatise speaks of 'the primacy of written proof and the mistrust which is prima facie inspired by oral testimony', which is seen as highly subjective.[12] Of the tradition of orality, the Roskill Report observed:[13]

> Documents are treated by the law with suspicion, and their importance tends to be undervalued...These rules were all clearly designed for an era when most of the population could be presumed to be illiterate. While their strict application has caused few difficulties in the general run of criminal cases, they seem increasingly inappropriate and burdensome in cases of fraud and dishonesty which themselves arise from business transactions which are the subject of written records.

Honoré has shown that neither kind of evidence is inherently more reliable than the other, although oral testimony has a tactical advantage. It is also

[9] R. W. Baker, *The Hearsay Rule* (Pitman, London, 1950).

[10] [1985] 2 All ER 1095, 1099.

[11] In *Teper v R* [1952] 2 All ER 447, 449.

[12] Dalloz, *Encyclopédie de Droit Civil su preuve*, cited Honoré, 'The primacy of oral evidence', in *Crime, Proof and Punishment: Essays in Memory of Sir Rupert Cross*, ed. C. Tapper (Butterworths, London, 1981).

[13] *Report of the Fraud Trials Committee* (HMSO, 1986), paras. 5.4–5.5.

necessary to establish the authenticity of documentary evidence.[14] There certainly are cases where the available documents are more reliable than oral testimony; where complicated transactions are involved, contemporaneous records must be more worthy of trust than what the persons involved may have to say in court, particularly if the events took place years before. This problem is typically dealt with by allowing the witness to use the document to 'refresh his memory',[15] and if he deviates from the facts set out in his own record, the court then faces the problem that it would rather rely on the document than what the witness says on oath.

Parliament has recognized that the major dangers of error in transmission and of concoction[16] are not present in all hearsay. In *Myers v DPP*[17] mundane records of car engine and chassis numbers compiled by the manufacturer were excluded although 'if the workmen...had testified, there would have been nothing to gain from cross-examining them; it would have established what was already known; that they had no incentive to make false records, and that the chance of their having made more than the odd error was remote'.[18] This kind of problem led to the introduction of the Criminal Evidence Act 1965, the beginning of a chain of attempts to devise a workable definition of admissible documentary hearsay. In those cases where there is a genuine danger of unreliability, why should it be assumed that a jury are constitutionally unable to grasp this fact and ascribe less weight to the evidence? They are expected to recognize the varying weights of the different sections of a statement on arrest which is partly exculpatory and partly incriminating.[19]

A significant factor in our traditional devotion to the hearsay rule lies in our obsession with cross-examination. Yet it is not clear why it is impossible to get across by other means that the absent witness may have had motives for lying or be generally unreliable. The traditional view is that cross-examination is an instrument which uncovers the truth; in *O'Loughlin and McLaughlin*[20] Kenneth Jones J refused to admit the documentary statement of an absent prosecution witness because the 'jury would have had no opportunity to judge the way in which [the witness] stood up to that testing

---

[14] Honoré, in Tapper (ed.), pp. 191–2.

[15] A procedure recommended by Lord Pearce in *Myers v DPP* [1965] AC 1001, 1035.

[16] For the rationale of the rule in detail, see Tapper and Cross, Evidence, p. 515.

[17] [1965] AC 1001.

[18] Birch, 'the Criminal Justice Act: documentary evidence' [1989] Crim LR 15, 18.

[19] *Storey* (1968) 52 Cr App R 334; *Pearce* (1979) 69 Cr App R 365; *Duncan* (1981) 73 Cr App R 359; *Sharp* [1988] 1 All ER 65. See below.

[20] [1988] 3 All ER 431.

process'. Another view is that cross-examination merely demonstrates 'the power of a skilful cross-examiner to make an honest witness appear at best confused and at worst a liar'.[21] The probability is that lawyers overestimate the unique potential of cross-examination to establish the truth.[22] Its importance in fact lies in the adversarial structure of the trial; counsel has such ability to limit what information is given in evidence-in-chief[23] through tight control of the witness's testimony that a balanced picture can emerge only where opponents can demand elaboration or explanation where appropriate. In any case, the adversaries are not allowed to pursue the objective truth. The scope of the questions permissible in cross-examination is tied to the specific case upon which a party relies. Cross-examination is issue-related, concerned with the reality of events only if they happen to coincide with the case pleaded. And, curiously, the logic of the hearsay rule persists even where the maker of the statement *is* in court and available for cross-examination; although the Civil Evidence Act 1968 in some cases allows the out-of-court statements of witnesses to be adduced,[24] in criminal trials they may not serve as evidence of the facts stated unless they fall into one of the exceptions.[25] At best, therefore, such statements may be admissible to prove consistency[26] or inconsistency, with a direction to the jury that the statement may not be treated as evidence of the facts contained in it.[27] Yet where an expert witness bases his or her conclusions on hearsay such as published research, the courts are content to permit reference to it[28] since there is at least *a* witness who may be cross-examined on its reliability or applicability. Yet this witness is not the maker of the statement, had no part in the research, and therefore has no direct knowledge of the manner of its execution.

The attempts by courts and legislature to devise exceptions which permit the reliable varieties of hearsay to be admitted have led to contradictory

---

[21] Birch, [1989] Crim LR 15, 17.

[22] See chapter 1.

[23] Chapter 1.

[24] Under s. 2; leave of the judge is required, and the other party must be notified to prevent his or her being taken by surprise.

[25] E.g. confessions by accused persons, or statements forming part of the *res gestae*.

[26] If within one of the exceptions to the general rule against admitting self-serving statements.

[27] *Golder* [1960] 3 All ER 457.

[28] *H v Schering Chemicals* [1983] 1 All ER 849; *Abadom* [1983] 1 All ER 364. The requirement from these cases that the expert witness make it clear when he or she relies on the work of others is frequently forgotten in practice; L. R. Haward, *Forensic Psychology* (Batsford, London, 1981), p. 185.

results; for example, the principle of the *res gestae* exception appears to be that the utterance, if spontaneous, is unlikely to be deliberately misleading. The danger of concoction remains if the maker of the statement has a long time to think about it, unless the event is of such overwhelming importance to him or her that his or her reaction is likely to be as genuine as one immediately contemporaneous with the event.[29] Some cases even refer to the absence of motive for concoction and therefore admitted the evidence,[30] but there are many cases where this reasoning has not been employed.[31] Advertence to the real likelihood of concoction would have the unsettling consequence of undermining the entire traditional rationale of the hearsay rule itself, and applying instead the dictates of common sense; this is not at present a widespread approach in decided cases. In any case, even where there is no realistic danger of fabrication, the dangers of uncertainty and misreporting remain. Ashworth and Pattenden[32] point out that the recent English cases on *res gestae* concern a participant in the event, so that guidance in relation to the evidence of spectators is in short supply. Given the finding that stress has a negative effect on human powers of description and recall,[33] the emphasis on spontaneity here may be misplaced.

Reliability appears to be the overriding concern of the exception to the rule which holds that declarations in the course of duty are admissible at common law. But this applies, for some reason, only where the declarant is dead.[34] This requirement forced the House of Lords in *Myers v DPP* to exclude perfectly reliable records kept by car manufacturers because the workmen who made them were still alive,[35] although such workmen, even if they could be identified, could not realistically be expected to recall the numbers of the engines they had made. Some common law exceptions are frankly risible, such as the dying declaration of the murder victim:

[29] *Andrews* [1987] 1 All ER 513.
[30] *Nye and Loan* (1977) 66 Cr App R 252.
[31] E.g. *Gibson* (1887) 18 QBD 537; *Sparks* [1964] AC 964; *Bedingfield* (1879) 14 Cox CC 341.
[32] Ashworth and Pattenden, 'Reliability, hearsay and the criminal trial' (1986) 102 LQR 292.
[33] B. R. Clifford and R. Bull, *Psychology of Person Identification* (Routledge & Kegan Paul, London, 1988); J. Shepherd, J. Ellis and G. Davies, *Identification Evidence: A Psychological Evaluation* (Aberdeen University Press, 1982).
[34] *Price v Torrington* (1703) 90 ER 1065.
[35] No relevant statutory exception existed at the time, and the House of Lords, while recognizing the anomaly, refused to extend the common law exception to records created by witnesses still alive, which would be tantamount to inventing a new one: [1965] AC 1001, 1027–8, *per* Lord Morris.

The general principle on which the species of evidence is admitted is, that they are declarations made in extremity, when the party is at the point of death, and when every hope of this world is gone; when every motive for falsehood is silenced, and the mind is induced by the most powerful considerations to speak the truth; a situation so solemn and awful is considered by law as creating an obligation equal to that which is imposed by a positive oath administered in a court of justice.[36]

Why this overwhelming pressure to tell the truth before departing this life applies only to people who are dying of murderous wounds, and allows their evidence only in prosecutions for homicide, is not clear.[37] At any rate, this reasoning demands proof that the deceased spoke in 'the settled, hopeless, expectation of death'.[38] Although the language in these cases is archaic, modern cynicism has not prevented the exception being employed today; there have been instances recently of victims who clearly would not live long enough to give evidence being asked to name the culprit in written statements in which they formally acknowledge that their medical advisers have assured them that there is no prospect whatever of recovery.

The response of the courts to being strait-jacketed in the hearsay rule, whose ancillary collection of exceptions does not mean that what is admitted 'is invariably reliable, or that what is left out is of no worth'[39] is, in some cases, to resort to bare-faced cheating to allow in evidence information which is thought to be valuable. Birch calls the device of defining the disputed evidence as non-hearsay in order to avoid losing it altogether a 'hearsay-fiddle'. The result is a string of incompatible decisions, an unidentifiable concept, and despair among lawyers who know the rule is immune to mastery.

THE 'CRAZY QUILT'[40]

Definition of hearsay

One of the areas where the borderline between hearsay and non-hearsay evidence is at its most elusive, and where it may be thought a good deal of

---

[36] *Woodcock* (1789), 1 Leach 500, *per* Eyre CB.
[37] Cf. A. Zuckerman, *The Principles of Criminal Evidence* (OUP, Oxford, 1989), pp. 203–4.
[38] *Peel* (1860) 2 F & F 21.
[39] Birch, 'Hearsay-logic and hearsay-fiddles: *Blastland* revisited', in *Criminal Law: Essays in Honour of J. C. Smith*, ed. P. Smith (Butterworths, London, 1987), p. 24.
[40] The hearsay rule and its exceptions have been likened to 'a crazy quilt made of

'hearsay-fiddling' goes on, concerns pictorial or graphic records. Mechanical print-outs and reproduction are of vital importance to criminal and civil courts, particularly as the advance of technology presents more and better scientific evidence which is generally reliable and convincing. Yet this is one of the worst minefields set up by hearsay adherents. Photographs are treated as original evidence and not hearsay. Yet it could be argued that a photograph of the murder weapon is not logically in the same category as the weapon itself. There are more possibilities for mistake or fabrication where a representation by mechanical device (here in the control of an individual) is allowed to replace the physical presence of the item itself. A picture of the scene of the crime cannot provide precisely the information available to the senses, which is why courts will occasionally adjourn to the *locus in quo*. But to treat photographs as hearsay would make trials unnecessarily elaborate, given that these difficulties in reality go to weight, and do not justify the exclusion of the evidence. However, the argument that the issue of reliability should go only to weight may equally be applied to all, or certainly some, categories of hearsay evidence which are currently inadmissible.

Given the starting point that photographs are not hearsay, the decision in *The Statue of Liberty*[41] provides a useful but inexplicably neglected[42] precedent on mechanically produced evidence. Two vessels collided in the Thames. The plaintiffs were allowed to use as evidence of the position of the vessels a film from a shore radar station showing radar echoes. Sir Jocelyn Simon placed such film in the same category as photographs. If someone had been reading a barometer, to make a judgment on weather conditions, he or she would be able to give evidence in court of those weather conditions, relying on the reading he or she took from the machine. Logically, there is no difference between that and using any record made by the machine itself in response to atmospheric pressure. The same reasoning applied in *Taylor v Chief Constable of Cheshire*;[43] a police videotape showing the accused in the act of stealing was erased in error, but police witnesses who had seen it and recognized the accused gave evidence describing the event and identifying D. It was held in the Divisional Court that their evidence did not involve hear-

patches cut from a group of paintings by cubists, futurists and surrealists': Morgan and Maguire, 'Looking backward and forward at evidence' (1937) 50 Harv LR 909; Birch, ibid., n. 6, however, prefers the analogy of the 'threshing room, in which some ancient flails are left propped up against the walls, their usefulness all but over, and shiny new machinery can be seen which has so many working parts that the major interest is to see which breaks down first'.
[41] [1968] 1 WLR 739.
[42] See below, cases concerning computer print-outs.
[43] [1986] 1 WLR 1479.

say, since a film of the crime is real evidence of it, and the officers were in the same position as eyewitnesses who see a crime as it occurs. Although the court was not in a position to assess the quality of the tape and therefore the margin for error the fact that it had to rely on the police officers to describe the clarity of the pictures went only to weight. But in *Cook*[44] the Court of Appeal resorted to a blatant 'hearsay-fiddle'. A photofit picture was compiled from the description of her attacker by the victim of robbery and indecent assault. The trial judge admitted the picture into evidence at the trial. The defence argued on appeal that it was inadmissible as hearsay, but the Court of Appeal disagreed, on the analogy with photographic evidence:[45]

> We regard the production of the sketch or photofit by a police officer making a graphic representation of a witness's memory as another form of the camera at work, albeit imperfectly and not produced contemporaneously with the material incident but soon or fairly soon afterwards...Seeing that we do not regard the photofit picture as a statement at all it cannot come within the description of an earlier consistent statement.

The analogy with photographic evidence, which is itself not without hearsay taint, is entirely unconvincing. The margin for error, suggestion and mis-understanding is almost endless. The notion that a police sketch or other realization of a description should serve as evidence of identification not only flouts the hearsay rule, but renders otiose the requirements in the Police and Criminal Evidence Act for carefully organized identification evidence. For example, in *Constantinou*[46] a photofit was made up from witness M's re-collection of an armed robbery. M's subsequent identification of D in a confrontation was excluded from the trial leaving no identification evidence against D apart from the photofit. Yet the picture was admitted in evidence against him and a conviction based almost entirely on it was upheld on appeal. This case involved a side-step not only of the hearsay rule but of the requirements in the 1984 Act that identification evidence should be of the most reliable kind. There is little point in the legislature stipulating the conditions in which identification parades should be held if identification can be achieved simply by presenting a photofit compiled out of court through the efforts of the eyewitness and a police officer.

The danger of distortion was regarded as significant in *Quinn and Bloom*.[47] The offence charged was keeping a disorderly house. Three striptease artistes

[44] [1987] 1 All ER 1049.
[45] Ibid., p. 1054, *per* Watkins LJ.
[46] [1989] Crim LR 571.
[47] [1962] 2 QB 245.

claimed that the act which they had been performing when police officers arrived had not been obscene, and offered in evidence a videotape in which they reconstructed their performances. The tape was held to be inadmissible, since it would be impossible for them precisely to duplicate all movements and gestures, especially as a snake was involved. It was conceded that during their oral testimony the witnesses could to some extent show by action or mime while in the witness-box roughly what they had been doing. The objection to the film centred on the risk that a full-scale re-enactment could be highly misleading, because of the scope for differences from the original. Re-enactments on videotape have been allowed in other cases, however, where the film fell into a known hearsay exception, or the danger of deviation from the event was not significant. In *Li Shu-Ling v R*[48] D had confessed to murder and agreed to participate in a filmed reconstruction of the event. It was hearsay, but fell within the admissions exception to the rule. His lack of acting ability did not affect the admissibility of the evidence, according to the Privy Council, but arguably went to weight. In *Thomas*[49] the road on which a chase involving D and a police car took place at night was filmed on a different occasion from a car driven by the same officers. For technical reasons this had to be done in daylight, but the trial judge held that the video was admissible at D's trial for reckless driving, because it enabled the officers giving evidence to describe the scene by reference to it. They would have been able to use a photograph for the same purpose.

Some computer print-outs are treated as real evidence, as in *Castle v Cross*[50] where the print-out from an intoximeter was held not to be hearsay. Yet in *Pettigrew*[51] the record of banknote numbers recorded by the Bank of England computer was treated as hearsay, even though no human had knowledge of the numbers since the machine itself sorted good and bad notes. The absence of an individual with personal knowledge prevented the documentary record from being admissible under statute,[52] but apparently did not suggest to the Court of Appeal that this was merely a mechanical reaction to physical stimuli as in *The Statue of Liberty*; in other words, that no statement had been made. There is certainly a closer analogy to a photograph in this case than there was in *Cook*. In *Wood*[53] the Court of Appeal treated as real evidence a print-out from a computer which scientists had used solely as a calculator. It had merely rearranged information to which

[48] [1988] 3 All ER 138.
[49] [1986] Crim LR 682.
[50] [1985] 1 All ER 87.
[51] (1980) 71 Cr App R 39.
[52] See below.
[53] [1982] Crim LR 667.

they could testify. In *Burke*[54] the pendulum inexplicably flew back in the other direction. A computer print-out showed the date and time of Vodaphone calls which connected D with his alleged co-conspirator. This was held to be a hearsay statement, which therefore must fall within a statutory exception in order to be admitted in evidence.

Rice[55] is a well-known case where the Court of Appeal was faced with two apparently insoluble problems. The first is that it is impossible to formulate a coherent distinction between hearsay and real evidence. The second is that strict application of the hearsay rule would make it impossible to identify valuable evidence as belonging to a particular person. The issue here was whether a used airline ticket, handed in after a flight and bearing the names of D and his co-accused, could be admitted into evidence. If admissible, it would serve as circumstantial evidence of their presence on the flight. The Court of Appeal treated it as a piece of real evidence. To avoid the rigours of the hearsay rule, such evidence must not be allowed to 'speak its contents', and so is not evidence of any statement such as 'my bearer is X' or 'I was issued to Y'; hence it is not evidence of to whom the ticket was issued, only that an air ticket which has been used on a flight and which has a name on it has more likely than not been used by a man of that name. The decision was followed in *Lydon (Sean)*[56] where a gun was found a mile from a post office which had been robbed. It may have been the one carried by one of the robbers. Near it were two pieces of paper, on which were written, 'Sean Rules' and 'Sean 85'. The trial judge allowed the prosecution to adduce these papers in evidence. The relevance of the writing was merely to indicate a relationship with someone called Sean.

These cases sit uneasily with decisions such as *Patel v Customs Comptroller*,[57] where the Privy Council refused to treat bags of coriander seed marked 'Morocco' as original evidence that they had come from Morocco. To admit the evidence would be to rely on a statement as to origin by some unidentified person. And if a ticket with a name on it is original evidence, why is not a record of car chassis numbers kept by the manufacturer an indication of the identity or description of those cars? In the Court of Appeal in *Myers*, Widgery J said that in *Rice* a foundation of evidence to show Rice was on the plane had already been laid, and, given that the carrier had a system for the retention and filing of used tickets, it seemed wholly artificial to deprive the jury of the assistance which a reference to the file of used

[54] [1990] Crim LR 401.
[55] [1963] 1 QB 857.
[56] [1987] Crim LR 407.
[57] [1966] AC 356.

tickets might give.[58] He argued that here the foundation for the identification of a stolen car had been laid by the evidence of its owner, and it would be artificial to exclude either party from consulting manufacturers' records 'and showing whether those records do or do not confirm the identification'.[59] He concluded that the admission of such evidence 'does not infringe the hearsay rule because its probative value does not depend upon the credit of an unidentified person but rather on the circumstances in which the record is maintained'. In the House of Lords, Lord Reid agreed that the proposition was undeniable as a matter of common sense, but the value of the evidence in its context did not alter the fact that it was hearsay.[60]

Following *Rice*, it would appear not impossible to argue that the documents in *Myers* were in fact real evidence of the symbols which appeared on a car engine rather than a statement of fact made by a person. The document would merely indicate that it was more likely than not to have been manufactured at the time. Yet the House of Lords regarded the engine number records as hearsay, and in *McLean*[61] the same view was taken by the Court of Appeal of a car registration number. The victim of a robbery dictated a car registration number to B, who wrote it down. The victim did not check the note, and so was not allowed to refresh his memory with it, and the writer could not give evidence of the number as he had no direct knowledge of it, and to allow him to testify to the number, or to use the note itself as evidence, would be hearsay.[62] There is still no statutory exception which would allow such a document to be adduced as hearsay evidence, although the more flexible version of *res gestae* offered by the House of Lords in *Andrews*[63] may provide a justification for admitting such obviously valuable evidence. In *Todd*[64] the problem was avoided by a 'hearsay-fiddle'. The defence disputed the admissibility of a document recording questions and answers alleged to have been made by D. The admissions were argued to be inadmissible under the Judges' Rules, which applied at the time. The prosecution put the document in evidence and sought to make it an exhibit. The Court of Appeal did not quarrel with the fact that the document had been admitted in evidence, saying that although it was not an *aide-mémoire* or a confession statement, it was 'something in between', which the jury could look at to decide whether or not to accept the police evidence.

[58] [1965] AC 1001, 1008.
[59] Ibid.
[60] Ibid., p. 1023.
[61] (1968) 52 Cr App R 80.
[62] Cf. *Fenlon* (1980) 71 Cr App R 307.
[63] [1987] 1 All ER 513.
[64] [1981] Crim LR 621.

Operation of the rule

The legal position where information is relayed through a disinterested inter-
mediary, whose task is to translate or transpose it, is far from clear. In
Attard,[65] an interpreter attended a police station interview, at which, it was
alleged, D confessed. It was held that only the interpreter could give
evidence of the confession as the police officer did not have direct knowledge
of it. This means that interpreters must be available for the trial as well as
the interrogation, and should either take notes themselves, or check the
police record at the time, so that they may refresh their memories when
giving evidence. An alternative approach would be to adopt an amanuensis
argument, treating an interpreter as no more than a mechanical device which
alters the form, but not the content, of the information which passes through
him or her. This was the reasoning of the Australian High Court in *Gaio v
R*;[66] again, a confession was obtained by police through an interpreter.
The interpreter gave evidence that he had truly and accurately translated the
questions and answers. The police officer then gave evidence of the
interrogation in which D had admitted killing his wife. It was held that there
was only one transaction involved in passing the information to the questioner. As long as the interpreter translates faithfully he is not a party to
the conversation, merely a mouthpiece. However, there must therefore be
evidence as to the accuracy of the translation. In *Taylor v Taylor*[67] the Court
of Appeal considered the stenographer's record of evidence given in court to
amount to a first-hand hearsay document created by the witness, the stenographer's role being only mechanical. The assumption that an account written at dictation is a first-hand hearsay statement by the maker is reinforced
by the wording of section 23(3) of the Criminal Justice Act 1988.[68]

Another controversial effect of the hearsay rule is to prevent the admission
into evidence of confessions to crimes other than those made by the defendant.[69] Although the common law appears to regard some statements against
interest as inherently more reliable than other hearsay statements,[70] there
appears to be no available exception in English common law to accommodate

[65] (1958) 43 Cr App R 90.
[66] [1961] ALR 67.
[67] [1970] 1 WLR 1148.
[68] See below.
[69] *Turner* (1975) 61 Cr App R 67, 78.
[70] At least, admissions by parties and declarations by deceased persons against their
interest.

third-party confessions.[71] However, in an American case, *Chambers*,[72] the confession was said to fall within the common law exception of statements against interest, but since the declarant was neither dead nor a defendant in the case, the decision amounts to an extension of the hearsay exceptions which English courts will not follow.[73] Birch appears content with the effect of this decision, which allows the nature and reliability of the third-party confession to affect its weight, not its admissibility.[74] The court said: 'The testimony rejected by the trial court here bore persuasive assurances of trustworthiness and thus was well within the basic rationale of the exception for declarations against interest. This testimony was also critical to Chambers' defence.'

The risk of highly unreliable confessions being adduced by defendants as evidence of their innocence is quite substantial, however, especially in relation to widely publicized crimes. These are notorious for attracting an inevitable string of false confessions. For example, the Lindbergh kidnapping in the United States resulted in over 200 confessions. At present these confessions appear to present no great practical problem to the police, as the subject can usually be eliminated from the inquiry because of insufficient knowledge of details of the crime.[75] However, new problems could be created if the person who is ultimately tried for that offence is allowed to cloud the issue by producing one or more of these confessions in his or her defence. It is quite obvious that the adversarial trial is incapable of dealing satisfactorily with such evidence; its structure is inappropriate to assess the proper weight to be attached to a third-party confession. Discussion of the circumstances in which it was made, and the apparent degree of knowledge of detail shown by the party, are collateral issues with which the adversarial trial cannot and will not concern itself. We have seen the narrowness of adversarial reasoning taken to its limit in *Blastland*.[76] A more inquisitorial procedure, however, could deal with such confessions more easily; completely untrustworthy confessions could be weeded out at an early stage, without inconvenient insistence on oral evidence on the manner in which they were given.

The rationale of *Chambers* is that what an individual says against him- or herself may fairly be presumed to be true. This assumption affects the law of

[71] See Birch, in Smith (ed.).
[72] *Chambers v Mississippi* 410 US 284 (1973).
[73] *Myers* [1965] AC 1001.
[74] Birch, in Smith (ed.).
[75] Gudjonsson, 'The psychology of false confessions', *Medico-Legal Journal*, 57 (1989), p. 93; he suggests as possible motives for such confessions 'a morbid desire for notoriety', feelings of guilt, and inability to distinguish fact from fantasy.
[76] See chapter 2 and below.

evidence in relation to admissions by parties, and declarations against interest by deceased persons. There is no basis in fact for the assumption; on the contrary, there is good reason to assume that a number of self-incriminating statements are highly suspect. The work of psychologists on the pressure on suspects during interrogation together with the effect of individual personality responses suggests that such statements should be treated with great caution.[77] Nevertheless, this dubious premise is the basis for the admissibility of confession evidence in criminal cases. The result is that the confession of the defendant in a criminal case is evidence of his or her guilt. Once the law adopts that position, it finds itself unable to deal coherently with statements by accused persons which do not fall neatly into the category of confessions, if, at the same time, they do not amount to previous consistent statements by the accused. Self-justifying statements made on being first accused of the crime charged have been argued to be admissible for the defence if consistent with the accused's present testimony,[78] but in that case they go only to credibility. They would therefore appear to have no relevance at all if the accused chooses not to give evidence. However, the practice has developed among prosecutors of allowing the entire statement on arrest to be read out irrespective of contents, forcing courts to deal, first, with the problem of apparently irrelevant exculpatory statements in cases where the accused does not give evidence, and of statements which are 'mixed', in that they are partly incriminating and partly exculpatory. There is a question of the role of the latter element in cases where the accused does not give evidence.

In *Storey*[79] D was questioned about the presence of cannabis in her flat and claimed that a man had brought it there against her will. The Court of Appeal held that her statement was admissible to prove, not the facts stated, but her reaction when first taxed with incriminating facts. In *Pearce*[80] a shop manager within a market was questioned several times over four days. His statements at the end of this period therefore could only with difficulty be regarded as evidence of his reaction when first accused, and the trial judge excluded those parts of his statement which did not constitute admissions. The Court of Appeal took the view that the excised parts were admissible as evidence of his reaction, from *Storey*, and the length of the questioning period went only to weight – the longer the time gap, the less weight should be attached to a denial. How the jury are to apply this evidence of reaction if the defendant elects not to give evidence is not explained. Phipson concludes

---

[77] Gudjonsson, *Medico-Legal Journal* (1989), and chapter 6.
[78] Gooderson, 'Previous consistent statements' (1968) CLJ 64.
[79] (1968) 52 Cr App R 334.
[80] (1979) 69 Cr App R 365.

that the only possible use of it is the illegitimate one, namely, to conclude that it is true.[81] The court was in the difficulty that although hearsay denials should not in theory be admitted as evidence of innocence, it is patently unfair for the prosecution to be able to adduce the incriminating part of a mixed statement on its own. If the suspect says on arrest, 'I did hit him, but that was in self-defence', to allow the prosecution to rely on the admission, but edit out the exculpatory element, would be grossly misleading.[82] The exculpatory part of the statement must therefore be admitted, even in cases where there is no question of the accused's credibility because he declines to give evidence. This was the case in *Duncan*,[83] where the accused did not give evidence at his trial for murder. He had admitted the killing to police, but his statement to them contained some evidence of provocation. There were no witnesses to testify to provocation at the trial, and therefore the issue was raised, if at all, only in his out-of-court statement, which at best was hearsay and in fact was adduced by the prosecution. The Court of Appeal recognized that the whole statement on arrest is admissible, and, rather than have the judge mystify the jury with an explanation of the part which is admissible as evidence of the facts stated, the admission, and that which is only evidence of reaction, he should explain that the jury should consider the whole of the statement, but give the admission more weight than the rest. This approach received House of Lords approval in *Sharp*.[84] Unfortunately, that judgment confines itself to approval of the *Duncan* treatment of mixed statements and offers no opinion on related matters, for example whether, if the accused chooses not to give evidence, an entirely exculpatory statement must be read. The prosecution would not appear to be under any duty to bring out an entirely self-serving statement to the police, and to refuse to do so would force the defence, if it wishes to use it as a previous consistent statement, to call the accused as a witness.[85] Cases so far have been concerned only with the significance of such statements where they have in fact been read out,

---

[81] Phipson, *Evidence*, 14th edn (Sweet & Maxwell, London, 1990), para. 12.63.

[82] This argument, employed by the House of Lords in *Sharp* [1988] 1 All ER 65, 68, would not appear to impose upon the prosecution a duty to read a statement made on arrest which consists entirely of denials. The defence, however, would be entitled to treat it as a previous consistent statement, but only if the defendant gives evidence.

[83] [1981] 73 Cr App R 359:

[84] [1988] 1 All ER 65.

[85] A curious effect of this would be that in fact the defence could, and possibly would, be under an obligation to prove the previous consistent statement by calling the police officer to whom it was made – a prosecution witness.

and concluded that they are evidence of the reaction of the accused but not evidence of the facts stated.[86] Phipson has an answer for the extreme case:[87]

> While it is clear that statements by defendants which do not contain admissions are commonly admitted in evidence, it is equally clear that the defendant is not entitled to require the prosecution to produce, or to produce himself, a 'carefully prepared written statement' produced to the police with a view to it being made part of the prosecution evidence.[88]

A run-of-the-mill case, however, will involve a flat denial made to the arresting officer, and there seems no reason to assume the prosecution has a duty to present that as part of its case.

A major anomaly is that, from *Pearce*, an entirely exculpatory statement is not evidence of the facts stated, and therefore does not discharge the defence's evidential burden in relation to any defence apparently arising from it, for example a claim of alibi.[89] But if the self-serving element of a *mixed* statement contains the basis of a defence, that statement, which must be read out in its entirety, does raise any defence referred to in it, so that defence must be put to the jury.[90] Such a result is inevitable, once it is settled that the jury must be directed that the self-serving part of the statement may be treated as evidence of the fact stated, even though it has less weight than the admission. Nevertheless, it is curious that an accused may, through evidence which is technically hearsay and is adduced by the other side, raise a defence of which he or she provides no other evidence. The House of Lords attempted to restore the balance thus: 'There is [no]reason why... where appropriate, the judge should not comment in relation to the exculpatory remarks upon the election of the accused not to give evidence.'[91]

These decisions appear to indicate a certain judicial desperation. It is apparently impossible to follow in all cases the strict logic of the rigid divide between evidence which goes to credibility and that which goes to the issue – a distinction entirely jettisoned here. The logical course would be to omit the exculpatory part of a mixed statement unless it amounts to a previous consistent statement by a defendant who gives evidence, because the philo-

---

[86] E.g. *Donaldson* (1977) 64 Cr App R 59.
[87] Phipson, *Evidence*, para. 12.63.
[88] Ibid., citing *Pearce* (1979) 69 Cr App R 365.
[89] *Pearce*, ibid.; *Barbery* (1976) 62 Cr App R 248.
[90] *Duncan* (1981) 73 Cr App R 359; *Hamand* (1985) 82 Cr App R 65.
[91] *Duncan*, ibid., p. 365, *per* Lord Lane CJ, cited with approval in *Sharp* [1988] 1 All ER 65, 67, by Lord Havers.

sophy of the law of evidence is that it has no relevance. But the result, as seen above, would be unfair and misleading. An additional difficulty is to communicate the logic of the hearsay rule to the jury; Lord MacKay argued in *Sharp*[92] that the concepts put before a jury must be capable of reasonably straightforward expression and application. The rules on hearsay as evidence of fact, and consistent statements as evidence of witness credibility, are far too complicated for that. Lord MacKay went on to quote the Lord Justice-Clerk Thompson in *Gillespie v Macmillan*: 'If law were an exact science or even a department of logic, there might be something to be said [for the Crown's argument]...But law is a practical affair and has to approach its problems in a mundane common-sense way.'[93]

The fact that a rule designed to promote reliability and ensure that the jury are not misled can, in some contexts, have the opposite effect is recognized in this series of cases. It may be a matter of celebration that the English courts have in respect of 'mixed' statements chosen the paths of common sense and fairness. But they have, in the process, been forced to abandon without authority the normal operation of the exclusionary rule, which prevails in other contexts irrespective of common sense or fairness. And in the case of an entirely exculpatory statement the adherence to the hearsay rule achieves an odd result – that the statement is evidence of the accused's reaction, the relevance of which is left unidentified – and not of the facts stated.[94] These inconsistencies of approach are a reflection of the difficulties created in the law of evidence by the hearsay rule and its exceptions.[95]

Just as impenetrable is the rule that statements which are adduced only to show the state of mind of either the maker or the hearer appear to fall outside the hearsay rule: 'It is well established in English jurisprudence, in accordance with the dictates of common sense, that the words and acts of a person are admissible as evidence of his state of mind.'[96] The most well-known case on this subject is *Subramaniam v Public Prosecutor*.[97] Threats alleged to have been uttered to D were held by the Privy Council to be admissible to show their likely effect on him, relevant because his defence was duress. The fact that the statement was made was significant to show what D's state of mind was likely to have been, rather than to prove the

---

[92] *Sharp*, ibid., p. 66.
[93] (1957) JC 31, 40.
[94] See above.
[95] *Sharp* [1988] 1 All ER 65, 68, *per* Lord Havers.
[96] *Lloyd v Powell Duffryn Steam Coal Co Ltd* [1914] AC 733, 751, *per* Lord Moulton.
[97] [1956] 1 WLR 965.

truth of its contents. Until *Blastland*,[98] there was no direct authority to show that statements could be admitted to show the state of mind of the maker of the statement, but the House of Lords has now given official sanction to the popular assumption that they can. The issue was addressed to some extent in *Ratten*,[99] but the Privy Council was content to allow the evidence in as part of the *res gestae*, which meant that the question whether or not the words heard by the telephone operator were hearsay did not have to be finally resolved. Mrs Ratten died of a gunshot wound. D claimed that his gun had gone off by accident while he was cleaning it. He claimed that he had summoned an ambulance, and that his wife had made no telephone call herself. She was dead by 1.20 p.m., when the ambulance arrived. The operator's evidence was that at 1.15 p.m. a call had been made to the local exchange from D's home, and that she heard a hysterical and sobbing woman say, 'Get me the police please.' The Privy Council inclined to the view that this evidence probably did not infringe the hearsay rule because the significance of it was that the call was made. The nature of the call and the apparent distress of the caller were inconsistent with D's account of events. The counter-argument was that the words uttered were not themselves necessary to prove either that the call was made or that the caller appeared distressed. Admitting evidence of the contents of the call allowed in an implied assertion that someone in the house (here D) was doing something unlawful and frightening, and therefore the operator was effectively testifying to a fact of which she had no direct knowledge.

It is frequently difficult, as in *Ratten*, to be clear about whether or not a statement is admitted to show that it was made, the relevance being that it shows the state of mind of the maker or the person who heard it, or whether its true significance lies in its contents. The danger is that an express or implied assertion will lie behind what is described as non-hearsay evidence. A case which can be criticized on that ground is *Wallwork*,[100] where a five-year-old girl was regarded as too young[101] to give evidence against her father on a charge of incest. The Court of Criminal Appeal held that although the child's grandmother should not have been allowed to give evidence of the particulars of a complaint made at the time by the child to her, since there was no question of the child's consistency, there 'would have been no objection to the grandmother saying "the little girl made a complaint to me"'. But if the statement is not admissible as evidence of either the facts complained of or the consistency of the complainant, it appears that its only function is to

[98] [1985] 2 All ER 1095.
[99] [1972] AC 378.
[100] (1958) 42 Cr App R 153.
[101] Now see chapter 4.

create prejudice.[102] Nevertheless, this approach is echoed in *R v Waltham Forest Justices ex parte B*;[103] complaints made by children to a social worker, child psychiatrist and guardian *ad litem* were admitted in evidence before magistrates despite the objections of the parents. The magistrates stated that they did not rely on the substance of the complaints as to their truth or otherwise, but they noted the complaints. Sir Stephen Brown P observed that in many child abuse cases the children's conduct is relevant, and that includes things they say to persons whose training puts them on inquiry when they hear them. But it is difficult to see why it is relevant that these agencies were put on inquiry; if evidence of a complaint of abuse is admitted and not used as evidence of consistency because the child is not a witness, there arises a strong suspicion that it is being used as evidence of its truth.

It may be possible to quote a child's out-of-court remarks, or describe the child's behaviour, to show a level of sexual awareness which suggests abuse by an adult. A commonly used term is 'inappropriate knowledge'; when a child is very young, abuse is the most likely explanation of highly sexual behaviour, whereas an older child might draw information from various sources. It is unlikely that this non-hearsay evidence will incriminate anyone, as its significance should be limited to the issue of whether or not abuse has occurred.[104] If the child's statement refers to facts in issue, the court should not, as in *Waltham Forest JJ*, allow it to be referred to in full because of the danger that the tribunal of fact will rely on the truth of its contents. In *Ames*[105] D's wife apparently told a neighbour that she was afraid that D was planning to cut her throat with a razor. She in fact died as a result of her throat being cut, and D was told of his wife's statement by the police. He then temporarily resiled from his story that she had committed suicide by cutting her own throat. But the danger of the jury relying on the contents of her statement was regarded as so great that the judge allowed the police witness only to say that as a result of a conversation reported to D, he confessed.

In other contexts the courts have created some unnecessary confusion on the proof of knowledge and the hearsay rule. In *Roberts*[106] the defence was

---

[102] Cf. Cross, 'Complaints of sexual offences' (1958) 74 LQR 352; A. Keane, *Modern Law of Evidence* (Butterworths, London/Edinburgh, 1989), p. 107. Cases to the opposite effect include *Guttridge* (1840) 9 Car & P 471; *Burke* (1912) 47 ILTR 111.

[103] [1989] FCR 341.

[104] However, in *Re X* [1989] 1 FLR 30, a child's distress in the company of 'Daddy', was suggestive, although only remotely so, of the identity of the abuser. See the discussion of implied assertions, below, pp. 211–12.

[105] [1963] VR 530.

[106] (1985) 80 Cr App R 89.

not permitted to call witnesses who heard the brother or D's co-accused make statements before the discovery of the body of the murder victim, which revealed detailed knowledge of the circumstances in which the murder had been committed. The trial judge, upheld by the Court of Appeal, agreed that if the only purpose of tendering the evidence was to show the state of the brother's knowledge at the material time, there would be no infringement of the hearsay rule. But he refused to admit it on the ground that to do so would involve a multitude of potential collateral issues, partly because there was a wide range of possible explanations for his knowledge, apart from his own guilt. Lord Bridge in *Blastland*[107] deduced from this judgment that the bare knowledge of circumstances of a murder of which another stands accused is not relevant without an accompanying inference of guilt. In that case the third party, M, was alleged by a witness to have returned home at about the time of the murder shaking, covered in mud and wet from the knees down. He told her at the time, and told others later, that a young boy had been murdered. Lord Bridge agreed that if statements were admitted solely to prove a person's knowledge, that would not be hearsay. But that knowledge would have to be relevant. Here M's knowledge as such had no relevance to the issue, unless it was considered together with an inference as to the source of his knowledge (that is, his own guilt). Taken on its own, knowledge that a murder has been done has no relevance to the issue whether or not the accused was guilty of the murder. To draw the inference of guilt from it would be to indulge in speculation, since there was a variety of possible explanations for M's knowledge. Unfortunately, the issues of relevance and hearsay have become confusingly entangled in Lord Bridge's judgment. After all, the defence was not trying to prove that a young boy had been murdered – the prosecution had already established that. The witnesses to M's statements were therefore not required to prove their contents, that the boy was dead; they were not testifying to a matter of which they had no direct knowledge. The inference of guilt did not arise from the statement itself as an implied assertion, but from the circumstances. The evidence was classic circumstantial evidence, which does not directly point to guilt but gives rise to an inference of another fact which does; the real objection to the evidence here was that the House of Lords considered circumstantial evidence against another to be irrelevant to Blastland's trial.[108]

It can be seen from the cases on state of mind or knowledge that there is scope for endless confusion about implied assertions and the hearsay rule. Strictly speaking, statements implied in words or conduct are subject to it;

[107] [1985] 2 All ER 1095.
[108] See chapter 2.

this was the view of Parke B in *Wright v Tatham*.[109] He gave as examples of inadmissible hearsay evidence, the payment of a sum resembling that wagered on the occurrence of an event as evidence to show it took place; payments by underwriters to an insurance policy to show that the subject insured has been lost; and the conduct of a testator's family in taking precautions as evidence that he was a lunatic. Parke B stressed the absence of the oath behind such implied statements, but if the conduct is not intended to be assertive of any fact the oath would appear to be unnecessary.[110] There seems little danger of fabrication, but the danger of inaccuracy would appear as great as with other kinds of hearsay.[111] Indeed, the danger of mis-understanding or misinterpretation may be more acute than for express hear-say statements. In theory, implied assertions are equally subject to the exclusionary rule, but there is endless scope for 'hearsay-fiddles' here.[112] However, it is difficult to play by the rules; *Ratten* was an example of how genuinely difficult it is to draw the line between conduct which is assertive and conduct which is not. In *Mawaz Khan and Amanat Khan*[113] lies told by both defendants to the police in similar terms suggestive of conspiracy were admitted as part of the prosecution case in chief. It was held that the stories were admissible, not as evidence of their contents, but to ask the jury to 'hold the assertions false and to draw inferences from their falsity'.[114]

Exceptions in civil cases

Although it is commonly supposed that the Civil Evidence Act 1968 'fundamentally changed'[115] the admissibility of hearsay evidence in civil cases, the fact is that an opportunity was missed. The statutory framework is over-complicated and over-restrictive and the fundamental reluctance of the legislature to open up civil cases to all reliable hearsay evidence has been exacerbated by the restrictive attitude of some judges in interpreting the Act.[116] There can be no doubt about the admissibility (with leave of the judge)

---

[109] (1837) 7 Ad & E 313.

[110] Weinburg, 'Implied assertions and the scope of the hearsay rule' (1973) 7 MULR 268.

[111] *Teper v R* [1952] 2 All ER 447; *Gibson* (1887) 18 QBD 537.

[112] See Weinburg (1973) 7 MULR 268; Birch, in Smith (ed.).

[113] [1967] 1 AC 454.

[114] Ibid., p. 462.

[115] E.g. P. Carter, *Cases and Statutes on Evidence*, 2nd edn (Sweet & Maxwell, London, 1990), p. 372.

[116] See statement in Tapper and Cross, *Evidence* (above, note 2).

of previous hearsay statements by witnesses.[117] The difficulty is in the implementation of section 2(1), regarding first-hand hearsay by parties not present as witnesses, and section 4(1), regarding documentary records containing information given by someone not attending as a witness. Both sections are subject to section 8 of the Act and RSC Order 38 in that it must be shown that the maker of the statement is unavailable to give evidence because he or she is sick, dead, unfit to attend, beyond the seas, cannot be identified or found, or cannot reasonably be expected to have any recollection of matters relevant to the accuracy or otherwise of the statement. There are uncertainties as to the meaning of these terms,[118] and how to prove that the witness is indeed unavailable on one of the approved grounds.[119] The requirements show that the preference even in civil cases is still very much for oral testimony. Yet first-hand documentary hearsay does not share with hearsay evidence of oral statements the problem of the accuracy of the reporting of the statement unless there is an issue of authentication.[120]

The exception in section 4, designed to cover business documents, suffers from the above-mentioned difficulties, but it is also a failure in drafting and in the way it has been dealt with in the courts.[121] The use of the word 'record', disastrously copied in the short-lived section 68 of the Police and Criminal Evidence Act 1984, gave judges plenty of opportunities to resurrect the hearsay rule. The Roskill Committee thought the distinction evolving in case law between records and non-records 'artificial and of doubtful value'.[122] In reported decisions the courts have been as restrictive in their interpretation of section 4 as they were of the 1938 Evidence Act,[123] despite the difference in wording, and it may indeed be the case that the wider terms of the 1988 Criminal Justice Act, which, ironically, make it in some cases easier to have hearsay admitted in criminal trials than in civil trials, are a response to this.[124] However, the decision that a file containing letters of complaint from customers who had been defrauded did not amount to a 'statement in a document...which is, or forms part of, a record' seems un-

---

[117] S. 2(2).

[118] E.g. 'beyond the seas', a description abandoned in the Criminal Justice Act 1988 for 'outside the United Kingdom'.

[119] The problem of proving these extraneous facts is dealt with below in relation to the Criminal Justice Act 1988.

[120] Law Reform Advisory Committee for Northern Ireland, *Hearsay Evidence*, p. 30.

[121] See above.

[122] *Fraud Trials Committee Report*, para. 5.16.

[123] See statement in Tapper and Cross, *Evidence* (above, note 2).

[124] Wolchover, 'Proof by missing witness – a postscript' [1987] NLJ 805.

objectionable.[125] More controversial is the finding that inspectors' reports for the Board of Trade are not records.[126] However, such reports contain mixed reported speech and opinion, and so may involve other issues of admissibility. There are some signs of increased flexibility; for example, in *Taylor v Taylor*[127] it was assumed that the transcript of a criminal trial would be admissible equally under section 2 or 4 of the 1968 Act. In *Nicholls*[128] it was conceded by the defence that sales receipts and debit advice documents were records,[129] although it disputed the non-availability of the maker of the statement. The definition given in *H v Schering Chemicals*[130] was that the document should either give effect to a transaction or contemporaneously register information supplied by those with direct knowledge of the facts. But *Cunningham*,[131] interpreting 'record' within section 68 of the Police and Criminal Evidence Act 1984, reverted to the *Tirado* restriction to a book, card index or 'primary source'. A second case on the 1984 Act provision is further evidence of the reluctance of judges to employ statutory hearsay exceptions. In *O'Loughlin and McLaughlin*[132] Kenneth Jones J held that a witness statement taken down by a police officer was not a record compiled by a person acting under a duty, since the police officer was only the witness's instrument, and therefore the witness was recording his own statement. This he had no duty to do. The judge was following *Barkway v South Wales Transport*,[133] which in fact interpreted significantly different language in section 1 of the Evidence Act 1938; also, there were other indications in the 1984 Act that he was wrong to use the amanuensis argument in this context.[134] In *Iqbal*[135] the Court of Appeal regarded an affidavit and signed statement as a record because it was a compilation of facts supplied by those with direct knowledge of the facts. A record should be preserved in writing, or some other permanent form in order that it is not evanescent.

---

[125] *Tirado* (1974) 59 Cr App R 80. But Pattenden takes a different view, 'Documentary hearsay and the Police and Criminal Evidence Act 1984' (1987) 51 JCL 90.

[126] *Savings and Investment Bank Ltd v Gasco Investments* [1984] 1 All ER 296.

[127] [1970] 1 WLR 1148.

[128] (1976) 63 Cr App R 187.

[129] Cf. *Jones* [1978] 3 All ER 1098, undermining the impression given by Lord Widgery CJ in *Tirado* (1974) 59 Cr App R 80, 90, that the terms suggests a ledger or card index for general perusal.

[130] [1983] 1 All ER 849.

[131] [1989] Crim LR 435.

[132] [1988] 3 All ER 431.

[133] [1949] 1 KB 54.

[134] McEwan, 'Documentary hearsay – refuge for the vulnerable witness?' [1989] Crim LR 629.

[135] [1990] 3 All ER 787.

A major problem confronting those who would reform the provisions on hearsay evidence in civil cases is that civil proceedings vary a great deal in their nature and complexity, so that the problems faced by one kind of tribunal are not necessarily shared by others. For example, the expressed preference for oral testimony is impractical for most commercial litigation. After all, it was the difficulty in proving elaborate fraud which led to the enactment of the new documentary hearsay provisions in 1988. It is unwise to hamper commercial courts with complicated hearsay provisions, even if they are relatively workable in courts dealing with simpler cases. The reality of the 1968 Act is that it appears to work reasonably well only because it is rarely invoked. In commercial cases it is not usually in the interest of litigants to object to the reception of hearsay evidence because both sides are likely to wish to rely on some hearsay; therefore its admission is agreed well in advance. Where objection is taken, severe practical problems arise. It may be that many files of documents have to be closely examined to ascertain who was the maker of the statement in each one. It may not be obvious from routine company documents who prepared them, or who made the statements of fact set out in them, particularly if they were prepared years before the proceedings. If the maker can be identified, the solicitors then have to investigate his or her whereabouts, in order to ascertain whether he or she is unavailable and could be subject to a section 8 notice, or whether he or she could be called, in which case the document might fulfil the requirements of a memory-refreshing document. All this is elaborate and time-consuming, at best. At worst, the maker cannot be identified and the document cannot be used at all, even if it appears to be part of a well-established routine of recording information, and therefore reliable. Ironically, even if the litigant manages to understand and apply the statutory provisions sufficiently to complete a section 8 notice, he or she may well then face the difficulty of an opponent who has not mastered them. The most common debate concerns the identity of the maker of the statement; a common mistake is to assume the same person as the maker of the document. This can lead to unnecessary and protracted arguments – and there is a risk that the tribunal will require elucidation as well – escalating the time and costs involved. There is now recognition from the Law Commission that the whole issue of whether and to what extent the hearsay rule should apply in civil proceedings needs urgent review.[136]

Cases dealing with the welfare of children are even less appropriate candidates than are other kinds of civil matter for the adversarial model of trial and the exclusionary rules. Many courts coped with this difficulty quite

---

[136] Law Commission, *The Hearsay Rule in Civil Proceedings*, Consultation Paper No. 117 (1991).

well by ignoring it, assuming that they were exempt from the rules of evidence generally, or the hearsay rule in particular. Recently it was made clear that they were wrong, and the chaos which immediately resulted from abandoning the convenient fiction, treating these proceedings, which might involve allegations of child abuse, in the same way as other civil trials necessitated speedy legislative intervention. For the hearsay rule was found to apply to some kinds of case and not others, and in those where the rule did apply, disparate statutory exceptions created more uncertainty. In care proceedings the hearsay rule *did* apply,[137] although many cases had been heard with all concerned apparently unaware of this difficulty. The statutory exception which applied to magistrates' courts and Crown Courts in relation to care proceedings was the Evidence Act 1938.[138] The hearsay rule was recently held to apply also to the matrimonial jurisdiction of the county court, which dealt with custody issues[139] and might therefore hear allegations of child abuse; to those cases the applicable statute was the Civil Evidence Act 1968.[140] There were other jurisdictions, or possible jurisdictions, which might hear allegations of child abuse of which the evidential position could not be described with any confidence.[141]

In *Re H and Re K* Butler-Sloss LJ explained that the considerable use of hearsay evidence in many child abuse cases hitherto had merely been instances of express or tacit agreement of the parties. Apart from wardship, the rule applied to all courts dealing with family matters, whatever the allegations which might be made. In reality, however, these courts had been operating in blissful ignorance of the problem. The risk created by the Court of Appeal decision in *Re H and Re K* was that lawyers would now oppose the admission of hearsay, particularly accusations made to social workers in disclosure interviews. The difficulty facing those wishing to establish any kind of child abuse if such statements could not be adduced was obvious; the Court of Appeal tacitly acknowledged the problem in deciding that the High Court exercising its wardship jurisdiction was exempt from all the rules of evidence, including the hearsay rule. There was little legal authority for this conclusion, which probably had more to do with common sense[142] than

---

[137] *Humberside v DPR* [1977] 3 All ER 964; *Bradford City Metropolitan Council v K (Minors)*, *The Times*, 18 August 1989.

[138] See McEwan [1989] Crim LR 629.

[139] *Re H and Re K* [1989] 2 FLR 313.

[140] Northern Ireland boasts a similar plethora of statutory hearsay exceptions in the Evidence Act (Northern Ireland) 1939 and Civil Evidence Act (Northern Ireland) 1971.

[141] McEwan, '*Re H and Re K*' [1989] J Cr L 106.

[142] Except that the result was a patchwork of different rules applying to different courts, depending on the jurisdiction.

precedent; but the reasoning is based on the fact that wardship is a non-adversarial, investigative procedure. Butler-Sloss and Croom-Johnson LJJ followed the *obiter dictum* of Lord Devlin in *Re K*: 'An inflexible rule against hearsay is quite unsuited to the exercise of a paternal and administrative jurisdiction. The jurisdiction is itself more ancient than the rule against hearsay and I see no reason why that rule should now be introduced into it.'[143]

Butler-Sloss LJ employed the same argument in *Re W (Minors)*,[144] where she claimed that wardship was a non-adversarial and administrative process which 'can be seen in its application to be different from other civil proceedings'. Unfortunately, despite its ancient origins, the fact is that wardship was not significantly different in terms of subject-matter or effect when dealing with cases of alleged child abuse, although custody and access proceedings, involving a dispute between two parents, may more easily be seen as adversarial.[145] In *Humberside* Lord Widgery CJ had concluded regretfully that the hearsay rule applied to care applications although they were 'essentially non-adversary, non-party proceedings'.[146]

Pending the major changes which will follow the implementation of the Children Act 1989, effectively ending the use of wardship by local authorities as an alternative to care proceedings, Parliament was sufficiently alarmed by the effect of *Re H and Re K* effectively to abolish the hearsay rule as far as child-centred hearings are concerned.[147] This allows the admission of not only the child's out-of-court statement but other kinds of hearsay, including welfare reports such as that prepared by the guardian *ad litem*.[148] It is not yet clear what will be the evidential position of the new-style care proceedings.[149] Although the 1989 Act unfortunately stops short of creating new children's courts, which would inevitably develop an investigative approach which would in any event render the hearsay rule entirely inappropriate, there is apparent in all the cases mentioned above and in the latest parliamentary interventions an anxiety about imposing adversarial principles in cases where

---

[143] [1965] AC 201, 242.
[144] *The Times*, 10 November 1989.
[145] E.g. *per* Cross J in *Re J* [1960] 1 WLR 253.
[146] [1977] 3 All ER 964, 967.
[147] Children Act 1989, section 96, as implemented by Children (Admissibility of Hearsay Evidence) Order 1990 (S.I. 1990 No. 143); however, problems remain in relation to the domestic jurisdiction of magistrates dealing with custody and access, maintenance and adoption. See White, 'Children and hearsay evidence' [1990] NLJ 390. The Order also refers to specific kinds of hearsay evidence which shall be admissible in magistrates' courts and which do not include, for example, medical evidence of a child's condition on examination.
[148] See *Practical Points* [1990] JP 479.
[149] Fortin, 'Care proceedings and the hearsay rule' [1989] J Cr L 11.

the sole issue is the welfare of a particular child. Lord Devlin, who had in *Re K* accepted that wardship could not be squeezed into the adversarial strait-jacket, felt that a judge sitting alone was perfectly capable of deciding what weight to give out-of-court accusations.[150] Butler-Sloss LJ went rather further, tacitly recognizing that an investigative procedure would dispense with all the rules of evidence, in fact arguing, through a somewhat idio-syncratic interpretation of section 18 of the Civil Evidence Act 1968,[151] that wardship was already in this position. Presumably this allowed dis-pensing with such rules as those relating to the competence of witnesses and the manner of examination of witnesses. Parliament has already accepted that the hearsay rule merely handicaps a court which attempts to identify the best interests of a particular child. The new hearings are to have full dis-closure of evidence and the institution of preliminary hearings, which will further undermine the orality principle and reduce the opportunities for surprise. In addition, party status is to be extended beyond its original limits, so that many cases will bear no relation to the two-sided battle which characterizes the adversarial trial; it is possible that in some cases as many as ten parties might be involved, and each could have a different perception of the child's best interests. Whatever personal animosity might exist between various members or former members of the family, all parties and the court express themselves as primarily concerned with the child's welfare, and therefore it is scarcely unfair to devise procedures which facilitate discussion of that single issue.[152]

Documentary hearsay in criminal cases

After the disaster in *Myers*,[153] where the prosecution found itself deprived of probably the most reliable possible evidence of the identity of cars alleged to have been stolen, a series of statutes attempted to devise an exception to the hearsay rule which would allow reliable documents, amounting to declarations in the course of duty, to be admitted as evidence to prove their contents.

The first, the Criminal Evidence Act 1965, was found wanting; confined to 'trade or business records', the provisions omitted reliable documentary information compiled by people in other kinds of work.[154] The next con-

---

[150]   [1965] AC 201, 242.
[151]   See McEwan [1989] J C L 106.
[152]   At the time of writing, rules of court under the 1989 Act have not been completed.
[153]   [1965] AC 1001.
[154]   *Patel* [1981] Crim LR 250; lists of prohibited immigrants compiled by the Home Office were inadmissible.

tender, section 68 of the Police and Criminal Evidence Act 1984, borrowed most of the language of section 4 of the Civil Evidence Act 1968. The uncertainty generated by the restriction to 'records' has been described above. The Criminal Justice Act 1988 now provides for the admissibility of documentary hearsay in criminal cases where the evidence complies with the definitions and conditions in sections 23 and 24. In fact the original Bill had gone beyond 'even the bold recommendations of the Roskill Committee on Fraud Trials' in envisaging a scheme where first-hand documentary hearsay and business documents would be generally admissible whatever the circumstances of the maker of the statement.[155] But opponents in Parliament forced the inclusion of conditions similar to those in the Civil Evidence Act 1968, whereby the reason for not calling the maker of the statement must be shown, save in respect of business documents not prepared for the purposes of pending or contemplated criminal proceedings.[156] This imposes the practical difficulties faced by civil litigants (in those rare cases where the civil statute is applied) on to criminal courts where the document is not a run-of-the-mill business record.

A nightmarish possibility also exists which appears not so far to have been addressed by criminal courts; it concerns the question how the reason for the absence of the maker of the statement is to be established. There is here a new potential field of operation for the hearsay rule if judges insist on oral evidence to prove that the witness is indeed unfit to attend, outside the United Kingdom and so forth. To apply the hearsay rule to the ancillary issue of the ground for non-attendance could lead to an endless regression where documents are adduced for that purpose in lieu of live witnesses whose absence would also have to be explained by oral evidence unless yet another statutory ground were satisfied. Given that the reason for absence is a collateral issue, and that the statute concerned was designed to allow more hearsay evidence to be given on the issue itself, it would be absurd to insist on strict proof here. *Nicholls*[157] is sometimes given as an authority for the proposition that non-availability has to be proved by oral evidence, but the Court of Appeal in that case did not go so far. The prosecution had argued that non-availability could be inferred from the nature of the document itself. This was rejected; the defendant was entitled to a trial within a trial and cross-examination of those concerned. The court certainly did not go so far as to say that hearsay would be unacceptable, for instance to show that the witness was medically unfit. In *R v Acton JJ, ex parte McMullen et al*[158] the Divisional Court held that 'fear' in section 23(3)(b) should be assessed

---

[155] Birch [1989] Crim LR 15.
[156] S. 24(4).
[157] (1976) 63 Cr App R 187.
[158] *Independent*, 4 May 1990.

from the point of view of the witness, and therefore did not have to be reasonable, as long as it related to the commission of the offence. It appeared to be sufficient evidence of the witness's fear that the prosecutor told the court about it. However, the ground for absence must be established beyond reasonable doubt.

The liberality of section 24, which does not insist on such grounds in relation to 'non-criminal' business documents is a welcome relief from such technicalities. Given the comparative rigour of the conditions governing the admission of first-hand hearsay, however, it is curious that this flexibility is attached to a surprisingly wide class of documents. For the definition of business document is drawn in terms which apparently include items that have virtually nothing to do with business of any sort, and which could be at least as unreliable as any other kind of document. After all, the section is designed to cater for hearsay on hearsay, whereas section 23 is restricted to first-hand hearsay. Section 24 includes as a business document one which was created or received in the course of a trade, business, profession or other occupation, or by the holder of a paid or unpaid office.[159] Documents *received* by businesses could go well beyond routine or otherwise reliable records prepared for professional purposes.[160] The only rider is that the supplier[161] of the information had or may reasonably be supposed to have had personal knowledge of the matters dealt with.[162] The width of the provision would appear to render an anonymous letter to the NSPCC a business document not requiring the maker of the statement to be called.

A further complication is that there is no specific time at which the document should have been received. Most, if not all, documents tendered for admission as evidence for the prosecution would have been at some point in the hands of the police or Crown Prosecution Service lawyers, and therefore 'received' by them. It cannot be the case that this fact alone renders them automatically prima facie admissible whatever their origin (although grounds for not calling the maker would probably have to be shown under section 24 (4)). There is no increase in inherent reliability by virtue of possession at some point by a particular professional body. Yet the wording of section 24 appears to be satisfied. It seems that such an argument (albeit a bad one) is the only answer to the *McLean*[163] conundrum, otherwise still unsolved. The

---

[159] S. 24(1)(c)(i).

[160] Letters to the editor of *The Times* appear to be included; see Birch [1989] Crim LR 15.

[161] Although the meaning of this word may appear obvious, s. 24 creates confusion by distinguishing the 'supplier' from the maker of the statement; see Birch, ibid.

[162] S. 24(1)(c)(i).

[163] Subject to *res gestae*, see above.

problem posed by the hearsay rule in that case does not appear to be dealt with by the provisions of the 1988 Act. Section 23 is the relevant section; the note of a car registration number taken by a bystander at dictation was a first-hand hearsay statement, although the eyewitness did not check it. In *Taylor v Taylor*[164] a transcript of evidence made by the court stenographer was regarded as first-hand hearsay, although the witnesses would not have read it through afterwards. And section 23(3) of the 1988 Act provides that where the maker is unavailable through fear or because he or she is kept out of the way the statement is admissible if made to, *inter alia*, a police officer; therefore it is assumed that such a statement is first hand.[165] But first-hand hearsay statements are admissible by virtue of section 23 only where specific reasons for not calling the maker of the statement exist. In section 23 these grounds do not include that given in section 24(4)(iii),[166] namely, that he or she could not in the circumstances reasonably be expected to remember the matters dealt with in the statement. If the bystander was professionally involved, the case might fall under section 24; but the most obvious professional to be involved is a police officer, and therefore the grounds for non-attendance would have to be shown. Here the inability to remember such a matter would be sufficient.[167] But, in general, *McLean* documents have not been brought within the statutory framework despite their vital relevance and probable reliability.

Documents admissible under sections 23 and 24 are subject to judicial discretion – to exclude, under section 25, documents which prima facie ought to be admitted, or to *include*, under section 26, those which prima facie ought to be excluded. The latter category relates to documents prepared for the purposes of criminal proceedings. Section 25 does not apply to committal proceedings; there is no discretion to exclude at that stage unless it is a 'prosecution'[168] (section 26) document, in which case the extreme caution with

---

[164] [1970] 1 WLR 1148.

[165] Although there is no stipulation in the subsection that the maker should have checked the statement, or any other requirement of accuracy of recording, there remains the discretion to exclude in the interests of justice; see below.

[166] Echoing Civil Evidence Act 1968, s. 8, and RSC Ord. 38, r. 25.

[167] If the position were reversed, so that a professional asks a passer-by to write the number down, it is not clear whether the case would fall within s. 24 or not. If the maker of the statement could be said to have 'created' the document through an amanuensis, it would be admissible, satisfying the grounds in s. 24(4)(iii). This was the argument of Kenneth Jones J in *O'Loughlin* [1988] 3 All ER 431, interpreting the different language of the Police and Criminal Evidence Act.

[168] Popular description, although such documents could conceivably be prepared by the defence.

which such evidence is treated affects even the issue whether or not there is a case to answer. The general principle affecting the exercise of both discretions is the interests of justice. Section 25(2) illustrates this by directing the court:

  (a) to the nature and source of the document containing the statement and to whether or not, having regard to its nature and source and to any other circumstances that appear to the court to be relevant, it is likely to be authentic;
  (b) to the extent to which the statement appears to supply evidence which would otherwise not be readily available;
  (c) to the relevance of the evidence that it appears to supply to any issue which is likely to have to be determined in the proceedings; and
  (d) to any risk, having regard in particular to whether it is likely to be possible to controvert the evidence if the person making it does not attend to give oral evidence in the proceedings, that its admission or exclusion will result in unfairness to the accused...

The wording here suggests that the possible unfairness to the accused resulting from his or her inability to cross-examine should be weighed in the balance with the relevance of the evidence and the difficulty of obtaining it by other means. Section 26 returns to the approach of section 68 of the Police and Criminal Evidence Act by creating a presumption against admission; the judge must be satisfied that to admit the statement is in the interests of justice, having regard to:

  (i)   the contents of the statement;
  (ii) any risk, having regard in particular to whether it is likely to be possible to controvert the statement if the person making it does not attend to give oral evidence in the proceedings, that its admission or exclusion will result in unfairness to the accused...and
  (iii) any other circumstances that appear to the court to be relevant.

Lord Caithness explained that the presumption in section 26 should prevent witness statements from being admitted as evidence of their contents in most cases. The difference between the discretions in the two sections appears to be partly one of degree, although presumably the principal danger to be addressed in relation to section 26 documents is that of manufacture. Lord Caithness gave the example of a case where the presumption in section 26 would be rightly displaced. It concerned a vital witness whose credibility was not in doubt but who died after making a statement to police.[169] Where

---

[169] HL Deb., Vol. 489, col. 99 (20 October 1987).

credibility is not an issue but the facts contained in a statement are of central importance and unobtainable elsewhere, it would seem that such statements should normally be admissible. Although an honest witness can make mistakes, and the loss of the opportunity to cross-examine is therefore always a disadvantage (hence the rule against hearsay) this may appear to be of marginal importance set against the relevance of the facts stated. Judges will take account of the centrality of the evidence in question. In *O'Loughlin and McLaughlin*[170] Kenneth Jones J, interpreting the discretion which applied to section 68 of the Police and Criminal Evidence Act 1984,[171] refused to admit the hearsay evidence of identification witnesses. He concluded that to try the accused for a very serious offence (the bombing of an army barracks) on the contested evidence of absent witnesses would be obnoxious and unfair.[172] It would be difficult for the jury to exercise judgment on the reliability of long, conflicting and unclear depositions. But in this case, where the witnesses had fled, there was no other evidence to link the accused with the offence, and the reliability of these witnesses was a vital issue.

An example of evidence which was less central, although contained in the statement of the alleged victim, and was admitted by way of hearsay, occurred in New Zealand in *Hovell*.[173] The Evidence Amendment Act (No. 2)[174] permits the admission of first-hand hearsay in documentary form, subject to a discretion to exclude if its prejudicial effect would outweigh its probative value or if for any other reason the court is satisfied that it is not necessary or expedient in the interests of justice to admit the statement.[175] In this case a woman of eighty-two complained of rape to the police, who took a statement. She gave a detailed account but was not able to identify her attacker. Medical evidence confirmed that she had been raped. The defendant admitted being at her flat at the material time, but claimed that he had been so drunk that he could remember nothing. The complainant died before the trial, and her statement to the police was used in evidence. The Court of Appeal upheld the judge's decision to allow it; the complainant had clearly not fabricated her account, and therefore the issue was solely one of identification. Although her statement was of major probative value on the nature of the attack the description itself was so vague that cross-examination would

---

[170] [1988] 3 All ER 431.
[171] Sched. 3, para. 2.
[172] He added that whatever discretion specific to the hearsay provision itself Parliament might provide, s. 78 of the Act would have allowed him to exclude the hearsay on the ground that to admit it would adversely affect the fairness of the proceedings.
[173] [1987] 1 NZLR 610.
[174] S. 3.
[175] S. 18.

not have made a significant difference. The Court could see no justification for restricting the operation of section 3 to less serious cases or more peripheral evidence.

Recently, the English Court of Appeal has considered the exercise of section 26 discretion. In *Cole*,[176] a witness to an alleged assault died before the trial. There were other witnesses to the violence, which was admitted by the defence, who argued that D had intervened to protect his daughter. The trial judge therefore concluded that it would not be unfair to the defence to allow the witness statement of the deceased to serve as part of the prosecution case. The account of the assault contained in it could be controverted, not only by cross-examination of the other witnesses to the incident, but by witnesses for the defence who would be free to present an alternative version. The defence replied that such an argument undermined the accused's right not to give evidence, since he would effectively be forced to do so in order to present a different account. The Court of Appeal was rightly unimpressed with this; the 'court cannot be required...to assess the possibility of controverting the statement upon the basis that the accused will not give evidence or call witnesses known to be available to him',[177] particularly as the court is not entitled to be told who, if anyone, the defence proposes to call. This decision prevents the accused from adopting a tactic such as refusing to give evidence and then insisting on the exclusion of hearsay evidence on the ground that he or she cannot now challenge its contents.

The case affords hope that courts are moving from their previously restrictive exercise of discretion with regard to hearsay evidence:[178]

> The overall purpose of the provisions was to widen the powers of the court to admit documentary hearsay evidence while ensuring that the accused received a fair trial. In judging how to achieve the fairness of the trial a balance must on occasion be struck between the interests of the public in enabling the prosecution case to be properly presented and the interest of a particular defendant in not being put in a disadvantageous position, for example by the death or illness of a witness.[179]

Judges must not make too much of the inability to cross-examine the maker of the statement; within the closely controlled procedures of the adversarial trial, it is always a disadvantage to be confronted with evidence-in-chief

---

[176] [1990] 2 All ER 108.
[177] Ibid., p. 116, *per* Ralph Gibson LJ.
[178] *O'Loughlin and McLaughlin* [1988] 3 All ER 431; *Martin* [1988] 3 All ER 440; *Cunningham* [1989] Crim LR 435.
[179] *Cole* [1990] 2 All ER 108, 115, *per* Ralph Gibson LJ.

without any opportunity to cross-examine. The terms of sections 25 and 26, then, must refer to those cases where the difficulty is particularly acute:[180]

> The mere fact that the deponent will not be available for cross-examination is obviously an insufficient ground for excluding the deposition, for that is a feature common to the admission of all depositions which must have been contemplated and accepted by the legislature when it gave statutory sanction to their admission in evidence.

The Court of Appeal view is that the contents of the statement are an important factor, and so is the quality of the evidence. But judges are unlikely to drop traditional preconceptions overnight; in *Acton JJ*[181] Watkins LJ remarked that s. 23(3)(b) 'let loose one or two unruly horses which the courts would have to be vigilant to control'.

The future of the hearsay rule

The nature of trials, both civil and criminal, is moving steadily further from the adversarial model. More pre-trial disclosure will reduce the importance of cross-examination. Inevitably, hearsay evidence will cease to be seen as unfair, and reliability of source will be more important in relation to each piece of evidence. The emphasis on cross-examination will gradually be confined to its proper place, that is, cases where the credibility or reliability of the witness is crucial. It may be that eventually, even there, relevant hearsay evidence will be allowed on the basis that characteristics such as the truthfulness, personality or powers of perception of an absent witness can be assessed by other (and perhaps more reliable) means than cross-examination. The hearsay rule inevitably goes in retreat with its arch-ally, the adversarial trial. The utter unsuitability of both in relation to cases of any complexity is clear; it is a pity that diehards fought so hard against the recommendations of the Roskill Committee and the original version of the bill which became the Criminal Justice Act 1988. It is certain that as methods of communicating and recording information alter, and they have been transformed in the last twenty years, the old methods of proof and evidential rules will increasingly be seen to be inadequate. The commercial world is smaller, but more complex, because of modern technology. It is futile to scramble in the

---

[180] *Scott v R* [1989] 2 All ER 305, 312–3, *per* Lord Griffiths; the legislation here was a Jamaican provision similar to the unamended provisions of Criminal Justice Act 1925, s. 13(3).

[181] *Independent*, 4 May 1990.

wake of such changes attempting to devise ever-more-sophisticated exceptions to the irredeemably archaic rule. All jurisdictions are finding that they
are dealing with elaborate frauds in both the civil and criminal contexts, and
these cases are characterized by mountainous quantities of documentation
with which the evidential provisions of many Commonwealth countries are
ill-equipped to deal. We have seen above that it is not only such cases which
are hampered by the hearsay rule; even 'classic crimes'[182] have fallen foul of
the rule to the benefit of those responsible.

There appears not to have been devised a workable set of statutory
provisions to cope with all these problems.[183] The inadequacies of English
civil legislation have been referred to the Law Commission, who will find
themselves faced with a challenging task; the Law Reform Commission of
Northern Ireland found it impossible to find a satisfactory solution in terms
of simplicity, certainty, cost or fairness except to abolish the rule altogether,
or subject it to a judicial discretion to exclude. Simple abolition has some
support in the Lord Chancellor's Civil Justice Review[184] and has actually
been implemented in Scotland in the Civil Evidence (Scotland) Act 1988[185]
despite the objection from the Scottish Law Commission to such a course.
The Commission's report stressed the value of cross-examination as an
instrument for exposing unreliable evidence.[186] But the government objection
to the Commission's solution, combining a notice procedure with discretion
to exclude, was that it could have the effect of simply reintroducing the rule
against hearsay.[187] Allowing the exercise of judicial discretion to be the only
barrier to hearsay evidence has the merit of flexibility, but opponents object
to the lack of certainty. Some critics also stress the alleged pro-prosecution
bias of judges who try criminal cases. But it is not obvious that such a
discretion is so very different from the present discretion to exclude evidence
which is irrelevant; allowing judges to exclude evidence on the basis that it is
not reliable, or could be adduced by other means, appears equally consistent
with a view that an experienced judge is able to distinguish evidence which
will take the case no further. And if the jury can cope with a direction that a
witness's previous statement is evidence only that it was said and may not be

---

[182] Of which the most famous and striking illustration must be *Bedingfield* (1879) 14
Cox CC 341, where the dying statement of Mrs Bedingfield, naming her husband,
was excluded.
[183] Law Reform Advisory Committee for Northern Ireland, *Hearsay Evidence*.
[184] *Report of the Review Body on Civil Justice*, Cm. 394 (1988), paras. 266–70.
[185] S. 2(1).
[186] *Evidence: Report on Corroboration, Hearsay and Related Matters in Civil
Proceedings* (Scottish Law Commission No. 100, 1986), paras. 3.31–3.34.
[187] Lord Advocate, HL Deb., Vol. 489, col. 1542 (12 November 1987).

used to prove the facts contained in it, they should be able to assess the probative value of hearsay evidence with comparative ease – and at present, of course, presumably do so when hearsay evidence (such as a confession) is presented by virtue of an exception to the rule. The other side are free to make any points they wish to devalue the force of hearsay evidence. The Law Reform Advisory Committee for Northern Ireland saw no problem as far as civil cases are concerned:[188]

> The main advantage of retaining some form of judicial discretion is that it enables hearsay evidence of probative value to be included when it does not come within any of the recognized exceptions, and conversely it enables hearsay evidence to be excluded even when it comes within a recognized exception... Parties should be entitled to adduce evidence of high probative value but should be protected from having to meet evidence of low probative value.

In chapter 4 we saw that the reluctance altogether to abandon adversarial procedures where children are the victims of crimes presents a problem of which the solution appears inevitably cumbersome, expensive and unpredictable in outcome. The reliance upon interviews conducted by non-lawyers as a source of testimony carries the risk that the final product will not be acceptable in court, sending all parties straight back to square one, with the child having to give evidence in the usual way, even if not necessarily in the body of the court. The insistence on orality which led to this is founded on assumptions which have little basis in fact; the most reliable evidence, particularly from children, is what is reported at the time. To accommodate this reality and to be fairer to the children, the Pigot proposals and the legislation which will be required to implement them must adapt existing procedures in an awkward and inelegant fashion which will reinforce Continental opinion as to national sanity. It is a pity that there appears to be no review body which feels itself entitled to stand back and examine the fundamental precepts of the trial structure with a view to establishing a simple and workable means of presenting evidence.

---

[188] Law Reform Advisory Committee for Northern Ireland, *Hearsay Evidence*, para. 4.11.

8

Conclusion: Future Directions

*I say that the adversary system is not the best system of criminal justice,
and that there is a better way...The American system, up to the time of
final verdict and appeal, puts all the emphasis on techniques, devices,
mechanisms. It is the most elaborate system ever devised by a society. It is
so elaborate that in some places it is breaking down. It is not working.*

Chief Justice Berger, 'The special skills of advocacy: are specialized
training and certification of advocates essential to our system of justice?'

In mock trials which compared inquisitorial and adversarial procedures,
Thibaut and Walker[1] found that whether or not the adversarial approach to
evidence gathering and presentation displayed an unbiased selection of facts
to the court depended on the balance of evidence in the particular case. If
the case was evenly balanced on each side, the bias in one party's presentation was offset by that of the other. In such cases the same number of facts
were generally gathered whichever procedure was used. But if the case was
unbalanced as between the two sides, the adversarial trial produced a biased
distribution of the facts. The version offered by the party who had the fewer
facts in his or her favour tended to over-represent the proportion of evidence
favourable to his or her case. If the actual imbalance, for example, was 25:75,
the distribution of evidence would be 36:64. This research seems to suggest
that inquisitorial systems are better at information gathering and representation. However, the authors also found that a person's perception of the fairness of a proceeding is not necessarily related to his or her success in it. The
adversarial system was perceived as fairer irrespective of the outcome; this
was true even of participants brought up in the Continental tradition. But

---

[1] J. M. Thibaut and L. Walker, *Procedural Justice and Psychological Analysis* (Wiley,
New York, 1975).

the apparent fairness of the adversarial trial to the experimental group may to some extent depend on a lack of appreciation of its full implications. The research was designed to measure the efficacy of information gathering, and therefore did not involve the more abstruse exclusionary rules, part of the repertoire of 'devices' deplored by Chief Justice Burger in the quotation above.[2] And that there is large-scale ignorance of the effect of adversarial reasoning on appeals is apparent from the 'gasps from peers as well as Yallop[3] himself, who was sitting in the public gallery',[4] when Viscount Colville of Culross explained it in the House of Lords:[5]

> There may in a criminal trial be evidence which is available and is known to one or other of the parties at that time which for one reason or another they choose not to use. In those circumstances, I do not think that some years later, because somebody considers that they were mistaken in their choice of not using it, the existence of that evidence would be grounds for reopening that matter by way of public inquiry.

In an adversarial trial, each party selects the issues and evidence he or she wishes to bring before the court; it is therefore his or her responsibility to ensure that the case presented is the most favourable possible from his or her point of view. The court's only duty is to provide a fair hearing. Thus, litigants are heavily dependent on the ability of their lawyers to present their case in the best possible light. Inevitably, this means those members of society who can most easily afford lawyers who know how to operate the system will be better served than others in this respect. However, it is impossible for any litigant to be absolutely certain a fatal mistake will not be made, and in general there is no room for appeal or complaint if a litigant feels that he or she – or the lawyers – threw his or her chance away. The Court of Appeal in criminal cases does have a power to order the production of and to examine fresh evidence, under section 23 of the Criminal Appeal Act 1968, but the exercise of its discretion is influenced, *inter alia*, by the availability of the evidence at trial.[6] In extreme cases, however, 'This Court ought not to consider itself bound by any hard and fast rule never to allow

---

[2] (1973) 42 Fordham LR 227. Although the Chief Justice excluded the English trial from the allegation that the adversarial trial put a premium on skill, adroitness and trickery, he thought the system in northern European countries such as Holland and Denmark more humane: ibid., p. 236.

[3] Author of *To Encourage the Others*, 2nd edn (Corgi, London, 1990), a study of the trial of Craig and Bentley in 1952.

[4] *Sunday Correspondent*, 12 August 1990.

[5] HL Deb., Vol. 106, col. 324 (14 June 1972).

[6] *Parks* (1962) 46 Cr App R 29; *Boal* (1964) 48 Cr App R 342.

further evidence to be called when the fact that it was not called was due to the mistaken conduct of the case....If it was plainly made out that justice required it, I think this Court would interfere'.[7] As far as the general run of cases, where the court would not interfere, is concerned, the legal system itself could be criticized only if the judge failed to do his or her job properly. Although to individual litigants this may appear unfair, the inquisitorial alternative, where it is essential that the judge uncovers all issues and evidence, may be as dangerous, since legal representatives are less able to influence the way the case is conducted. In the adversarial system there is the opportunity, at least, to have one's case presented to its best advantage.

The perception of fairness identified by Thibaut and Walker must be maintained, since systems of justice require public support. It could even be enhanced if trial structures become more flexible than they are at present. For the appeal structure militates against this perceived fairness, as does the operation of exclusionary rules of evidence which 'run contrary to fact in many cases'.[8] The answer is not to adopt the full-blown Continental system, but to modify the English one to create a 'mixed' system on the lines of the Scandinavian countries; the appeal system already provides a discretion in the matter of fresh evidence, and this could be operated more flexibly. There are developments in that direction following on from the cases of the Birmingham and Guildford IRA bombings. Trials also should be more flexible; procedures should be modified to allow the judges a greater role in calling witnesses and asking questions. Counsel's editorial control of examination-in-chief would therefore be curtailed and witnesses could be permitted to give evidence more freely, as Scandinavian witnesses do. After all, the Pigot proposals and current Criminal Justice Bill,[9] which will allow a videotaped interview with a child to replace his or her examination-in-chief, countenance a conversation in its place which will bear little resemblance to the manner of testimony currently elicited by counsel. The importance of cross-examination would diminish where the witness is not tightly constrained in giving his or her account. With it should go the overthrow of the principle of orality, already doomed by the move towards more disclosure of evidence. The hearsay rule would then be seen in its true colours, as no more than a rough, commonsense guide to the relative reliability of evidence. Allowing witnesses more freedom to explain themselves would deprive counsel of their vital role in relation to the evidence laid before the court, but

---

[7] *Perry and Harvey* (1909) 2 Cr App R 89, 92, *per* Walton J; quoted with approval by Scarman LJ in *Lattimore* (1975) 62 Cr App R 53, 55–56.

[8] Cohen, 'Freedom of Proof', in *Facts in Law*, ed. W. Twining (Steiner, Wiesbaden, 1983).

[9] See chapter 4.

there is support for it. Frankel wrote: 'We should be prepared to inquire whether our art of examining or cross-examining, often geared to preventing excessive outpouring of facts, are inevitably preferable to safeguarded interrogation by an informed judicial officer.'[10] Such views are anathema to the traditional British advocate; his or her point of view is expressed in typical terms by Sheriff Stone: ''strictly controlled questioning' has certain advantages – the witness is taken step by step and point by point through material facts, in a planned and orderly way.[11] This prevents the witness from rambling. 'If some witnesses were simply asked to say what they know about the facts in issue, the rules of evidence and the expertise of the advocate would disappear....[he or she] might state damaging facts, which there was no obligation to reveal, by law.'[12]

It might be no catastrophe if this field of expertise were to disappear, allowing courts to focus on the facts and the law. Less emphasis on orality would also have the effect of undermining the division between evidence on the issue and evidence which goes only to credibility, since that is a function both of the hearsay rule and the need to avoid prolonged and complex oral trials. Once that distinction bites the dust, we can avoid the hypocrisy of the claim that the accused's criminal record is evidence only of his or her credibility on oath. In a less formal atmosphere, lawyers might even go so far as to accept that the current style of cross-examination is not necessarily the most efficient way to assess witness credibility. In any event, as Egglestone argues, cross-examination as to credit should be confined to the witness's reliability in respect of the facts to which he or she has deposed.[13] More enlightened use of expert evidence might assist the court to reach an accurate assessment of that; and experts should not be assigned to one party or the other, but be recognized as impartial, disinterested witnesses whose ability and knowledge should be available without restriction to the tribunal of fact.

Exchange of information before the case comes to court is becoming more important in both civil and criminal cases. In criminal cases the imbalance between the prosecution duty to disclose and that of the defence is increasingly being seen as a barrier in complex cases to convictions which would be entirely deserved. The changes already operating in fraud cases are only the beginning of a process of reform born of disillusion with the notion that the presumption of innocence necessarily means that the defence is

[10] Frankel, 'The search for truth: an umpireal view' (1975) 123 U Penn LR 1031, 1053.

[11] Although that depends on the level of preparedness of the advocate.

[12] M. Stone, *Proof of Fact in Criminal Trials* (W. Green & Sons, Edinburgh, 1984), p. 273.

[13] Egglestone, 'What is wrong with the adversary system?' (1975) 49 ALJ 428.

entitled to take the prosecution entirely by surprise.[14] The right to silence must, therefore, be to that extent curtailed. Adversarial theory is inconsistent with any process whereby one side effectively assists the other, yet no useful purpose is served by a system of trial which involves the presentation of two cases which have little or no common ground. This makes some duty to disclose inevitable. Extending it, however, ensures a drift away from the emphasis on orality; this means considerably less scope for 'advocacy' to win the day in a 'climactic and continuous trial'.[15] In Jackson's model for criminal trials,[16] an independent magistrate would be involved at a pre-trial stage to ensure full disclosure of all evidence, and to compile it in a report. This would be presented in advance of the trial to the triers of fact. The witnesses would be questioned at the trial by lawyers for the prosecution and defence, but also by the triers of fact, who would have power also to summon witnesses, such as the independent magistrate if clarification of the report is required. Counsel would therefore have little opportunity to control through questioning technique the evidence given by witnesses. The result would resemble the processes investigated by Leigh and Hall Williams in northern Europe.[17] The meticulous review of evidence which involves all parties, including the defence, in the Netherlands, for example, means that most disputes of fact are settled at an early stage. Information requested by the defence is freely provided; there is no sign of the confrontational approach with which English lawyers are familiar. As a consequence of the consensus likely to develop early on in each case, there are relatively few contested trials and few acquittals.

The evolution of civil procedure already shows a more marked progress towards a more inquisitorial style. If the wishes expressed in the House of Lords that more information be available to a judge before trial so that he or she needs less guidance once in court[18] are carried out, many issues of fact and law would effectively be decided in advance, subject to dissuasion by the advocate on 'the day'. Those with little faith in the English judiciary tremble at this prospect. Curiously, civil courts have shown reluctance to order disclosure where fraud is alleged, because 'keeping one's card close to the chest might be justified in order to preserve the element of surprise to assist

---

[14] Another of the 'devices' referred to by Chief Justice Burger.

[15] Egglestone, (1975) 49 ALJ 428.

[16] Jackson, 'Two methods of proof in criminal procedure' (1988) 31 MLR 249.

[17] L. H. Leigh and J. E. Hall Williams, *The Management of Prosecution Process in Denmark, Sweden and the Netherlands* (James Hall, Leamington Spa, 1981).

[18] See chapter 1: Lord Templeman in *Spiliada Maritime Corp v Cansulex Ltd* [1987] AC 460; *Banque Keyser Ullmann SA v Skandia (UK) Insurance Co* [1990] 3 WLR 364.

in showing that the defendant has been fraudulent.'[19] The irony of these remarks, given the abandonment of such reasoning in criminal fraud trials, is inescapable. In other commercial litigation, it is not clear to what extent judges are able to familiarize themselves with the cases they are due to hear; counsel are frequently producing skeleton arguments at the last minute because of pressure of work, and judges themselves have drawn attention to their own predicament. Harman J, for example, observed recently that such proposals showed the House of Lords to be 'wholly out of touch with reality'. He went on:[20]

> Lord Templeman[21] observed that he hoped that in future the judge will be allowed to study the evidence and refresh his memory of the speech of...Lord Goff in the quiet of his room and without expense of the parties. He will not be referred to other decisions on other facts, and submissions will be measured in hours, not days. An appeal would be rare and the appellate court slow to interfere. This matter came on before me at two o'clock on Monday. I am delivering judgment at a quarter to four on a Thursday afternoon. I do not regard any minute of the time that has been taken before me as wasted...Lord Templeman's observations bear no relation to any conceivable way in which this matter could have been conducted. Where I should have found the time to read the evidence, which runs in the exhibits to some hundreds of pages and in the affidavits alone to 134 pages, I cannot imagine. The result is that Lord Templeman's wishes are wholly incapable of performance and have not been performed.

The Children Act 1989 creates a system whereby the number of parties with individual points of view may be considerably extended. There will be full disclosure of witness statements as between the parties and to the court. There will be preliminary hearings involving a magistrate and the clerk, who will decide, for example, whether expert reports are required. The guardian *ad litem* will advise the court as to the child's best interests and his or her report must be supplied to all parties before the full hearing. It is to be hoped that the new procedure will achieve its objective of more com-promised solutions being found so that a hearing is unnecessary. In any event, the court should require less oral evidence and argument, sparing interested parties a great deal of distress.

The recent recognition both at first instance[22] and in the Court of Appeal[23]

---

[19] *Richard Saunders & Partners (a firm) v Eastglen* [1990] 3 All ER 946, 951, *per* Judge Dobry QC.

[20] *Re Harrods (Buenos Aires) Ltd* [1990] BCC 481, 486.

[21] In *Spiliada* [1987] AC 460, 465.

[22] *Richard Saunders v Eastglen* [1990] 3 All ER 946.

[23] *Holden v Chief Constable of Lancashire*, *The Times*, 22 February 1991.

that the practice of exchange of witness statements prior to trial should be adopted in all forms of civil litigation (even in jury trials) 'save in exceptional circumstances'[24] provides authoritative confirmation that current changes in procedure represent a developing policy to move in the inquisitorial direction. The Master of the Rolls has spoken of a 'sea change over the last quarter of a century in the legislative and judicial attitude to the conduct of litigation which took the form of increased positive case management by the judiciary.'[25] Certainly the conduct of litigation is currently changing rapidly and fundamentally as a result of these procedural shifts and most specifically in those implemented in very recent years.

It is important to note that the most consistent justification for the change of approach is to shorten trial time, save costs and maximize earlier settlements.[26] It is not the most voiced selling point of reform that the new style of trial is fairer to the parties or more likely to produce a just result, concepts themselves open to debate. In other words, the concentration of effort from the judiciary and the Rules Committee has been to examine the economics of litigation and improve efficiency in dispatching cases through the system. The emphasis has not been to consider what style of procedure is the most desirable for the parties from the viewpoint of protecting their legal interests. However, the result of these developments is fundamentally to change the essential nature of the civil trial both in form and in substance, diluting the importance of the advocate's role and the lawyer's personal expertise and ability to influence the outcome; it involves an inevitable retreat from adversarial principle. A witness's evidence will effectively be 'settled' by his or her lawyers in advance of the hearing, and presented in a coherent and comprehensive form wholly unlike the product of many examinations-in-chief, and bearing little resemblance to the witness's own manner of communicating. This runs the risk that the judge's perception of the witness's credibility, should the case come to trial, will be more than ever influenced by the way the witness stands up to cross-examination. Some lawyers fear the effect on the witness of stepping straight into a hostile onslaught without first getting 'the feel of the court' through a friendly interrogation by his or her own side. The exchange procedure as it is at present therefore distorts the natural balance of the adversarial trial.

The individuality of the lawyer's role thus is to be replaced by the more methodical and mundane requirements of careful preparation and the production of a paperwork case – 'lever-arch litigation' – as practised widely in Europe. This will inevitably undermine the position of the Civil Bar and

---

[24] Ibid.
[25] Ibid.
[26] Ibid.; *Banque Keyser Ullmann SA* [1990] 3 WLR 364, 380, *per* Lord Templeman.

will probably have a more fundamental role in dismantling the distinction between barristers and solicitors than any more direct and specific legislative reforms ever will. Once important cases are perceived as being won or lost on paper and prior to trial the difference between the style and role of the lawyers is eradicated where the decisive work takes place on the desktop, whether in a solicitor's office or counsel's chambers, rather than in the cauldron of the court. The overall wisdom of these radical reforms remains to be assessed, but the basic assumption that money and time will be saved cannot be accepted without argument, as the observations of Harman J make clear.[27] Furthermore, it may be that the emphasis on pre-trial preparation and paperwork (which are very expensive) will give an unfair advantage to the wealthier litigant. The massive costs of commercial litigation are certainly as much to do with the preparation as with time in court. However, the die appears to be cast and the process is probably irreversible; problems of evidence should now be addressed in that light.

In chapter 6 it was observed that the duty of the prosecution and its agents to observe higher standards of conduct than is necessary in the case of the defence amounted to an implied acceptance that the parties in a criminal case are not independent in the strictly adversarial sense. But in an inquisitorial system there is a danger that the prosecution, never wholly independent of the state, is not independent either of the court which will try the case: 'The essential element of the inquisitorial system, when compared to the accusatorial, is the blurring of the distinction between the function of prosecution and that of judgment.'[28]

Erikson argues that in a Continental system the members of the judiciary who conduct criminal investigations, prosecutions and judgments are colleagues in the same profession. They form a separate brotherhood which is distinct from that of the lawyers who defend the accused and never prosecute or go on to become judges. The danger, however, is that securing convictions is just as dear to them as it is to police officers; despite this risk, the apparent impartiality of Italian investigating judges, brought into investigation at an earlier stage in proceedings because of criticism of police methods of obtaining convictions in the 1950s and 1960s, led to them being given sweeping powers which would have been politically unacceptable in a police force. In England, judicial criticism of police methods is not unknown, although not an everyday occurrence. Erikson suggests that separation of powers makes it more likely than it is in an inquisitorial system. There, a judge would find it difficult to suggest that a colleague had lied on

---

[27] *Re Harrods (Buenos Aires)* [1990] BCC 481.
[28] Erikson, 'Confessions in evidence: a look at the inquisitorial system' [1990] NLJ 884.

oath and ought to be prosecuted. Such problems suggest that England would be unwise to institute a 'career judiciary' in the Continental sense.

In Scandinavia and the Netherlands, however, there appears to be virtually no distrust of or complaints against the police, prosecution or magistrates among defence lawyers; the early involvement of all parties in the investigative process encourages a co-operative atmosphere in which evidence is tested and discussed, and therefore mutually accepted or discarded, long in advance of trial.[29] It is not clear whether the roots of this consensual approach are in a tolerant national temperament and culture, or actually flow from the nature of the procedures themselves. Sir Peter Imbert, the Metropolitan Police Commissioner, has suggested[30] that the British look closely at the French system of using examining magistrates, partly because of criticism of police methods in certain notorious cases, but also because there may be advantages in harmonizing legal processes across Europe. Certainly one of the practical problems facing Crown Prosecution Service lawyers at present is incompleteness of evidence, and this might be reduced if they were involved at an earlier stage, as suggested in a *Times* editorial[31] which argued that they ought to be able to question suspects and witnesses themselves. *The Times* rightly pointed out that at present the police have to anticipate the likely requirements of the Crown Prosecution Service, but as time goes on, it may be that police officers will become sufficiently used to the criteria applied to collect and organize the evidence as directed. Given the Italian experience, it would appear unwise to tinker with the relationship between the police, the prosecutor and the court without at the same time establishing a mechanism whereby the defence also participates in investigations. However, this would not be practicable without the radical reorganization of defence lawyers, and therefore possibly of the legal profession generally.

If such a system were successful, there should be fewer trials and fewer shock verdicts. The English system already has an impressive repertoire of devices with which to encourage a criminal defendant to opt out of a contested trial altogether,[32] but other possibilities have been tried, although within a traditional adversarial prosecution system, such as the 'night prosecutor program' of Columbus, Ohio. Here the victim and defendant give their uninterrupted version of events to a volunteer law student mediator, who suggests options which would avoid trial. If no agreement can be reached, the trial goes ahead. Mediation has been suggested also for civil cases, on the basis that since so many cases are concluded by a settlement

---

[29] Leigh and Hall Williams, *Management of Prosecution Process.*
[30] *The Times*, 18 July 1990.
[31] Ibid.
[32] See Ashworth, 'Criminal justice and criminal process' (1988) 2 Br J Crim 111.

reached at the courtroom door (a very expensive stage at which to abandon suit) cost might be saved if negotiations are brought about by a third party far earlier.[33] Earlier negotiation, even without a mediator, is made more likely in any case by the greater disclosure taking place in complex civil cases. Parties are much better placed than before to assess the strength of the case against them. One of the principal aims of the new House of Lords directions on disclosure is to encourage earlier settlement. The argument is that the courts would consequently hear fewer cases, leaving more time for the scrutiny of documents relating to those cases which will fight. If such procedures become the norm in civil cases, there should be less need for mediation or arbitration, which is currently being suggested as another avenue of escape from the expense and uncertainty of adversarial trial. Rutherford argues[34] that arbitration can be 'versatile, efficient, cost effective, and satisfactory', but there are advocates who maintain that the exact opposite is the case.

Although, as we have seen, many recent departures have diluted quite considerably the adversarial properties of the English system of legal adjudication, the unpredictability of the trial on the day is still unfair to some potential litigants who are unable accurately to assess the strength of their case. Yet, paradoxically, it may encourage those with little merit because something may be achieved by surprise or some other tactic. And, as we have seen, a weak case may appear comparatively stronger in an adversarial contest than an inquisitorial one. There seems to be no reason in principle why, in England, we should be reluctant to consider further developments away from traditional methods. It has been shown throughout this book that in many respects neither civil nor criminal trials are pure embodiments of adversarial principles, although they deviate in different ways from the classical adversarial pattern. England has never had a pure adversary procedure, but there is reason to believe that it is moving farther from it in both the civil and the criminal context. Unfortunately, this drift is not recognized; if it were, the insistence on retention of exclusionary rules of evidence which are appropriate only within an adversarial system would inevitably diminish.

[33] See Rutherford, 'Back to the future' [1990] NLJ 1600.
[34] Ibid.

Index